OWYHEE TRAILS
The West's Forgotten Corner

OWYHEE TRAILS
The West's Forgotten Corner

By

MIKE HANLEY

With

ELLIS LUCIA

MAPS AND DRAWINGS BY MIKE HANLEY

The CAXTON PRINTERS, Ltd.
Caldwell, Idaho
1999

First printing December, 1973
Second printing September, 1974
Third printing September, 1975
Fourth printing January, 1980
Fifth printing August, 1988
Sixth printing November, 1999

Library of Congress Catalog Card Number 75-140118

International Standard Book Number 0-87004-281-5

Printed and bound in the United States of America by
The CAXTON PRINTERS, Ltd.
Caldwell, Idaho 83605
165555

To my forebears and all the other pioneers
who made this book possible.

CONTENTS

Page

LIST OF ILLUSTRATIONS ix

ACKNOWLEDGEMENTS xiii

FOREWORD xv

INTRODUCTION xxi

SHADES OF THE OLD WEST 1

CROSSROADS OF THE OWYHEES 22

THE TRIBES STRIKE BACK 45

LONGHORN TRAIL FROM TEXAS 78

POOR FOOD, TOUGH HORSES 101

LAST INDIAN UPRISING 124

THE LEGEND OF BIGFOOT 148

MUTTON FOR THE HUNGRY MINERS 161

THE COLORFUL BASQUES 183

FRISKY TIMES IN SILVER CITY 198

Page

DOG TOWN GROWS UP 232

WHEN THE PONIES RAN 250

MOONSHINE OVER JORDAN 256

THE COUNTRY DOCTOR 265

BLACKSMITHS WERE A SPECIAL BREED 274

THE BATTLE OF SOLDIER CREEK 280

RUNNING OF THE MUSTANGS 288

GOINGS ON 296

INDEX 308

LIST OF ILLUSTRATIONS

Page

Open country in southeastern Oregon 6
Succor Creek wends its way through the Owyhee
    Mountains 8
Owyhee Canyon — looking downstream 9
The town of Jordan Valley lies just a mile from
    the Idaho border 10
High formations of eastern Oregon's Owyhee canyon ... 12
Birch Creek in the Owyhee Canyon 14
White bluffs, known as the "Rome Coliseum,"
    stand near the Owyhee Crossing 16
Grave of Baptiste Charbonneau 17
Lakes where Indian
    tribes once roamed 18
Jordan craters 19
Jordan craters, the site of great lava beds 19
The author holding an old flintlock rifle 20
The Owyhee river of eastern Oregon 21
Dewey, Idaho, a mining town in the Owyhees 25
Mr. Irwin proudly shows off his fine trotter
    before the ornate Dewey Hotel 28
An old safe, broken open, found beside the stage
    road to the Owyhees 31
John Baxter and his wife 34

Page

A freight outfit near the post office in Silver City 35
A jerkline outfit hauling mining equipment to
    Idaho City 36
The Jesse Anderson store as it appears today 38
Stage coach on road to Silver City 39
Site of old Camp Lyon as it appears today 42
Old miner's shack 43
Nomadic Indians of the Owyhees....................... 48
A Bannock war chief, in full regalia 49
The enlistment poster for the "Oregon Volunteers,"
    with four officers of the group 51
Camp Lyon as it was in 1866 55
The rocky bluffs made natural fortifications for
    the Red Men 59
Sagging barn at Ruby Ranch 62
Sim Glass in front of Inskip Station's fortified
    house in 1911....................................... 63
Nee-keah-peop, member of the Bannock tribe 66
Colonel Coppinger and his staff at Camp Winthrop
    in 1868 71
A box canyon in the Owyhees......................... 72
William J. McConnell 74
Willie Dorsey, a Paiute Indian, and his wife, Nora 75
Cattle grazing on the Owyhee rangelands 80
Map of Cattle Drives of David Shirk from Texas
    to the Idaho Mines 81
Con Shea and his wife 83
Dave Shirk.. 87
Dave Shirk and his wife, Frances, about 1926 94
Pete French... 97
A typical early cow camp, near Cow Lakes 100
Pick Anderson... 102
The Agency Valley, as it appears today 109
John Devine, early cattleman 114
Henry Miller 115
Map of Bannock Indian War............................ 125
Indian braves, probably Bannocks 127
Chief Buffalo Horn of the Bannocks 129
Sarah Winnemucca 134
Stone buildings of the old Ruby Ranch, near Danner ... 137
State Line ranch house, refuge during Indian outbreak.. 139

Page

A Bannock brave 146
Drawing of Bigfoot on the rampage 153
Farewell Bend on the Snake River 157
Flock of sheep near Owyhee Crossing 163
Tom Turnbull 166
Jim McEwen with his new bride, Mima 173
Bill McEwen herding sheep on Steens Mountain, 1910 ... 174
A group of Scot herders 178
Tim Lequerica 189
John Lequerica 194
John Lequerica working with sheep in the pens 197
Map of the Silver City Mining District 200
View of Silver City just after the turn of the century 202
Freight wagons rumbled through the streets of
    Silver City 204
Silver City in winter 206
A drilling contest, during July 4th celebration, 1898 209
Labor Day parade, 1898 210
Silver City had a huge Chinese population 213
A celebration near Silver City 217
Colonel Dewey 218
DeLamar, an Owyhee mining town 219
One freighter tries to pass another at lower DeLamar 222
The Jack (or J. W.) Stoddard house at Silver City
    with its ornate gingerbread trim 224
Silver City residents, in Sunday best 225
The rough and tumble crew of the Trade Dollar mine 227
Many rustic old buildings still stand in Silver City 229
Silas Skinner with his wife, Annie 233
Map of the Jordan Valley area 235
Town of Jordan Valley, near the Oregon-Idaho
    border 236
Main Street, Jordan Valley, in the early 1900s 237
The old Jordan Valley Hotel 238
A fine antique collection 239
Mr. and Mrs. J. R. Blackaby, Blackaby general
    store, 1890s 242
Typical early family (the Cowgills) of Jordan Valley 244
Modern residents of Jordan Valley in oldtime
    costume 247
Bally Beers, the most famous race horse in
    the Owyhees 253

Page

Bally Beers finishing in his usual place — first 254

A race to the finish line — Bally Beers and Shrimp 255

Sketch of moonshine equipment 257

Mike Hanley examines old bottle used for
     moonshine 259

A load of moonshine wrecked near the Sheep Ranch 261

A country doctor and his family 267

Pharmacy which was headquarters for
     Dr. Walter William Jones 271

Interior of Dr. Jones' pharmacy today 272

Oxen being shod at Dave Summerville's forge in
     DeLamar 275

Setting a wagon tyre is an art few are now able
     to practice 276

Ernest Stites 279

The Soldier Creek area 284

Mike Hanley III, the author's father 285

A pair of wild horses warily eyes the photographer 289

Spirited mustangs gallop along a rocky defile,
     trying to escape capture 291

A small band of mustangs flees from the onlooker 294

Ed Hanley and Jack Dalton with his wife in
     Alaska, 1898 297

The author brings juniper posts from Idaho with
     a six horse team and wagon 300

Uncle Bill Hanley with his niece Martha at the
     Bell A ranch 301

The mud wagon type coach plunging through a
     narrow creek 303

Omer Stanford "rolls his own" in front of a
     rebuilt stagecoach 305

ACKNOWLEDGEMENTS

SPECIAL APPRECIATION and "thanks" is expressed to the following people who contributed in various ways to make this book possible:

Mr. and Mrs. J. M. McEwen, Mr. and Mrs. Everett Miller, Ernest Stites, Ernest Fenwick, Ambrose Maher, Joe Swisher, Frank Swisher, Bob Strode, Tim Lequerica, Aurora Madariaga, Floyd Acarregui, John Lequerica, Mr. and Mrs. Fred Eiguren, Mr. and Mrs. Mike Hanley III, Reub Long, E. R. Jackman, Mr. and Mrs. Cameron Cliff, Walter McEwen.

Julian Calzacorta, Rodney Hawes, Norman Jess, Everett Jones, Dr. Walter W. Jones, P. O. Duncan, Leonard Duncan, Vernon Warn, Charles Loveland, Mr. and Mrs. Bill Loveland, Bob Dowell, Jerry Shea, Aileene Staples, Mr. and Mrs. Frank Gusman, Ted Cowgill, Mrs. Milton Anawalt, Clinton L. Anawalt, Mr. and Mrs. Jeff Anderson, Dr. Merle Wells, Omer Stanford, Ralph Stanford, Mildretta Adams, Mrs. Pascual Arritola, Mr. and Mrs. Pete "Larrinaga," Jim Elordi.

Mrs. Clemens, Charley Dowell, Mr. and Mrs. S. K.

Skinner, Mr. and Mrs. Robert Skinner, Bill Ross, Glenn Wolcott, Tim Mills, Gabriel Elordi, Jerry Stankie, Mr. and Mrs. Bill Schwartz, Mrs. Bill Moore, Joe Zatica, Joe Studio, Joe Telleria, Bill Maher, Art Cherry, Mr. and Mrs. Pete Fretwell, Irene Simpson, Mary Hanley, Martha Hanley, Claire Hanley, Clifford Northorp, Bill Hawes, Terry Ackerman, Sr., Idaho Historical Society, Wells Fargo Bank.

Frank Pitts, Dave Vail, United States War Department, Dr. Lee Johnson, Norman MacKenzie, Fred Scott, Walter Bowden, John Turner, Alfred McConnell, Tom Whitby, James Turnbull, Mr. and Mrs. George Potts, Mrs. Dick Staples, Marion Wroten, Mrs. Pilar Tucker, A. J. Page, Charley Cronin, Preston Onstead, Ellis Lucia, Mrs. Tex Payne, Leonard Davis, City of Winnemucca, Sara Baker, Mrs. Tom Skinner, Virginia Stanford, Mrs. Vinson, The City of Jordan Valley, Verma Anderson.

MIKE HANLEY
Jordan Valley, Oregon

FOREWORD

IN THE MASSIVE telling and retelling of the taming of our Western frontier, commonly now called The Old West, what strikes me as amazing is the phenomenon of innumerable rich veins and sparkling pockets of adventure and folklore, struggle and pathos, love and heartbreak, that have been passed over, remaining raw and untold.

The late Lucius Beebe, that colorful literary genius who loved the West of the nineteenth century with a passion, described these as "the tailings." He was indeed well aware of them, as was his good friend Stewart Holbrook. Mr. Beebe observed that I, too, enjoyed "working the tailings," and that I found them of great interest and fascination. Many authors and publishers, and their readers, tend to re-plow the same furrows and follow well-worn trails. But I see little worth, nor can I well up much enthusiasm, over yet another book about Jesse James, Billy the Kid, the Little Bighorn, or the trek of Chief Joseph — unless, of course, a rare vein of raw material has somehow come to light.

Therefore, it was a genuine thrill to discover the efforts of Mike Hanley, a young rancher of the Jordan Valley who for many years has been working the tailings of that once bustling and little-known territory which is one of the most remote sections of the West. It is sometimes called the I-O-N- Country, where the three states of Idaho, Oregon and Nevada mesh together. In plowing through old records and talking with old-timers, Hanley struck some fertile deposits and staked his claims.

Mr. Hanley is unique for his time and place. While many of his generation outwardly reject the past (and therefore their own heritage) as "dead and gone, having nothing to do with today," Mike has developed an intense interest in and knowledge of what went on in his region and in the Pacific Northwest. He believes that the preservation of this heritage is most important. Mike has lived and breathed Western history, both fact and legend, all his life as a fourth generation descendant of the celebrated Hanley family of Oregon who first settled in the 1850s in the Rogue Valley near historic Jacksonville. The Hanleys later became influential ranchers developing the sprawling stock lands east of the Cascade Range. His great uncle, Bill Hanley, was a pioneer rancher, entrepreneur, politician, salty philosopher in the mold of Will Rogers, and a powerful influence in Oregon affairs into the first quarter of the twentieth century. So Mike Hanley came by it naturally, growing up with the saga of the West all around him, not as something read in books or seen in the movies.

At the tender age of nine, Mike's father took him along on the cattle drives and round-ups. He camped, ate, slept, and rode with the buckeroos, among them grizzled old-timers whose memories extended back to the wild days of the roaring frontier towns, the Indian wars, the gold and silver strikes, and the days when Pete French and John Devine rode the range.

He leaned against the old chuck wagon, itself a relic of the Old West frontier, night after night as the buckeroos swapped yarns. His imagination was whetted by the tall tales and pieces of true history related by former jerkline freighters, miners, ranchers, and drovers who lived through it. Stories of saloon fights, the red light districts, and cold-blooded killings weren't "shocking things," only life as it happened, and the father did not attempt to shield the boy from them.

During long winter evenings Mike heard more stories from his parents, his grandparents, aunts and uncles, and from a colorful ranch hand, Frank Swisher, who entertained the kids in the bunkhouse to the background music of a screechy gramophone. The Hanleys often explored the sites of past events. One of Mike's early memories was hearing his father tell about an encounter with the Rogue River Indians at the Hanley homestead cabin, then his mother digging about and coming up with a spear-head sunk in the cabin foundation and a bar of lead for making bullets. A boy isn't likely to forget such pieces of evidence, tied to reality.

But there was something unusual about this. Not only was Mike's imagination fired up over what he heard, but he had the good sense, even at a tender age, to do something about it. One night at a campfire, the boy tore the label off a tomato can and began noting down some of the stories. He's been doing it ever since, even while in college. He courted his girl while poking through archives and historical collections in Boise. He has interviewed and swapped yarns with most every old-timer in his region, realizing that he must hurry, for they were fast dying off and closing the doors forever on valuable information about the past. He explored on horseback most of the Owyhee back country of old mines, Indian encampments, military forts, scenes of skirmishes, stage roads, caves, and buckeroo hangouts. He found Indian and pioneer writings on the faces of high bluffs, and camped where cavalry troopers had bedded down, awaiting the dawn to attack an Indian encampment. Barren meadows and open desert came to have vivid new meanings. Often Mike returned with belt buckles, buttons, mule shoes, old tools, pieces of harness, and other artifacts, sufficient for beginning a small museum, which he intends to do.

Outside his ranching chores and herding his cows (Mike wishes history could be more profitable), Hanley spends much time rebuilding wagons of the past from decaying frameworks given him by friendly ranchers who know his interest and from abandoned barns or yards. His mounting collection includes a stagecoach, a Conestoga freighter, and a military wagon. Such authorities on the eastern Oregon country as Reub Long and the late Herman Oliver observed that young Hanley (he is now slightly beyond 30) knows more about the heritage of his region than anyone alive, and furthermore, he is still young enough to contribute much more to its preservation through what appears to be an intense lifetime interest. He was well aware, for example, of the grave of Charbonneau, Sacajawea's son who saw the Pacific Ocean as a babe in arms with the Lewis and Clark Expedition, long before it became common knowledge in 1970, and on his own initiative, built and erected a sizable historical marker over the site.

The story of the I-O-N region, which Mike likes to call the Forgotten Corner, has never been adequately told. It has remained largely the land of the mysterious Owyhees. Yet a century ago, traffic through this region was tremendous with the activities of thousands of miners, Chinese laborers, freighters, stagecoach operators, road builders, saloon keepers, bawdy house madams, Indian tribes, ranchers and roustabouts. Silver City, Idaho, was the scene of some of the West's greatest mining strikes and was almost as rich as the Comstock. But Silver City has been over-shadowed by Virginia City, Alder Gulch, Tombstone, Central City, Leadville, and other brawling camps. Jordan Valley is better known for its late-coming Basque population than as a hub of freighting, ranching, battles with the Indians, and gunplay, where rugged individualists like Silas Skinner, Con Shea, Pick Anderson, Dave Shirk, and Hill Beachy were familiar figures. It was once a great horse racing center, and the home of a tough and kindly country doctor who braved flooding rivers and deep snowdrifts to reach his patients.

As an author and student of Pacific Northwest and Western history and folklore, Hanley's material excited me for its freshness and vitality. But this is primarily Mike's book. He got it all together, and it is told largely with his own words and his own viewpoint as to the way things were in his region. Hopefully, between the two of us, we have parted the veil that has lain over the I-O-N Country; a land that people just drive through on their hurried ways to Reno and Boise, but where important things happened — and not so very long ago.

ELLIS LUCIA
Portland, Oregon

INTRODUCTION

Dear Mike,

Owyhee Trails comes kind of close to me because of my association and the association of my family with the Hanleys over many and many a year. When my mother was a girl, she worked on the Hanley Ranch near Jacksonville for your great grandfather, Mike Hanley. My people lived at Christmas Lake at a stopping place and watering hole on the desert. Christmas Lake was on a road traveled by the Hanleys when they first came to the country east of the Cascades. Bill Hanley, a very famous rancher in Harney County, often stopped at our home when I was a small boy.

So, Mike, I am going to try to say something about how much I liked what you have written.

It is so necessary that someone who has learned the early history write it down as you have done so that it will not forever be lost. Your description of the big desert country with its rimrocks and sagebrush and river valleys could only be told by someone like you that had lived amid these things.

xxii INTRODUCTION

The stories of the pioneering, mining camps, Indians, and the Army have long needed to be told, and you have done a grand job of getting together these many tales.

And so, Mike, thanks to you for writing this book which will be read with much interest, not only by the people who live in "The Forgotten Corner," but by everyone interested in the West and who may pass our way.

Your friend,
/s/ "Reub"
R. A. Long

"They'll be changing our old names that tell people the whole history of the country: Squaw Flats, Yaninax, Bake Oven, Rawhide, Stinking Water . . . so many others given by the boys, often for things that happened there. All means something. Every one a story."

— BILL HANLEY
in *Feelin' Fine*

SHADES OF THE OLD WEST

ONE DAY NOT LONG AGO, near Jordan Valley where I ranch, a meandering rancher stumbled upon two cattle thieves butchering a beef along a remote old road leading to the Owyhee Crossing at Rome, Oregon. The rustlers, or poachers as they're now sometimes called, were so startled seeing the rancher come into view that they dropped the meat and took off in a small plane they'd landed on the dirt road.

There could be no forming a posse to track them, as in the old days, but the rancher managed to get the plane number. It was traced to Salt Lake City, some four hundred miles away across two state lines. The trail went cold there, for the plane had been rented and the men gave aliases. But it pointed up a critical problem for modern cattlemen in my section of the West, which stretches clear down into Nevada and over into Idaho. It's a sizable chunk of real estate, much of it unchanged and only slightly less wild than when Indians roamed this land and the ranchers had trouble with cattle thieves on the sparse frontier.

Much of the West is still plagued with rustlers, and the ranchers suffer heavy losses through mechanized robbery. The long rope and the running iron have given way to refrigerated trucks, motorcycles, campers, pickups, and planes. When we talk to those on the "outside" about cattle thievery, they think we've been seeing too many television Westerns. Fact is, in Jordan Valley, we don't have to watch TV to know that rustlers are in action. Most Americans feel that the West of the cowboy has faded into the past, fully tamed and principally legend now. But it's not true; the Old West is dying hard, with its boots on, and outraged cattlemen feel that rustling is as great a threat as it ever was. The thieves are much more difficult to catch — not to mention the fact that the courts have gone soft on them.

Old-time rustlers usually located a herd and drove it away from home range, then rebranded the cattle. Many cows were also butchered outright. The story goes that if it hadn't been for "The Wrench," the Pacific Land and Livestock Company cattle, most of the homesteaders of Harney County, Oregon, might have starved to death. The same applies to many other places. Some ranchers, feeling sorry for the homesteaders and hoping to keep losses controlled, gave beef to tide them over. But regardless of the motives, the law didn't deal lightly with rustlers in those days. Where there was little formal law, the cattlemen dealt with thieves in their own way. Many cases were solved over the sights of a Winchester at the far end of a long trail through the sagebrush.

The American West has changed since then, with the shift of people to the cities, but great stretches of land untouched by bulldozers and housing developers still sprawl in all directions. The ranches are scattered far apart and the old basic problems are still there, now enhanced by fast mechanized equipment, high production costs, and prices that have skyrocketed in the market place. It's inspired modern rustlers to butcher beef critters on the spot, some making a good business out of it. The ranchers suffer the losses, often running into thousands of dollars, perhaps their profit for the year. This big land of ours, too, is difficult to patrol because there's so much of it. Talk about Nature; we've got her running out our ears.

The standard procedure is for the thief, or thieves, to drive along an isolated road and shoot a beef. If it's a small animal, he loads it into his truck or camper to be butchered later. Or more likely, only the hind quarters are taken, so that he can beat it fast before someone surprises him. With a great invasion of the eastern Oregon-Washington country by campers and sportsmen, many of these folk know the back country roads and trails almost as well as we do. They can sneak a supply of meat with ease from the herds on summer range.

Calves are stolen by motorcycle riders who run down the calf, hogtie it, and stuff it into a sack lashed to their cycle. These cycles and the four-wheel drive vehicles can get around the rough country nearly as well as you can on horseback. Then, there are the bigtime rustlers who are in it for the bucks, working with huge refrigerated trucks equipped with hoists. They methodically butcher several beefs at a time, then market them in the big cities through their own special outlets.

The losses are far from small. One year we turned twenty-five replacement heifers loose on Juniper Mountain. When we gathered in the fall, they were all gone — no trace, never to be seen again. In one case, two thieves stole nineteen head and were about to slaughter them when caught. They admitted other butcherings of about seven head for a Seattle restaurant. And a California rancher reported a loss of thirty thousand dollars in one year and seventeen hundred head gone from his herd and those of his neighbors. The ranchers got together, hired a private detective to patrol some four thousand miles of back roads at night, and cut the losses to nearly zero within a year.

Trouble is, the courts looked upon rustling as a petty crime, not to be taken too seriously. In the late 1960s and early '70s, it became next to impossible to convict a cattle thief at all; and if he was, he got off with a light sentence and might just go right back to work. In the old days, the tough vigilantes who roamed our territory would have given those boys a fair trial, then hung 'em. Rough justice, they called it. The law of the Old West didn't tolerate horse and cattle thieves. You could steal another man's woman and maybe get away with it, but not his horse or his stock. No so today. It's a standing comment that a man can get more time for stealing a two-bit ring from a dime store than for stealing livestock. One rustler I know about had enough larceny charges against him to tally seventeen years in the State Pen, yet within three months he was out on parole and back in business with a considerable nest egg from his past activities. In another case, two rustlers drew thirty-day jail sentences and three-year probation terms.

Brand inspection laws are weak, for another thing, and there is a lack of uniformity and cooperation among the states. In this remote section, three states meet and two others aren't far away. Very few thefts are detected by brand inspectors anymore, simply because anyone stealing beef isn't likely to have it inspected. But in the winter-spring of 1970, the cattlemen east of the Cascade Mountains were beginning to strike back. They met as they'd done in the old days (although not in secret) to tighten up things with the law enforcement authorities for more road inspections of trucks hauling livestock and closer surveillance of hunters, anglers, and campers leaving ranges where livestock was grazing. They sought the help of state police, county sheriffs, brand inspectors, game wardens, and even loggers. Groups of ranchers were deputized. Aerial surveillance, even at night, was used to reduce the losses. The planes had radio contact with ground forces to report anything that looked suspicious, for the situation of thievery, fires, and vandalism had gotten out of hand.

That's why I say, from personal experience, that cattle rustling is as bad as in the old days. In many ways it's "the second time around" for the ranchers. Jordan Valley has seen wild times before, from Indian wars to gold strikes, stagecoach holdups and gun fights over mining rights. I guess we're still the Old West by big city standards, but from what I hear and read, I hope it stays that way. . . .

Jordan Valley is tucked away in what might be called the far corner of Oregon, much as the Pacific Northwest is often referred to as the far corner of the United States. I like to call it the Forgotten Corner, for we're three hundred fifty miles from the Willamette Valley where the heavy population is, and the rest of the state is often inclined to forget that we even exist. This is sometimes called the I-O-N Country, where Idaho, Oregon, and Nevada come together. We're about as far from "town" as you can get anymore in this country, outside Alaska: right on the border of Idaho, one hundred miles from Boise, five hundred miles from San Francisco, four hundred miles from Portland, four hundred miles from Salt Lake, and even a good distance from the "centers" of our own locality. The southern part of Malheur County is well removed from the sphere of influence around Vale, the county seat. Vale, Ontario, and the surrounding towns have most of the 23,169 people in the county. Malheur is the second largest county in Oregon (the biggest is Harney) and sprawls for 9,871 square miles along the Idaho and Nevada borders. That's outdoors in a grand style, and it's seen a lot of hard riding action, although

Photo by Bureau of Land Management
This vast expanse of open country of southeastern Oregon was once the scene of much turbulence in the search for gold and silver, Indian wars, the rush to the Idaho mines, and the coming of the early cattle kings.

like most else, this too has been generally overlooked.

The valley region where we have our ranch is the hub for this vast area of sage, tall rye grass, broken buttes, and surprising canyons that became the hideouts for outlaws and renegades in times not so long ago. It's bordered on the north by Cow Creek, the Mahogany and Spring Mountains, and the Owyhee breaks. Some of the scenery can hold its own for awesomeness with most any place in the world. On the south and west flows the meandering and mysterious Owyhee River, and to the east are the great Owyhee Mountains, primitive and foreboding for greenhorns who don't know the country.

Visitors find it passing strange that we have a touch of Hawaii in this far-removed region. The river and the mountains take their name from those distant Pacific islands. In 1818 the North West Fur Company sent an expedition under the leadership of Donald McKenzie to see what he could do about increasing the Columbia's inland trade. Upon reaching the head of what appeared to be a large river, McKenzie sent three Hawaiian Islanders down it to investigate the area for beaver and the possibilities of navigation. The Hawaiians never returned and were presumed lost or killed by Indians, probably the latter. The river was called the "Sandwich Island River" and from this came the name "Owyhee," as those natives referred to their homeland. It is one of those strange twists of history that becomes unbelievable to succeeding generations.

The Malheur River and the county also get their name from early explorations and encounters with the Indians who held this land for many centuries. Malheur means "bad time" and that was what a party of trappers from old Fort Boise found when they came to this valley. The Red Men killed several of them and took their furs. The survivors named the river in remembrance of the encounter, and the county took its name from the river. It was a part of Baker County, Oregon, until February, 1887, when Governor Sylvester Pennoyer signed the bill which divided the massive eastern Oregon county, thus creating Malheur.

The area where the town of Jordan Valley, once called Baxterville, has long been the hub, is about sixty miles long, one hundred miles square, and embraces some six million acres of land. Its elevation is forty-two hundred feet, with a fall of about one hundred feet from north to south. The town is at about the center, one and a half miles from the Idaho line and one hundred and one miles from Nevada over U.S. Highway 95, which snakes across the valley and on into Idaho. The highway crosses into Nevada at McDermitt, near Fort McDermitt Indian reservation.

Succor Creek wends its way through the rugged canyon it has cut through the centuries in the rock of the Owyhee Mountains of southeastern Oregon. Spectacular scenes such as this are repeated many times through the canyon, which is reached by paved and gravelled road from Ontario or Jordan Valley.

Photo by Bureau of Land Management
Owyhee Canyon — looking downstream.

In that border town there is a famous saloon and eating place straddling the line. You can gamble and play the slot machines on the Nevada side of the building, but not on the Oregon side; and years ago, before Oregon adopted liquor-by-the-drink, you could quench your thirst only on the Nevada side too. A line painted on the floor designates which part of the place is Oregon and which Nevada.

The incorporated town of Jordan Valley, with about two hundred people, consists of a couple of grocery stores, a souvenir gift shop, two cafes, a park, two motels, a campground and a few miscellaneous buildings, some of them landmarks of local history centering around the Basques. I guess we're known more for our Basque population than anything else. The town stands on the banks of Jordan Creek, named for Michael M. Jordan who discovered gold in the creekbed in May, 1863, and then got himself killed the following year by Indians near Three Forks, where the main Owyhee River is formed.

It is all beautiful, craggy country: a world of broken lava, sagebrush and tumbleweed, sudden chasms, and the green oases of the ranches and farms. Less than a thousand people live on those ranches, and thousands of head of cattle, sheep and horses. As a rule, the winters aren't cold, spring arrives early, and the summers aren't too everlastingly hot. The earth is rich alluvial soil; the farms and ranches grow healthy fields of grain, wild hay, and alfalfa. The range lands are rich with native and foreign grasses, which are being increased by a management program of the ranchers and the Bureau of Land Management.

There's a wealth of variety in this valley and its surrounding mountains, pinnacles, rolling hills, and deep ravines. If old-time miners and pioneers were to come back now, they'd find it much the same as when they left. I like best seeing it from the saddle, riding slowly through the sagebrush, picking my way

Oregon State Highway Department Photo

The town of Jordan Valley lies just a mile from the Idaho border and has known much Western history. This view, from Pharmacy Butte, looks toward Idaho, with the Owyhee range and South Mountain in the right background.

into the canyons with walls hundreds of feet tall, and climbing to the high places, pretending to be looking for a stray, but truly just enjoying the country and letting my mind wander. Or riding out with my wife, Judi, looking for Indian signs and relics of the past. Sometimes I sketch these places, just for kicks, trying to show the way things were. One thing I enjoy about buckerooing out on the range is finding traces of the Indians. Not many buckeroos even notice such things, but they leap out at me. I guess it's because the Hanley family lived so much of this Oregon history and I've heard about it all my life, so that the points of interest take on special meaning.

When two cowboys squat on the ground and sketch a map of landmarks to tell where they're going, they call it "horseback geography." When I gaze at the high bluffs and broken formations done in fiery red, yellow and orange strata, I call it "horseback geology." Scientific terminology never meant much to me in geology classes, for I enjoy the spectacles of this earth without having my mind cluttered by technical jargon to ruin it for me. One of the most rewarding experiences of this desert country is to ride into a river canyon and look up at the layers of lava forming the canyon walls. Try to think of the great changes, the mighty upheavals, represented by the layers. To me, that's geology!

The highest peak in our region is War Eagle Mountain, which towers in the east over eight thousand feet above all the surrounding country. From the top, on a clear day and with the help of a telescope, you can see half the world: the great Teton Range in Wyoming, the southwest corner of Montana and Yellowstone Park, the Wasatch Range in Utah, a peak or two in Washington, and parts of Nevada, California, and Oregon, where the wonderful Steens Mountain rises from the desert floor to 9,670 feet above sea level. The view from War Eagle is the same one that excited

Oregon State Highway Commission Photo

High formations of eastern Oregon's Owyhee canyon dwarfs man and horse at their base. The formations, carved by water and the wind, form a spectacular display of the works of nature.

early explorers. And while much of our country has been altered and polluted at a reckless pace, our valley remains unblemished.

Hudson's Bay trappers searched for beaver in streams within the shadow of this great mountain. When the wagon trains were traveling the Oregon Trail in the 1840s, they passed along the banks of the Snake River which is close at hand. War Eagle Mountain seems almost alive, having witnessed all that went on in the deserts and canyons below. I guess if it could talk, I wouldn't be writing this book.

There were big happenings, too, right on its very

slopes. Prospectors struck gold on its western drainage in May, 1863, and before long booming mining camps sprung up on each new strike, among them the queen — Silver City, Idaho, scene of the second richest silver strike in the West. The boom days ended finally, but not before many skirmishes with the Red Man and the arrival of cattle and sheep herds, driven onto the ranges surrounding War Eagle. The herds provided meat for the hungry miners, but when the mines closed down, the herds remained, for the grassland was good, and thus furnished a new industry for the region. There is little activity on War Eagle now; it seems at times lonely and desolate, but it still holds mineral secrets awaiting the miner's touch.

South of War Eagle stands South Mountain with its clear cold streams, fir and quaking aspen, and a haunting beauty of another kind. In spring the grass is high and lush, the choke cherry trees are in bloom, and the slopes bright with larkspur, penstemon and wild peonies. South Mountain has its own story to tell. It once supported its own large mining camp and a steam-powered sawmill spewing lumber for all the camps until the gold and silver petered out. Then the houses and other buildings were torn down, and the lumber hauled for rebuilding in the valley below. The only remaining sign today of South Mountain City, called "Bullion City," is a slag pile from the smelter. But two thousand miners worked there over a century ago in that large gold and silver mine. The ore was hauled out by ox-drawn wagons, slowly making their way to Winnemucca, Nevada, from which it was shipped to San Francisco and by ocean vessel to Wales for final processing. On the mountain's north slope there was a running battle between the Silver City Volunteers and the Bannock Indians of Chief Buffalo Horn. The famous chief and two volunteers were killed.

Folks still comb the Owyhees, even though the mining gave way to livestock years ago. They dream of a big strike, finding the end of the rainbow. Old log cabins and rock shelters are scattered all over this country. Each year holders do assessment work on their claims and a few dig in the tunnels or shore them up. They're marking time, waiting hopefully for the day when the price on gold, silver, or other minerals will climb, then they hope to open up again. In 1968, the U.S. Bureau of Mines listed Owyhee County, Idaho, as producing only one ounce of gold. The value of that and other minerals totaled seventy-three dollars. It's likely there was more which went unrecorded, but it wasn't much. That's quite a comedown for what was once one of the richest places in the nation.

Juniper Mountain, also to the south, never excited the miners much because of its volcanic origin, while the rest of the Owyhee Range is mainly mineral-producing granite. Juniper Mountain is separated from the main range by the deep canyon of the North Fork of the Owyhee River, with its dramatic cathedral-like walls that hold the drama of centuries. On the south, Juniper is cut off from the surrounding desert by the

Photo by Bureau of Land Management

The vast expanse of southeastern Oregon's meandering Owyhee River is primitive and foreboding, with broken buttes and surprising canyons which were hideouts for outlaws and renegades not so long ago. This view is of Birch Creek in the Owyhee Canyon.

Middle or East Fork, and these two forks join a third stream, South Fork, to form the main Owyhee River which dumps into the Snake. The rivers, the canyons, and the rugged mountain became a natural stronghold for the Indians, a stout fortress that the white volunteers and the Army never conquered. At Three Forks, the troopers lost a cannon while rafting it across the river swollen by the spring runoff. The rushing water broke up the raft and the cannon sank to the bottom.

Three Forks became a strategic crossing on the route to and from the Idaho mines, Nevada and California. The Army built a fort there to protect the ford, but the Indians soon drove the troops away and travelers had to fend for themselves. Approximately thirty miles below Three Forks, the river travels through open country, then again enters a narrow canyon. Most of the California-Nevada traffic came this way through the place called Rome. Its name seems just as strange and far-removed as Owyhee, but at least I'll have to give credit to those pioneers for originality. West of the Cascades I've noticed many Bear and Beaver creeks, some within a few miles of each other. But early travelers gave Rome its peculiar name because the white chalk bluffs reminded them of the pillars of that ancient city. Nearby is the famous Owyhee Crossing, the busy gateway to the treasure mountains and the scene of much early-day action, being in danger from constant Indian attack. One of the worst incidents happened six miles away where half a hundred defenseless Chinese laborers bound for the Idaho mines were killed by marauding Indians.

Jordan Creek dumps into the Owyhee a mile above the old crossing, end of the trail for the stream which has its headwaters above the base of War Eagle Mountain. Following the creek east toward the Owyhee Range, you retrace the tracks of the miners headed for the camps. The wheels of the heavy wagons that hauled in the supplies and the ore out carved a clear

Photo by Bureau of Land Management

These strange white bluffs, known as the "Rome Coliseum," stand near the Owyhee Crossing and were a landmark to pioneers traveling the route, reminding them of the structures of ancient Rome.

route which is still visible and easy to follow, in the lava.

Cow Creek joins Jordan Creek at the site of the old Ruby Ranch, which played an important roll in the valley's past. Hill Beachy, father of the Northwest Vigilantes, raised a barn here (which still stands) for his short-lived Idaho Stage Company, its stages bound for California over the old Chico-Ruby City road which Beachy built. The ranch house and corrals were of native lava which also provided staunch fortifications against Indian attacks. The Indians hit the ranch many times, and travelers who stopped there often spent a sleepless night keeping the warriors back in the shadows. The story that Indians won't attack at night is pure Hollywood fabrication, for they sure did at the Ruby Ranch.

One of the most famous early travelers coming to the Ruby Ranch arrived in May, 1866, on his way to

The grave of Jean Baptiste Charbonneau, colorful son of Sacajawea who came west for the first time as a baby with Lewis and Clark, is located near the old Ruby Ranch, early stagecoach station and scene of many an Indian battle.

the Montana gold fields of Alder Gulch. He became ill, contracted pneumonia and died, to be buried at this place. His name was Jean Baptiste Charbonneau, the son of Sacajawea, born during the westward trek of the Lewis and Clark Expedition, and first arriving on the Pacific shore in 1805 as a babe in arms. Yet here he reached the end of the trail, in this little-known corner of the West. The grave can be found, for I clearly marked it a few years ago as an historical point of interest that should be preserved. There is now, in 1972, a National Historic Landmark marking the spot.

Cow Lakes, upstream from the mouth of Cow Creek, are formed by a lava flow which dammed the waterway. These shallow lakes are used today for irrigating the surrounding lands. Planted trout were in the lakes and anglers had good success, but then came a spell of extra-warm years which killed off the fish. Salmon also used to climb the rapids between

the twin lakes, as they did other tributaries to the
Owyhee, but like so many places, dams downstream
put an end to them. Matter of fact, one of the last
bear shot in the Jordan Valley area was killed long
ago, in 1870, as it fished for salmon in the Cow Lakes
rapids. Now the hottest fishing place in the vicinity
is Antelope Reservoir south of the community of
Danner, originally called "Ruby" for the Ruby Ranch.

Near Cow Lakes are the Jordan Craters, where tunnels and cones form what is one of the most recent lava
flows on the continent. It has so far been little changed
by erosion and vegetation growth, for geologists believe the craters and lava fields to be only about five
hundred years old. Indian tales seem to substantiate
this, describing to early arriving whites a not-too-
distant time when fire and smoke poured from the
ground. The craters and lava flow cover some sixty

Oregon State Highway Photo

A modern ranch near Cow Lakes where Indian tribes once roamed.

Oregon State Highway Photo

Some sixty square miles of the Jordan Craters are pock-marked with cones, tunnels, and blow-holes in what is believed one of the most recent lava flows on the continent. This is one of the craters. Jordan Craters are rated as having a geological value equal to Craters of the Moon in Idaho.

Oregon State Highway Photo

The little-known Jordan Craters are one of the natural features of the Owyhee Country, the site of great lava beds which are evidence of violent eruptions many centuries ago.

square miles pock-marked with tubes and tunnels,
hard charcoal-like mud, blow holes, cones, pinnacles,
towers, monoliths, and monuments which seemingly
stretch forever and give off muted colors at sundown.
The area is said to have a geological value equal to
Craters of the Moon in Idaho.

Upstream from the lakes, where U. S. Highway
95 crosses Cow Creek, is the community of Sheaville,
named for Con Shea who introduced cattle into the
Owyhees in 1867. The animals were Texas longhorns
and this place became the base for his unique operation for twenty years. A killer winter broke Con Shea.
His ranch was split up and what was his land now
supports several ranches, but at least his name is preserved in memory of this first cattleman, at this way-
point to the mines.

West of the highway, about one mile on the south
bank of Cow Creek, is the site of old Camp Lyon,
one of the most active military posts of eastern Oregon
and headquarters for the First Oregon Cavalry during
the troubled 1860s. When the Army first moved in,
troopers found themselves cutting logs at the head

Ellis Lucia Photo

The author holding an old Hudson's Bay trade gun from the time of the early white
explorers in the Owyhees. It is a flintlock and was found in the vicinity of Jordan
Valley.

of Cow Creek shoulder to shoulder with the gold-seekers they were sent to protect, who were felling trees for cabins and mine shoring. There's nothing left of Camp Lyon now, except a ryegrass knoll and a lot of memories.

From here, at the head of Cow Creek, it's east across the high ridges and back to the foot of War Eagle Mountain. This is my country, big, rugged, sprawling, wild and free, with signs of the Old West all around you. And you appreciate it best when you see it from the back of a horse. . . .

Oregon State Highway Department Photo

The Owyhee river of eastern Oregon cuts its way through high cliff formations to form one of the most rugged and colorful river canyons in the Northwest. The floor of the canyon, offering little free access to people, is many miles long, following the carving whims of the river.

CROSSROADS OF THE OWYHEES

GAZING AT THE TOWERING rugged sandstone bluffs and the faded writings of Indians and white men on the rocks, I have often wondered what the natives really thought when they looked down upon the first small bands of strangers struggling through the sagebrush and across the rocky cuts and washes. Or for that matter, when they noticed the first strange "canoes with wings" that reached the shores of the Pacific Northwest. Perhaps very early, the wisest of their chiefs realized that their days were numbered, that these strangers with the pale skin would eventually drive them from their lands. Whatever their feelings, it was soon made clear that the white men meant to destroy the Indians and their free way of life.

This particular section of the West has for centuries been a busy crossroads. Fragmentary history, legends and pictographic writings go back many thousands of years, probably much farther than we realize. In a cave over near Fort Rock, for instance, Indian sandals were uncovered and carbon-dated back nearly 10,000 years. Writings and artifacts uncovered in scattered parts of this land originated many centuries ago. For generations the Indian tribes — Paiutes, Snakes, Shoshone, Bannocks — all roamed in complete freedom across these plains and mountains. The signs of their trails, fords and campgrounds are found everywhere throughout this region.

Bands of fur trappers were poking about the inland Oregon Country as early as 1818, among them parties of Donald McKenzie and Peter Skene Ogden of the North West Company. Fifteen years after McKenzie's expedition, Captain Benjamin Bonneville and his men passed this way during their strange meanderings of the inland West. But these were small groups of whites; the Shoshone, Bannock and Paiute tribes continued their nomadic ways without outside interference. Except for an occasional trapper or two, the Owyhee Country remained much as it was when McKenzie named it.

After the discovery of gold in California, all the West got the fever. During the late 1850s and early 1860s prospectors fanned in every direction. They had a hunch there must be treasure somewhere in this territory. Parties set out from California and the Willamette Valley to seek new strikes, for the older gold fields had been taken up or depleted. The Mother Lode had been largely prospected and the rich placer areas claimed. There were good strikes in southwestern Oregon at what became Jacksonville, drawing the California miners north. Thoughts turned, too, to the legendary "Blue Bucket Diggings," the "lost mine" of the Stephen Meek wagon train which supposedly existed somewhere near the Oregon Trail east of the Blue Mountains, maybe not too far from War Eagle Mountain.

In 1862, a party of fifty men from the Willamette

Valley made an extensive search for the Blue Bucket mine along the Snake River to a point above Catherine Creek in Owyhee Country. Eight of the men became disillusioned and turned back. At the mouth of the Owyhee, they ran into another party and told of their disappointment. The eastbound band, shrugging off this tale of woe, decided to try their luck in another direction. They crossed the mouth of the Boise River and tracked far into the hills to discover the rich Boise diggings around Idaho City, which became one of the wildest camps in the Pacific Northwest.

The word spread like a prairie fire. By the following spring, the Boise Basin was swarming with determined miners. Others contended it was too crowded, that they needed more elbow room, and if there was gold here, it stood likely to be elsewhere, too. In nearby Placerville a party of twenty-nine was organized by one Michael Jordan to look for the Blue Bucket. Early on the morning of May 18, 1863, the party, with about sixty horses and mules, came upon a small stream. They decided to establish a camp, rest, and prospect for awhile. Before unpacking his mule, one man panned a little gravel and obtained about a hundred colors. He let out a whoop, and within ten minutes, every man was frantically digging, panning, and getting colors. Twelve days after the strike, laws for the district were established. The creek and district were named for the two leaders, Mike Jordan and W. T. Carson. But before spreading news of the find, members of the party staked claims to all the land the law would allow.

Some twenty-five hundred miners pulled out of the Boise Basin for the Owyhee fields. Others were flooding in from the south and the west. That summer a new town was born, called Booneville for another of the original party, perhaps a descendant of the famed wilderness scout. Booneville was poorly located at the mouth of the canyon where there was little space for growth. Later, it was renamed for Colonel W. H. Dewey, who held extensive mining interests in the area. He was a native of New York who came to the Owyhee that first year and long rode tall in the territory.

Because of Booneville's drawbacks for expansion, a second town sprang to life farther up the creek, where there was more space and good clear spring water. Ruby City became the first Owyhee County Seat and also spawned the area's first newspaper, *The Owyhee Avalanche* which remained there a year. Again, there wasn't enough room for growth in what was rapidly developing into one of the richest gold and silver mining areas on the continent.

Dewey, Idaho, was one of the string of mining towns in the Owyhees leading to Silver City. It was originally called Booneville and later renamed for Colonel W. H. Dewey, who had extensive mining holdings there. Mine is at the left and the huge hotel, Colonel Dewey's pride, may be seen at the right.

The first residents of Ruby City tied up all the property, placing exorbitant prices on the few development sites. During that initial summer, about two hundred fifty men were living there, and a like number at Booneville, while another five hundred were scattered over the Carson mining district. When Colonel Dewey could get nowhere with the greedy "hog-'em" real estate crowd, he decided to join with others to build a third town. In the spring of 1864, Silver City was born, destined to become within a short time one of the most flamboyant and harum-scarum mining camps of the Pacific Northwest. It was located near the eight thousand foot level, on the slopes of War Eagle at the head of Jordan Creek, and almost atop the fortune the mountain held. Silver City was also sheltered from the violent winds that sometimes swept the mining region and all-in-all, became immediately popular. Dewey encouraged growth by constructing the first wagon road that spring from Silver to Ruby and also starting work on the Reynolds Creek road. Travel was heavy up and down the canyon, and when further progress came to the Silver-Ruby road, the *Avalanche* gleefully noted the improvement:

"The Half Way is in full blast, and the weary traveler between Ruby and Silver will be glad to know that the carrying of a flask is no longer an necessity."

Competition between the two towns was bitter since they were only a half mile apart, but Silver City held the stronger poker hand by far, being close to several spectacular mines. Eventually most of Ruby moved up to the new location, including the *Avalanche*. There were riches to be had. Among the first strikes were the lush Oro Fino assaying at seven thousand dollars a ton in silver and eight thousand dollars a ton in gold, and the Morning Star. The Carson district became famous for its lodes, with some two hundred fifty mines in the surrounding hills. Deposits were of the fissure type, divided into two veins, the

War Eagle and the Florida Mountain. And the strikes weren't confined to the Silver City diggings alone; South Mountain soon supported Bullion, with its mounting population of around twenty-five hundred.

The ore was beyond belief. Silver's Poorman Mine became legendary, assaying from four thousand to five thousand dollars a ton after the initial strike was made in 1865. At about a five hundred foot depth, the famous Poorman Nugget was uncovered, weighing five hundred pounds. Its solid mass of ruby and silver crystals was so spectacular that the giant nugget created a sensation at the 1866 Paris Exposition, and was awarded a gold medal. Ore from these diggings was so very rich that it justified shipment clear to Wales for special processing, and British companies began development work in the Carson district.

Silver City grew and prospered, with a population of around five thousand at its peak. In 1866, the town managed to take the Owyhee County Seat away from Ruby, holding onto it until 1934, when the center moved to Murphy. Although ranking second only to Virginia City, Nevada, as a silver producing area, the town never rivaled the epitome of luxurious nineteenth century grandeur known on the Comstock. Its inhabitants weren't the type, but even so, the queen of the Northwest camps had its own shining moments of crystal and brocade.

There were more saloons than drygoods stores, two newspapers, two major hotels, and eighteen pleasure palaces. Theatrical troupes and entertainers placed the camp on their regular circuits, much to the prospectors' delight, for lonely Western miners loved the theater. Whenever a troupe was due, the barber shop which boasted baths as a "specialty," with a photograph of the bathtub appearing in its advertisements, had a sudden upsurge in business. The saloons, always busy, held a certain elegance with their handsome, highly polished back bars. So did the Idaho and War Eagle

Life in Dewey and other mining towns of the Owyhees wasn't all rough and tumble. There was style of the Victorian age, even on this frontier. Here, a Mr. Irwin proudly shows off his fine trotter before the ornate Dewey Hotel.

hotels. The two hotels were haphazardly put together, the Idaho varying from one to three stories in its different sections and the War Eagle helter-skelter, having been started from the small cabin of an early settler. The Idaho, which still stands, was the more popular, especially after word got around that the War Eagle was haunted by the ghost of a young girl who died there.

Idaho's banking system was pioneered in Silver City and in Idaho City, through the efforts of Christopher Moore's C. W. Moore & Co., which grew into the Boise County Bank. The camp became a small city — the Masonic Temple straddling Jordan Creek, a courthouse, joss temple, school, general and hardware stores, assay office, restaurants, and houses and cabins scattered through the hills. The Catholic Church was dedicated to "Our Lady of Tears," appropriate for boom-and-bust, while from a higher level of ground, the Episcopal Church looked down on the turbulent scene of covered wagons, freighters, bawling oxen and cursing teamsters, miners and roustabouts.

Workers of the rival mines staged full-scale wars in and out of the tunnels. Stories spread, too, of diamonds found in these hills, bringing on "the great Owyhee diamond craze." And everyone turned out to view the meteor which soared over the camp in 1867, some folks believing it marked the end of the world. Miners described its size by the most familiar thing around, "as big as a whisky barrel."

The *Avalanche* and the *Tidal Wave* dutifully reported the comings and goings of the district, with personal observations of the editors thrown in for good measure. The *Avalanche* became Idaho's first daily newspaper and also had the first telegraph news wire in the state. The telegraph line was opened in 1874, from Silver City to Winnemucca, and the following year connected with Boise. In 1876, its wire hummed with the startling news of Custer's Last Stand over in Montana.

Silver City survived the collapse of the Bank of California in 1875, but past glories faded as the mines ran out. Some fifty million dollars had been mined in the vicinity. By the Great Depression, only a handful of people lived in the once fabulous camp. Today many of the buildings remain, surviving time and heavy winter snows to be visited by tourists and lovers of the Old West.

The only way to the mines at first was by horse or mule, or hoofing it. Commerce moved on pack animals along the steep, rocky trails. It became a prime necessity to improve the so-called roads. As long as fabulous strikes kept their minds occupied, prospectors thought little about road conditions. But when the camps began taking on the appearance of permanent settlements, merchants and miners alike grew concerned over the inconvenience and high cost of transporting goods into the mountains. Freight on the pack strings cost from sixteen to twenty cents a pound. In turn, the packers had to pay high rates for feed. Hay cut in the bottom lands sold from two hundred to three hundred dollars a ton, delivered at Ruby City. Oats and corn were packed from Umatilla, Oregon, and went for as high as forty cents a pound. Later, a road was opened to Jordan Valley and hay was hauled to Ruby City, bringing one hundred dollars a ton.

There was a mounting demand for better roads and transportation to the mining communities. Land grant acts by the federal government encouraged road building, but also attracted the land-grabbers. There had been frontier federal land acts since 1823, when a bill was passed granting public land to Ohio if the state would build a wagon road. There were two more grants in 1827, then the practice was abandoned until after the Civil War. Between 1863 and 1866, five road companies obtained grants. One of them was the Oregon Central Military Road Company construction of a road, never realized, between Eugene and the eastern border of the state. The act was approved by Congress on July 2, 1864. It pioneered the way for several other Oregon companies. One of them was the Willamette Valley and Cascade Mountain Wagon Road Company which had ambitious plans for routes east of the mountains.

It's not hard to understand why land grant road projects were eagerly received by company organizers, when you discover how generous the government was with land they were to gain for their good works. Alternate sections were promised, with three sections to the mile and "within six miles of said road." The land grabbers misrepresented the amount of work done on the roads and took the land anyway. Of the five wagon grant roads in Oregon, not one of them lived up to terms of the grant, and for the most part, they built no roads at all. (One inspector lost the road thirty miles out of Albany when it was supposed to be completed far beyond that point.) Altogether, they got away with about one million, eight hundred thousand acres in Oregon before being investigated.

When the Willamette-Cascade company came under investigation in the 1860s, it was learned that they picked up thousands of acres through the motions of a half-hearted survey crew. The survey party was

Ellis Lucia Photo

An old safe, broken open, was dumped beside the stage road to the Owyhee. It is one of the many relics of the days when the mining towns were booming.

made up of men on horseback with a wagon, moving at about ten to fifteen miles a day. Passing through timber, they merely blazed the trees and in open country, broke down sagebrush too high for the wagon to pass over. They located fording places of the streams and were supposed to place stakes about a mile apart to mark the route. The survey party traced the "road" for three hundred fifty-eight miles, from Cache Creek east to Washoe, but the investigation disclosed that next to no actual work was done. The party merely followed Indian trails and pioneer routes and "never made any pretense of doing any work or building a road."

"Their surveys followed the Indian trails through the creek bottoms and valleys and over mountains and table lands, from one section to another," said the investigation report. "Trails were passable for Indian ponies but which no wagon or vehicle could pass, and over which none has ever passed from the day of the survey to this. These trails were not graded anywhere but one place near North Crooked River and another on Buck Creek, and this work was of so slight a nature that no trace now exists. The brush was not cut from the sides the trails, the banks of the streams crossed were not cut down or made passable, and often even a horseback traveler would have to hunt up and down the streams for a crossing, and many of these streams were at all times utterly impassable for all kinds of vehicles. When the country through which this section of road passes was settled up, the settlers, for their own convenience and from necessity, were compelled to build roads from one settlement to another, and these roads are the only roads now in that section, and the only roads ever used by the traveler."

At the head of Barren Valley, the so-called construction party came upon a branch of the road to Fort McDermitt, following it for about six miles. After crossing the Malheur River, they picked up an old emigrant trail which dated from 1845, when Stephen Meek guided a wagon train of two hundred families in an attempt to reach the Willamette Valley over what became known as the Meek Cutoff. Following the Malheur River, Meek became lost, causing much suffering among the weary pioneers. The train wandered over the Harney Valley as far south as Wagontire Mountain, then finally found the Deschutes River and followed it to the Columbia, back to the Oregon Trail. Yet that strange trek led to the discovery of gold in the Owyhees, for along the way the emigrants uncovered nuggets in a stream and hammered them out on the wagon tires to use for sinkers in fishing. Probably the most expensive sinkers ever used by an angler. Realizing their find, the men marked the spot — supposedly with a blue bucket — and from this sprang the legend.

So the road company followed the Meek Cutoff from Cottonwood to the Snake River. The outfit received some seventy-six thousand, eight hundred acres of land for the road, but didn't do a lick of work to earn it. Yet despite the crookedness, the land grant acts helped to settle the country, for land could be purchased on easy terms, at one dollar twenty-five cents an acre and even less. When the company was in financial trouble, I've heard of this land going for ten cents an acre. The mere fact that the land passed from public to private ownership offset the poor roads, or no roads at all. This added more land to the tax base for state and county governments. Had the land grants not been offered, the counties in eastern Oregon would find a larger percentage of their total areas owned by the federal government. Ranchers who have trouble with the Bureau of Land Management and the U.S. Forest Service would agree that there should have been more land grants to break the stranglehold Uncle Sam now has on the rancher, making him dependent on public domain for a living.

Photos courtesy Mildretta Adams

John Baxter and his wife. Baxter operated the first post office in Dog Town, later to be called Baxterville and finally Jordan Valley.

Yet not all road builders were land grabbers. In the Owyhee, with the boom of trade spurred by the many mines, there was a growing need for more and better roads. Miners felt that better roads would reduce the inflated prices. Flour was twenty-four dollars a hundred, bacon one dollar a pound, and most other provisions priced accordingly. Freight from Sacramento cost fourteen cents a pound, most of it being packed by burro and mule into the Owyhee.

Under the inflation, pressure was brought upon the Idaho Territorial Legislature to grant franchises for better roads. Several public spirited citizens stepped forward. The first franchise of 1864 was granted to three partners — Mike Jordan, W. H. Dewey and Silas Skinner — for a toll road from the Owyhee mines to Boise, extending over a fifteen year period. That same summer, the three partners also widened the existing trails from Booneville toward the Snake River, across the divide and via Reynolds Creek. They charged three dollars per team and wagon, one dollar for horse and buggy, and twenty-five cents for a saddle horse. But they had to move quickly, for others saw opportunity in the same idea. S. W. Childs, for one, built a toll road from Ruby City to Camp Lyon and the mouth of the Owyhee, connecting there with a road from Boise City to Umatilla, Oregon, on the banks of the Columbia where steamboats would take passengers and freight down to Portland. Only trouble was that steamboat prices, too, were very high.

Skinner wasn't to be outdone, so laid plans for another toll road from Ruby. In 1864, John Baxter settled in a stone cabin on the banks of Jordan Creek. As traffic increased, more shacks sprang up. The place became known as Baxterville, although the teamsters called it "Dog Town" because of all the mongrels darting out to scare the teams. It was a rest stop, watering

Idaho Historical Society

Everything moved in and out of Silver City and the other mining camps of the Owyhees by heavily-loaded freighters, bound for Boise or Jordan Valley. This freight outfit making ready to head out, paused near the post office (middle building on right).

Another jerkline outfit, this one hauling mining equipment to Idaho City. This photo is an excellent illustration of the way in which the horses were trained to step over the chain, pulling to keep the outfit on the road as they negotiate the turn.

hole, and shelter for travelers, and it eventually grew into the town of Jordan Valley.

The miners were overjoyed that Skinner was improving the road. Observed the *Avalanche*:

"By this road, it is just twenty miles to Baxter's Ranch, and the only direct or even passable one to the valley and the Owyhee Crossing on the Nevada and California roads. It is built on the north side of the creek, thus giving it the full benefit of the sun to keep it dry. Mr. Skinner informs us that the company will keep it in good traveling order the entire year."

Dewey, Jordan, and Skinner — their names were becoming familiar ones in the Owyhee country. Colonel Dewey had emerged as a builder in his own right. But this Mike Jordan wasn't the same one who struck gold in the creekbed. The first Mike Jordan had joined some volunteers that busy summer of 1864, pursuing Indians who had made a raid on the Owyhee, and was killed in a skirmish along the Owyhee River. Mike Jordan II was Skinner's partner, but suffered a similar fate at the hands of the Red Men near Gusman Ranch in November, 1867.

As for Mike Jordan III, he later owned a toll road from Devil's Wood Pile on Reynolds Creek. This was in the age when motor vehicles were first invading the Owyhees. Jordan III who lived halfway between didn't know what to charge these new contraptions. When the first one came along, the owner bragged about his car and how much horsepower it had. Mike charged fifty cents a team, so he took it from there and the bill came to eighteen dollars. The fellow never did come back, and I'll bet he didn't do anymore bragging around toll stations.

Silas Skinner became known as the "Owyhee Road Builder." Like thousands, he was drawn in the early 1860s to the West Coast by the prospects of fortune. He signed on as a sailor from his home on the Isle of Man and came around Cape Horn in terrible storms, then up to San Francisco. He jumped ship as did most of the crews (the harbor was cluttered with abandoned vessels) and headed for the Mother Lode. But the excitement had moved inland; news of rich diggings drifted into San Francisco from Nevada and the territories of Idaho and Montana. Silas went to the Comstock, but found it all taken up, nothing left for a newcomer. So he headed for the mines that everyone was talking about in Idaho, accompanied by two other prospectors and a burro.

Arriving at Ruby City, "Sam" Skinner saw again that the country was swarming with would-be millionaires. He decided, however, to try his luck as a prospector. Buying provisions for his venture, he was stunned at the terrific prices. Merchants told Skinner there was nothing they could do about it because of the expense of freighting over the existing trails.

Skinner thought that over as he hunted for gold. Since he wasn't having any luck, he figured maybe he could do better with toll roads. It was the beginning of a celebrated career. But Skinner had his opposition, among them Colonel D. H. Fogus and a man named

Hall, who discovered a good ford at the river's three forks, fifty miles above the Owyhee Crossing, and made plans to develop a major route to Nevada across their ranch. It was estimated this route via Antelope Springs would shorten the distance to Star City, Nevada, by about fifty miles. Its only drawback seemed to be that Three Forks was a favorite crossing for the Indians, including warriors raiding along Jordan Creek. A ferry for the crossing was therefore considered impractical.

"Private enterprise can hardly be expected to build roads, bridges, ferries, develop the country generally, and raise and equip and pay a company of men to protect laborers and travel," commented the *Avalanche* editor. "The route is a most important one and should have a permanent camp of soldiers."

Ellis Lucia Photo

The Jesse Anderson store near the old Chico-Silver City stagecoach route as it appears today. Store is in vicinity of Ruby Ranch.

Passenger travel to the Owyhee mining camps was by such conveyances as this stage, shown here on the road halfway from Murphy to Silver City.

Before toll could be charged, the law required that the mail be hauled over a new route. When a determined stagecoach with mail reached the southside of the Owyhee Rim, the road company promoters were confronted by a one hundred fifty foot drop. The stage was lowered down the bluff with ropes and the mail went through to the Owyhee and the Boise Basin. Company officials thereby could swear that the legal requirement was fulfilled, but didn't volunteer any details. The franchise was issued and the road opened in 1866.

The Indians constantly harassed the Three Forks crossing. A detachment of troops was sent to establish a permanent camp, but the Indians made things too hot for them, firing from the advantage of rim rock and high bluffs. The Blue Coats quit the position in favor of Camp Winthrop on Soldier Creek, some sixteen miles north. By the time the Indian wars had ended, the transcontinental railroad was nearing Winnemucca, Nevada, and the Fogus-Hall road was abandoned in favor of Skinner's safer southern route, through Jordan Valley and the Owyhee crossing at Rome.

This was Sam Skinner's second toll road, opened to wagon traffic May 19, 1866, after he obtained his franchise from the Third Idaho Legislature. But the trip was dangerous because of Indian raiders. Although the road created more free flow between mining camps, mines, and the "outside," it didn't by any means eliminate the inflationary prices, which had originally inspired the former sailor to break these new and better trails. Some prices dropped, but flour reached thirty-two dollars and twenty cents a hundred pounds in 1867, eggs three dollars per dozen, picks eight dollars each, shovels four dollars apiece, and heavy miners' boots twelve dollars a pair.

Travel by commercial conveyance was also expensive, although safer than going it alone. Stagecoaches, wagons and pack trains solicited the miners' business. The Chico and Idaho Stage and Saddle Company carried U.S. Mail and charged fifty dollars a fare from Ruby City to Chico, California. Actually, the bill came to sixty-six dollars, with extra charges for bedroll and "passenger provisions." Forty men had made the first trip in 1865, which took them twenty-seven days. Thanks to the road improvements, this was later cut to thirteen days.

The Indians made a valiant attempt to stop the whites from invading their domain, but the magnetic pull of quick riches was too powerful. The Red Men swooped down on travelers and set way stations ablaze with their war parties. Sometimes renegade whites rode with them. The Oregon Steam Navigation Company kept the Indians stirred up to force passengers and shippers to use their Columbia River steamboats. The Army moved in to protect the roads, the scattered ranches, the crossroad settlements, and the travelers, but the natives out-maneuvered them. It would be years, at the cost of many lives, before the country could be considered absolutely safe for travel.

Mounting traffic meant continual repairs. Sam Skinner and his partners, Mike Jordan and Peter Donnelly, inspected the route each week, for the heavy wagons and teams broke down the grading in many places. The inspections were risky, since the Indians were always around. David Shirk, who hauled vegetables and cord wood from his little wood ranch at the head of Blue Gulch, six miles from Ruby City, went along with Skinner on one inspection. Skinner warned him that they might encounter Indian braves and "asked me if I was timid or would stand fire."

Shirk answered that he'd never been in a real skirmish and wasn't sure how he'd react, but that he was willing to take a chance. He didn't think he'd live up to his name, however, for he admired Sam Skinner as "one of the most remarkable men I have ever met." They struck out on saddle horses, with one pack animal carrying their blankets and provisions. By noon they reached the Sheep Ranch, consisting of a rock house, with roofing of rye grass and dirt, and a small shed used as a stable. The place was vacant; they decided to make it headquarters for that night, left the pack horse, and spent the afternoon clearing rocks from the road toward the river.

Skinner was obviously on the lookout for Indians and took precautions in staking the animals and bedding down. Neither man could sleep. After a long silence, they began to talk, then suddenly heard one of the horses blowing. Skinner leaped from his blankets, followed by Shirk. Sure enough, the Indians were prowling around the place. The men decided to hold their lead, but the raiders knew white men were in the cabin and tried setting fire to the grass roof. Small slots or "port holes" had been cut in the rock walls on all four sides of the cabin. The pair began shooting from first one window, then another, trying to confuse

Site of old Camp Lyon as it appears today. A major U.S. Army post once stood on this site, from which cavalry troops were dispatched to attempt to subdue the Indian tribes.

the attackers as to how many were inside and keep them at a healthy distance. Even so, the warriors got close enough to put a torch to the roof.

Shirk suggested they make a break for the willows along the creek, but Skinner maintained that their chances would be reduced considerably if they did, that it should be a "last resort." The roof fire burned slowly, and they managed to get it out. Then the Indians set fire to dry grass behind the cabin, again threatening the building. However, the men had wisely filled two old camp kettles with additional water and quenched the blaze.

"By keeping up a fire from our rifles and revolvers, we had no further trouble in keeping the Indians at a safe distance," Shirk later wrote. "And from the looks of the ground about the cabin on the following morning, I am satisfied we sent more than one of the savage devils to their happy hunting grounds."

Next morning a squad of soldiers from Camp Lyon arrived at Sheep Ranch. The troopers were on a reconnoitering expedition. By then the Indians had gone, taking the three horses. The troopers tracked the band as far as the river, but never overtook them which didn't surprise Shirk who commented "that was generally the case when there were no citizens with them."

"These small squads," added Shirk, "were usually sent out under command of a sergeant, but as a rule, not having lost any Indians, accomplished little or nothing."

Skinner and Shirk managed to return up the valley to the Bachelor Ranch where they heard of the killing of Mike Jordan, Skinner's partner, and his brother at the old Farnham Ranch (Gusman Ranch). They found the bodies "scalped and horribly mutilated."

"In fact," added Shirk, "they were so cut to pieces that we had to gather them up in a blanket to bury them."

They found the Indian trail and backtracked it a way, becoming firmly convinced that it was the same raiding party that had attacked the Sheep Ranch.

Shortly after this incident, Skinner married an English girl, Anna Callow. The couple and six children

Ellis Lucia Photo

Boarded up and inhabited only by ghosts of the past, this old miner's shack still stands along the route to the mining camps of the Owhyees.

made their home in Owyhee County where Skinner's
stature as a fearless, resourceful, honest business man
grew steadily. A lover of fine horses, he imported some
of the best thoroughbreds seen on the Pacific Coast,
and bred and sold them. Finally, he sold his road,
became seriously ill, and moved to the Napa Valley
in California where he died. His road continued serving the Jordan Valley even after mining declined in
the Owyhees in 1875, in the wake of a general national
depression. Then in 1878, the Owyhee County Com-
missioners purchased the entire Idaho portion of the
route to the old mines.

THE TRIBES STRIKE BACK

AS THE SEARCH for gold became frantic, the Indian tribes of the Owyhee grew more hostile. You couldn't blame them. They suffered deeply when the whites chased them from their traditional hunting grounds, and they retaliated as more miners swarmed through Jordan Valley to the diggings.

The natives rampaged across the prairie and through the hills, and many a miner and dreamer of wealth met his Maker far from home, in this battle-scarred land. At Flint, a tombstone epitaph tells the entire story of the Great Adventure of "going West" by the pioneers:

WILLIAM L. BLACK

BORN SOUTH CAROLINA
MAY 31, 1802
MOVED TO ALABAMA 1817
TO CALIFORNIA 1849
TO IDAHO 1867
64 YRS. 4 MO. 24 DAYS

If you read between the lines, that simple marker tells the story of one man's dreams of a golden future, of following the rainbow toward an elusive pot o' gold, and of his hopefully quick death at the hands of an Indian raiding party. It might have been my great grandfather, for he, too, traveled the golden trails and came near to having his scalp lifted by the natives. If Bill Black had settled in California, or stayed home, he might have lived to a ripe old age. But the pull of the Idaho and Owyhee strikes brought him into what became the most dangerous section of the West. He was ambushed at Flint, en route to Silver City.

Around the campfires, when the cowhands were jawing, the old Western code was often brought up — that "the only good Indian was a dead one." Even today, that attitude persists; there are many folks who have little use for the Red Men who once owned all this country. Yet my sympathies have always lain strongly with the Indians who were defending what was rightfully theirs by long possession. I think they got a raw deal and are still getting the short end of the stick.

Scientists and historians are convinced that thousands of years ago there was a land bridge connecting what is now Alaska and Siberia. Over this bridge probably came the ancestors of the Indian tribes that populated much of America. The Maya, Inca, and Aztec peoples reached high levels of civilization while their Greek, Roman, and Egyptian counterparts half a world away developed the basic civilization of the white man.

To the north, from Mexico to the Arctic Circle, hundreds of tribes lived in a variety of ways. Some were farmers; others were hunters or fished the many streams, rivers, and seacoast inlets. Their settlements and ways of life depended upon the land in which they lived. Indians of the Southwest, for example, erected huge permanent apartments carved in the cliffs or of adobe brick. Farther north on the Western plains, the tribes were nomadic, shifting constantly to follow the great migrating herds of buffalo through all that lush grass. They were free to roam, there were no fences, no boundary lines, and these hunting grounds were their means of survival. Yet the white man steadily, surely, killed them off by direct warfare, surprise attacks, the spreading of smallpox and other white diseases, smashing their winter camps, slaughtering the herds, and finally forcing the Indians onto crude reservations, often far removed from their native homelands.

Through restless pressure the settlers, traders and miners prodded the tribes to war and the Indians realized that time was running out, that they had little choice other than to fight. They were further aggravated by the white man's forked tongue, his failure to honor treaties, and by the corrupt Indian agents who were often cruel and grasping. Chief Big Road of the Sioux summed it up at a tribal council when asked to give his opinion of the white man's conduct.

"Brothers," he declared, "last year when I stood before you, I was thin. Today I am fat — and the reason I am fat is because I have been stuffed full of white man's lies."

Missionaries had tried to impress the good qualities of the whites upon the Indians. From the time when Lewis and Clark came to the Pacific, the Indians tried to help the newcomers. But now Drowning Bear of the Cherokees commented on the Bible: "It seems to be a good book . . . strange that the white people are not better, after having had it so long."

The tribes were pushed into this forgotten corner of the West and were determined to hold it at all cost. But again it was the same story; discovery of the yellow

Smithsonian Institution and Oregon Historical Society scenes like this were familiar, as nomadic Indian tribes wandered through hills and mountains of the Owyhees. Coming of the whites in search for gold and silver disrupted the Indian peace which had been known for centuries and sent the tribes on the rampage.

gold brought the rowdy miners deep into Indian territory.

"The whites will now come," said young Chief Winnemucca after an incident involving the kidnapping of two Indian women and the killing of their captors. "Let us prepare."

The first settlers into the Jordan Valley and the Owyhee were in constant danger from the Snake,

A Bannock war chief, in full regalia, photographed in Idaho.

Paiute and Bannock Indians. The tribes were pent up, hitting wagon trains along the Oregon Trail near the Snake and Burnt Rivers. About the most dangerous section was between Fort Hall and the Grande Ronde Valley, across southern Idaho. Old grave markers are scattered throughout the region, and there are thousands of graves where the markers have disintegrated or disappeared. One old-timer said that in several places near the mouth of Sinker Creek he uncovered rusty pieces of wagon iron, evidence of some long-forgotten tragedy. Near Huntington, a single cross marks the common grave of thirteen emigrants who died in an Indian attack. The phrase "killed by Indians" is often seen on the markers of pioneer cemetaries.

The State of Oregon, with the Indians "on the rampage," organized a force called the "Oregon Volunteers," since the federal troops were busy with the Civil War. The volunteers furnished their own horses, costing one hundred twenty-five dollars to two hundred fifty dollars each, and were given an allowance of forty cents a day, under a Congressional Act of 1861. The system was discontinued three years later, with enlistments of the first six companies expiring that fall, returning the men to civilian life, for by then federal troops were available for the West. The previous spring, the Oregon Volunteers launched their biggest offensive against the Snakes under General Benjamin Alvord, commander of the District of Oregon. Two simultaneous expeditions were ordered. One column started south in April from Fort Dalles under Captain John M. Drake; the second, commanded by Captain George B. Curry, was out of Fort Walla Walla, moving south through the Grande Ronde Valley, then slicing southeast along the emigrant trail.

A little over two weeks later, Curry was still looking for Indians, and going through some of the roughest,

Major W. V. Rinehart

Lt. Col. John M. Drake

Col. George B. Currey

(OHS Collections)

Brig. Gen. Benjamin Alvord, circa 1864. (OHS Collections)

The enlistment poster for the "Oregon Volunteers," along with four of the officers
of the unofficial group. The campaign led by Currey and Drake in the Owyhees
did little to curb the Indian uprisings in the area.

driest country in the West. After days of forced marches without food or water, he reached a certain spot where he wrote:

"I arrived (at this place) on the morning of the 25th about 10 A.M. This creek, which I named Gibbs Creek in honor of his excellency Governor Gibbs, is a small creek which, wandering through traprock canyons a distance of about twelve miles from its headspring to the southwest, falls into the Owyhee about five miles below the mouth of Jordan Creek. As I found good grass and water here I halted, and sent Captain Rinehart with twenty men back to the camp of Captain Barry, at the mouth of Owyhee one hundred miles downstream with orders for Barry to come."

The camp established on May 25 was named Camp Henderson, for an Oregon Congressman. On June 13, 1864, scouts from Camp Henderson were fired upon by Snakes who chased them to within eight miles of the camp. The troopers had at last made contact with the "enemy." The following day there was a lively skirmish and the troopers got the worst of it. Henderson was never used again, for on June 16, Curry struck the camp, marching south toward the Steens Mountain. Yet the site is easily located today where U.S. Highway 95 crosses Crooked Creek southwest of Jordan Valley. The First Volunteers carved their names along with Curry and Rinehart on the red sandstone bluffs. Other travelers later added their names in what has become a permanent record of the past, having withstood more than a century of weathering.

The campaign by the Volunteers did nothing to curb the Indian menace in the Owyhees. If anything, it only irritated the situation. Some people, especially in the East, were beginning to voice concern for the Indian tribes. President Lincoln, in his 1864 message to Congress, urged a more enlightened Indian policy that would provide for the "welfare" of the tribesmen while protecting "the advancing settler." But the Indians weren't ready for welfare then, if ever, and the Eastern mouthings found little acceptance in the West where settlers advocated a "get tough" policy to "clean 'em out." So far as people in the Owyhees were concerned, the Indian was a "murdering savage" and the settlers were embittered against them, even when it involved the "heathen Chinese" who had come to work in the mines.

"Another wholesale Indian slaughter has occurred west of the Owyhee, just above the mouth of Jordan," reported the *Avalanche*. "Fifty Chinese were on their way to Idaho City and all but one were murdered by the brutal Indians. Their bodies were mutilated in the most shocking manner. They had thirteen horses and a full compliment of mining tools — the former were taken, the the latter, the picks, were stuck through the bodies and the heads of the victims. The victims were mostly scalped and cut in a sickening style. It is believed that there were between two hundred and three hundred Indians — part on foot and many on horses. Had white men been there they would probably have shared the same fate. Here's another fine text for the skimmed milk philanthropists to exercise their excusatory powers and justify these ignorant savages who don't know any better, who don't know that murder is wrong, who merely slaughter a few pioneers now and then for fun — which is their right. O, Mush."

Paiute warriors under Chief Egan were blamed for the attack on the Chinese, in addition to many others throughout the territory. Egan was a hard-riding, hard-fighting war chief who set this eastern Oregon country aflame and was generally feared. He had good reason to hate the whites. He was born a

Cayuse and saw his parents killed in a massacre when a boy. He fell into the hands of a Paiute family who raised him and gave him the name *Ehegante* or *Ezichyue-gah* meaning "blanket." When he grew to manhood, Egan chose for his wife the daughter of *Shenkan*, a Paiute chief.

The best news in a long while came to the mining camps with word of General Lee's surrender on April 9, 1865. Maybe the nation would get straightened out and the government could turn attention to the troubles in the West by sending sufficient military strength to crush the Indians once and for all. But a second item in the *Avalanche* marred the good news:

"The Civil War is over, but on April 15, our great President, Abraham Lincoln, was assassinated. The news has been slow to reach us, but has not lessened the sadness felt by near all in this camp 'Ruby City.' On this, the 29th of April 1865, the merchants have closed their business."

A delegation of northern California citizens sent a petition to General George Wright, commander of the Department of the Pacific, requesting military protection for the route from Red Bluff to the Idaho Territory. General Wright responded by ordering construction of a number of posts to protect the roads to the Owyhees. In June, 1865, Second Lieutenant Charles Hobart was ordered from Fort Boise to establish a post on the road leading to the Owyhee mines. The selected site was in the Idaho territory but only a mile from the Oregon line, twenty-four miles from Ruby City on the Humboldt-Chico route.

The new outpost became one of the most important in this busy yet sparsely settled territory. It was garrisoned by companies A, B, and D, the First Oregon Cavalry, and a detachment of Company G, First Oregon Infantry, and was named in honor of Idaho's

Photo Courtesy Pilar M. Elorriaga

Camp Lyon as it was in 1866 when it was the military headquarters for the
Owyhee district.

second Territorial Governor and Superintendent of
Indian Affairs, Caleb Lyon. A year later in June, 1866,
Major General Henry Wager Halleck and his staff were
on an extended inspection tour of Western fortifications in Nevada, Idaho, and Oregon. They called at
Camp Lyon on what was a mighty big day for the
remote outpost, since General Halleck was a man of
much prestige and fame within the military. He was
former General-in-Chief of the Union Army until
replaced by General Grant. At the time of his Camp
Lyon visit, he commanded the Divison of the Pacific.

More camps were set up to supplement Camp Lyon
in what would be a major move against the Red Men.
Camp Alvord was established on the east side of the
Steens Mountain, in the Alvord Valley. Camp C. F.
Smith was secured on White Horse Creek, north of
the Quinn River Mountain; Camp Three Forks at
present-day Three Forks; and Camp Winthrop near
the head of Soldier Creek. Under Colonel John J.
Coppinger, a block house was built at Three Forks
to make it a "summer camp," when travel was heaviest,
and then Coppinger ordered the site at Soldier Creek
turned into a winter camp. Both posts were to guard
the new road from Silver City to Nevada and
California. But the Three Forks post proved impractical, for the Indians were too strong there and kept
things hot by pouring lead and arrows from the bluffs,
so it was abandoned in favor of the post on Soldier
Creek.

There were other outposts, too; a regular network
involved in this mammoth operation to subdue or
annihilate the Idaho-Oregon tribes. These posts were
under the jurisdiction of Fort Harney in the north,
originally called Camp Steele for the general who commanded the Columbia Department in 1866. Located
at the entrance of Rattlesnake Canyon, fourteen miles
east of Burns, the name was changed in 1867 to honor
another Oregon military officer of the previous decade,

William Selby Harney who was in command of the Department of Oregon in 1858/59 but was then recalled for his seizure of San Juan Island from the British in July 1859.

Many campaigns against the natives originated from Camp Lyon. The policy was generally one of search and destroy, if the Indians refused to surrender.

"His Excellency Governor Lyon arrived in Ruby City one week ago last evening," reported the *Avalanche* of November 25, 1865. "The Governor made an address to a crowded assemblage in Magnolia Hall. His Indian policy is just the thing. Says he will either fight or feed them, and for this purpose has requested, with all hopes of success, two regiments of cavalry. He says he does not expect to reduce them to a state of peace, except by offering them the terms of peace or death; and if they will not quietly accept the one, the other will be forced upon them. This is good talk."

After a month of preparation, on July 2, Hobart took out his first expedition of forty-four enlisted men, following a trail of stolen stock from Jordan and Reynolds creeks. The trail led to the Malheur River in a circuitous fashion, for the Indians were trying in every way to throw the troopers off their track. Nearing the Malheur, advance scouts came suddenly upon three Indians gathering berries. The natives fled into the brush, leaving their horses. A search was made, in hopes of finding the trio so that they couldn't get back to the main party. Camp was hurriedly set up beside a small creek dumping into the Malheur, with good bunch grass and a high mountain to the rear. The command then pushed forward, trying to reach the main Indian party before the berry pickers. On the way to the river, three more Red Men on horseback were spotted and the horses captured, but the Indians got away.

All afternoon the troops pursued the Indians, finding several recent camping places, but never catching them. Then the trail became confused, and faded, with the stock appearing to be scattering in many directions. The command was divided into several parties which combed the land for several miles, but there were no further signs of the thieves, so the soldiers returned to the camp.

An hour before daylight the guard reported Indians nearby. The stock was driven in, boots and saddles sounded, and the howitzer drawn into position. The Indians, learning that their presence was known, began blasting the camp with a heavy barrage from all directions, and most effectively from that mountain bench. A canister charge was hurled at them, driving the warriors back, but then some of the mules and horses broke from the men, galloping toward the bench.

Hobart ordered a small party to go after the stock, for the expedition was facing disaster in this first encounter with the natives. The Indians gave them a rough time; retreating warriors shouted to their companions across the way to "cover" them, and Indian rifles again began pouring lead down on the troops who were expecting a frontal attack. One private was wounded, but "a few discharges of spherical case and canister causes them to retreat over the mountain."

The stock was returned to camp and the troopers pushed forward for about five or six miles of running fight with the marauders.

"They managed to escape down a steep rocky canyon, leaving in our hands the body of one Indian, whom they were unable to take off, his arms and ammunition, and nine horses," reported Lieutenant Hobart. "Three other dead Indians were carried off by them, together with their wounded, how many in number I could not say, the country being so cut up with canyon breakoffs from the main ridge, that an Indian could elude pursuit by going into them. The

horses captured were covered with blood, and I think
quite a number of Indians must have been wounded
as the fire of our men was quick and very well
directed."

The Indians, estimated to be around seventy
mounted and many others on foot, scattered into the
canyon. Those afoot kept to the high ridges, out of
range where the terrain would be tough for mounted

Photo by Bureau of Land Management

The rocky bluffs with their hidden caves made natural fortifications for the Red
Men. Often the Indian warriors disappeared without a trace, much to the frustration of U. S. cavalry and volunteers from Silver City.

pursuit, and completely disappeared. But Hobart had his suspicions.

"I think white men must have been among them," he wrote, "for they told us in good English to '*Come on you sons of bitches we can whip you anywhere.*' They had considerable soldier's clothing among them and appeared to have plenty of arms and ammunition. I am of the opinion that some of the Boise Indians were among them as the gun captured is one of those that was stored in the Quartermaster's storehouse at Fort Boise."

The warning was spread that any white man caught with the Indians would be shot.

The first encounter had been a failure, from the Army's point of view, and the command returned to Camp Lyon with at least two wounded men and the loss of two horses and a mule.

Yet enthusiasm over the Army taking on the Indians was short-lived in the mining camps. The miners wondered if they weren't better off with the Volunteers, for the Blue Coats didn't seem to know much about Snakes and Paiutes or how to fight them. It was a helluva big country; prospectors, settlers, traders and small ranchers were scattered all over, and the troopers had difficulty patrolling a rugged land that the Indians knew so well. The braves, finding that they could out-trick the military, became bolder, making more frequent raids on mines and ranches. The Army was almost powerless to halt the hit-and-run depredations.

Sometimes, too, the troops handled things in such a way that it did nothing to improve their image. Silver City miners slapped their thighs and guffawed over one particular incident which went the rounds of the saloons. The *Avalanche* told of a small detachment of troops scouting along the Owyhee. In the dim light of late afternoon, they spotted "what appeared to be a batch of Indian wickiups inhabited by at least one hundred fifty of the noble savages. A portion of the troops remained on lookout, while the balance went to Camp Lyon for reinforcements. Quite a force turned out; after traveling all night they reached the scene of the anticipated hostilities. Forming in order of attack, they made a fierce — if not terrible — charge on a cluster of curiously shaped rocks! How ridiculous this may seem; anyone traveling through this country is subject to deceptions of like character. It is to be regretted that the present instance was not otherwise ordered."

Yet if this appeared hilarious to the Silver City crowd, the experience of an old Indian fighter, G. W. Inskip, was unfunny indeed. He wrote the *Avalanche* from Ruby Ranch on November 28, 1865:

"On the evening of the 18th we were visited by a band of cutthroats (commonly called New York wharf rats) in the shape of U.S.A. Regulars. They stole everything they could get their hands on about the ranch — flour, rice, sugar, coffee, potatoes, liquors, hay to sleep on, and robbed the corral of the fence posts and wood pile for fuel — and when I called on an officer to put out a guard to stop such depredations, he said it was a wet, bad evening, but he would make it all right in the morning. But when morning came, I was told by the same officer that they were going out to fight the Indians, and I should not begrudge the soldiers a little 'straw'."

Inskip was informed that he could trade with the soldiers for anything they had, save their guns, but next morning the officer ordered everything returned, and refused to pay for what the men had stolen. Inskip estimated it would run about one hundred dollars. One of the troopers deliberately fired his gun inside the house, striking a collar beam and rafter, frightening everyone, and spraying splinters over a table where eight men were eating. Inskip asked that the man be

Ellis Lucia Photo

This sagging barn at the Ruby Ranch, also known as Inskip's Station, was built by Hill Beachy, proprietor of the Idaho Stage Company and father of the Northwest Vigilantes. Old rock wall was also erected as corral and part of fortifications.

removed, but the C.O. only told the trooper it was impolite to shoot in the house. It turned into a wild evening, the drunken troopers stealing not only from the innkeeper but from each other, fighting, and breaking up the furniture. Only two soldiers remained sober and tried to control their companions.

"I think these men are more to be dreaded than the native Indians of the country," Inskip concluded. "I also believe that New York sent them out here to get rid of them, and placed them in a weak territory where we need help instead of a den of thieves."

The *Avalanche* editor was angry: "Regular, volunteer or citizen who act as stated deserves the severest punishment. The officer who permits or participates in such conduct should be dismissed from the service in disgrace. These soldiers' acts are in no wise excusable."

Sim Glass, Jordan Valley pioneer, was photographed before the Inskip Station's fortified house in 1911 where he nearly lost his life during an 1866 Indian attack. Dark marks in wall behind Glass were bullet holes.

Fed up to here with the military, the mining crowd decided to take matters into their own hands. They would clean up on the red devils and show the Army. A "war meeting" was called for St. Valentine's Day, 1866, at The Challenge, Bill Sommercamp's saloon at the corner of Washington and Second streets in Silver City. The purpose was to organize a force of volunteers. R. Tregaskis was elected president of the sponsoring organization, after all had had their say and registered their beefs against both Army and the Indians. A committee of five was appointed to collect money and provisions and to send Ed Bohannon to

Boise to tell the Governor what they were doing. Residents of the Boise Basin were invited to join up and "anyone who has lost stock of any kind can have it by going out with this company and capturing it, but not otherwise."

The miners meant business. A corps of twenty-five men was to be selected "to go Indian hunting." A bounty was placed on scalps, to be paid from the treasury, of one hundred dollars each for buck scalps, fifty dollars for "every squaw scalp," and twenty-five dollars for everything "in the shape of an Indian under ten years of age." And, "each scalp shall have the curl of the head and each man shall make oath that the scalp was taken by the company."

The Owyhee Volunteers, soon as they were outfitted, hit the trails to educate the Indians. The motley gang soon discovered it was tougher than it looked; they gained considerable insight into the problem of trying to subdue the natives and also keep the citizenry happy. Moreover, they were ill-equipped, stockmen and ranchers failed to loan them the promised animals, and the Indians were slippery and difficult to find in the rough terrain.

"One of the party that went to Sinker Creek after horses returned last night with one little old mustang," J. A. Lytle wrote the committee. "Word (is) that the balance of the party will be in today with three more. This is all they could get after searching the countryside for nearly a week. They report that the ranchers and stockmen have secreted all their animals that are for service, and that it is impossible to get the required number for your use without resorting to force which they do not feel authorized to do. Now my advice is for you to try to get transportation of some kind at Camp Lyon, and if you fail there, store your supplies and return to town with your arms. We can stand Indian raids as long as the stockmen of this country. . . ."

While the Owyhee Volunteers were having trouble

finding any Indians to fight, the cavalry had them in their sights in abundance. In mid-February thirty-five troopers under a Lieutenant Pepoon rode from L. Hall's ranch in Pleasant Valley tracking warriors who had made off with some stock. They went six miles up the north side of the Jordan River, then crossed, heading south for about five miles where they found a beef slaughtered by the thieves. The trail swung west, the column following it another five miles and then making camp near sundown. At daylight, they hit the trail again, pressing forward for eight miles to find four head of cattle abandoned by the Indians, perhaps as a decoy. Pepoon had the feeling the thieves weren't far off. Using a telescope, he spotted an Indian rear guard directly ahead and had a hunch the main party was close by. The column charged at full gallop. Pepoon was right: the Indians tried to outrun them, but the cavalry closed the gap and the warriors were forced to abandon the stock about two miles from the Owyhee under a steady fire from the Long Knives.

Some Red Men were on horseback, others on foot. Three Indians quit their horses and ran. On the river bank another leaped from his mount, then shot the animal. The renegades crossed the river as Pepoon's command came on fast. Some hid in the willows along the bank, others scattered through the sagebrush, hugging the ground to escape detection. An Indian at close range put a shot through the neck of Trooper Pat Raney's mount, the animal dying in a few minutes. Trooper E. Miller returned the fire, hitting but not killing the warrior who got Miller in the side with an arrow. Then another trooper rode right up to the Indian and severed his bowstring. The wounded native took one look at the troopers surrounding him and fell over dead.

The skirmish ended and the cavalry unit camped that night at the river bank. Some Indians hit the camp about ten o'clock, but it was a brief encounter, the

Nee-keah-peop, member of the Bannock tribe, was photographed by William
H. Jackson at Fort Hall in the 1870s. He is typical of the Indian warriors who
tried in vain to turn the invading whites from their lands.

pickets driving them off. Then just before dawn, some squaws came down to mourn the dead Indian.

That day the expedition scoured the land for about six miles up the Owyhee's middle fork. They found fresh signs of natives in sizable numbers and also came upon large bands of stock. Pepoon realized he didn't have enough men to handle the cattle and fight Indians, so decided to drive the stock back to Hall's ranch, send for a howitzer and reinforcements, and return to the field as quickly as possible, since the Indian band was a large one and on the move.

While Pepoon's force was tracking Indians up the Owyhee, a band of twenty-five hit the Ruby Ranch the night of the 18th. There were six men there, some of them travelers passing through — Frank Osgood, R. B. Gibb, H. B. Carter, J. D. Osborne, a man called Thomas, and proprietor Inskip. The attackers kept up a sporadic fire throughout the night, and no one got any sleep. The men concluded the Indians were well armed, since the lead flew around the house and its small stone fort in a "lively manner."

At one point, the defenders hoped things might taper off, for they believed a leader had been killed, perhaps an old chief. When a heavily loaded shotgun was discharged, the shocked silence that followed lasted seemingly for hours. When the Indians hit again, the distinctive voice shouting the commands was missing. At the end of the long night, the warriors ran off the last horse in the corral, set fire to the hay, and burned a wagon before disappearing.

Osborne struck out after daylight for Camp Lyon. Shortly after he left, five civilians rode up as a rescue party. Later in the day, Captain White and thirty troopers arrived at the Ruby to hear Gibb describe the skirmish as a "lively night."

But the Indians weren't about to quit the area. A couple of nights later, David P. Brown and Moses Mott who were making plans to return in a few weeks to their homes at Humboldt headed for Inskip's place with two yoke of oxen and a wagon. Eight miles from the Ruby Ranch, the Indians attacked and within minutes, the two men were dead, their bodies mutilated. Later, the remains were taken to Lockwood's ranch in Jordan Valley for burial.

The *Avalanche* editorialized:

"Aside from the loss of property, here are two more victims of those bi-ped hyenas. Two more good men have given their lives in pioneer pursuits. Thus are the arguments painfully multiplied in favor of more troops and the utter extermination of the Indian tribes. Can it be that we are much longer to record the humiliating facts that the Government will not protect her pioneer citizens? That there are thousands of soldiers for old established settlements and none for the new? That the men who more than any others are bringing to light the hidden wealth of the nation and living a life approximating torture, are to receive no encouragement? That the savages who delight in stealing and burning his property, taking his life, scalping his lifeless corpse, cutting his heart out, etc., are to be fed and clothed for so doing? As they do nothing else. How long? Ye red rapists, how long?"

Throughout the spring and summer the Owyhee country was aflame. More parties of Chinese were killed, nearly one hundred in two raids, only five escaping and a Chinese woman taken captive. Two Mexicans were also killed in Ives Canyon.

The whites taunted and degraded the Chinese in the camps, but now the *Avalanche* took a noble view:

"Major Marshall is now making a raid after the Chinamen murderers on the west side of the Owyhee. If the Major overtakes them and is not overpowered, may the Lord have mercy on their miserable souls — if they have any — for the troops will have none."

The determined Owyhee Volunteers meanwhile continued chasing Indians, although they seldom found any. Sometimes they saw where they had been, but not even a sign, more times than not. Mounts were in short supply, so the Volunteers often had to walk, dragging along a half dozen pack animals. It was a wonder they weren't wiped out by mounted Indian raiders, but fortunately the warriors didn't find them.

"The boys campaigned it for two weeks," reported the *Avalanche* of one expedition. "They waded streams in icy temperature and had no luxurious time. They labored hard and deserve great credit. That they killed no Indians was not their fault. They are anxious to return if horses can be obtained. A quantity of flour, coffee, ammunition and cooking utensils belonging to the expedition is left at Hall's ranch for future use."

Government Indian policy frustrated and angered the citizens who lived in terror of attack at any moment. The federal government was trying to defeat the Indians, then herd them onto reservations. Governor Lyon proposed to appropriate land claims of several farmers for a reservation "to colonize a few renegade Snakes" in the vicinity of the Warm Springs Ranch. But the Indians, it was found, used the reservations as sanctuaries for continuing their attacks against the settlers. White renegades were working with them in hit-and-run raids on stock, the Indians then pulling back to the safe shelter of the reservation. In one graphic case, a posse tracked thieves with thirty-six horses from Muddy, most of them stolen from the Canyon City stage line, right to the edge of the reservation.

"If the agent in charge of these Indians cannot keep them on the reservation," commented *The Idaho Statesman*, "the only source left for the settlers along the line of the road is to 'take them in' on sight. After a few illustrations of that character, the balance of them will learn to remain where they belong."

Trouble with renegade whites grew more serious and the Army tightened its patrols to cope with the situation. Stories circulated that steamboat interests along the Columbia were provoking the Indian raids to turn the traffic to the river boats. Major L. H. Marshall of the 14th Infantry was assigned to Fort Boise. He saw at once that he was short of men and supplies to cope with conditions in the field, so he reassigned units of the First Oregon Cavalry, pulling them east from south-central Oregon camps like Alvord. He ordered no sympathy be shown for renegade whites in league with the Indians — that they be hanged on the spot. Camp Alvord was abandoned, the companies assigned to patrol Squaw Creek area. Other units were reassigned to Camp Lyon and along White Horse Creek at Camp C. F. Smith.

The cavalry under Pepoon and Captain Walker was eager for another brush with the warriors. Their chance came in May during an expedition to the Owyhee. The area was crawling with the natives, but the troopers couldn't make hard contact in this guerilla-type warfare. The Indians, it appeared, didn't much fear the Army, for at the *Avalanche* reported "the cursed devils still hang around Dr. Inskip's." The cavalry tried again to locate a large war party, this time Major Marshall riding alongside Pepoon. At last they found the warriors, about five hundred strong, at Three Forks and the Indians drove the troops off, costing the Army four men, their artillery tents, and some provisions. The troopers dug in on the west bank, with the tribesmen across the way. At least half the braves had rifles — not an arrow was fired — so the soldiers had to build breastworks from the lava rock with bullets flying around their heads.

Leading the band was a fine-appearing chief, colorfully dressed in red trappings and astride a big white American horse. The command ordered the troopers to "get him" and under a barrage of rifle fire, they

Colonel Coppinger and his staff at Camp Winthrop in 1868. The cannon the Colonel is sitting on is probably the one lost in the Owyhee River at Three Forks and later recovered by the cavalry.

knocked him from the mount. This only stiffened the Indians' resistance, as the women rushed forward to carry off the body, their wailing heard loud and clear across the river, above the noise of the guns.

Now the troopers tried to get the howitzer over the river, but the raft made of driftwood capsized in the rush of water and the gun went to the bottom. One of the men on the raft swam to the side held by the troops, but the other mistakenly reached the enemy bank. The hostiles roped him around the neck and dragged him through the brush. Marshall thought

Oregon State Highway Photo

Nimble-footed warriors scrambled quickly over the rocks of natural "forts" such as this where they could fire down upon pursuing troops and sometimes trap them in box canyons similar to this one. Sage and junipers also provided good cover. In 1866 some fifty volunteers from Silver City under a Captain Jennings were trapped in a box canyon much like this and had to be rescued.

they might retrieve the howitzer, but they couldn't. It was recovered later by a Colonel Coppinger who had his picture taken at Camp Three Forks, sitting on the barrel of a cannon which very likely was the same one.

The Indians were so well armed that Marshall felt it would be "madness and murder" to attempt a crossing, especially after losing the howitzer. He reported only the one man lost that day (as opposed to another report that four were killed) and swore he would keep after the braves all summer and into the winter if necessary.

Once again the miners and settlers grew heatedly

critical of the way the cavalry was handling the Indian menace, and firmly believed they could do better. A new group of the Volunteers was activated early in the summer of 1866, bent on pursuing the Indians into their stronghold on Juniper Mountain. Major Marshall was opposed to the Volunteers entering the field, for they would only be an additional headache for the Army. The foolhardy Volunteers might fall into a trap and the Army would have to go to their rescue. In any case, the troopers would have to protect this ill-equipped force wherever possible. Yet Marshall was powerless to keep them from going after the Indians, for he couldn't impose martial law on the civilians.

The Volunteers appeared to be as foolish and disorganized as Marshall had predicted. Many of the ragtail force viewed the expedition as a holiday, in contrast to the troops who saw it as serious business that could well cost a fellow his life.

Juniper Mountain was rugged and unpredictable terrain, fully known only to the natives. It was indeed an advantageous fortress from where warriors could raid ranches, camps and wagon trains. The Army had avoided any direct assault on the stronghold, keeping to the perimeter, for the mountain seemed impregnable. The Volunteers concluded that the troopers were cowards, that they would show the Army boys by "taking the bull by the horns" and invading the Junipers.

Fifty men under the command of a Captain Jennings rode out from Silver City, to cheers and shouts of "good luck" and "get the red devils." Then they dropped out of sight, as though swallowed by a bed of quicksand. Three weeks went by before a pair of ragged, starving scouts got back with a note from the command asking for help at once. The Volunteers were surrounded by about five hundred warriors on a small volcanic plain, encircled by rimrock and near the

Idaho Historical Society

William J. McConnell led one of the rescue parties trying to reach trapped Volunteers from Silver City during an Indian engagement. McConnell was one of the leaders of the vigilante movement and later became governor of Idaho.

Crutcher crossing of the Owyhee. They were trapped and might all be dead before a rescue party could reach them. The scouts had managed to slip away in the night and made it back to Silver City.

Three rescue parties were hurriedly organized, hoping to reach the Volunteers before disaster. One of the parties was led by a familiar figure, William J. McConnell, stockman from the Payette Valley who commanded the Idaho Vigilantes, cleaned up Idaho City, became second governor of Idaho, and then a U.S. Senator. By late afternoon, they reached the trapped force and found them happily in good condition, although nearly out of food and ammunition. They were well entrenched behind breastworks of lava, had water, and were proudly flying Old Glory from a willow pole.

The Indians had sucked them into a trap in a box canyon as Major Marshall feared, evidence of the greenness of the Volunteers. Just what happened then, from the Indian point of view, was made clear in 1963 when an old Paiute named Pawonto, a medicine man, commonly called Willie Dorsey, took George

Idaho Historical Society

Willie Dorsey, a Paiute Indian called Pawonto, was a boy when his tribe trapped the Jennings Volunteers. In 1963 he took a group over the battleground. Willie Dorsey was about one hundred three years old in 1964, when he and his wife, Nora, one hundred, voted for the first time on the Duck Valley Reservation.

Crookham and others over the battleground. Willie claimed that he was one hundred four and as a boy was with the tribe when they trapped the Jennings Volunteers. Using his twenty-eight year old great grandson as interpreter, Willie showed the group a cave where the Indians stored their supplies and on the rimrock another cave where "we threw a Shoshone brave, with his horse on top of him."

The Indians were camped in the box canyon, a place known long to the Paiutes as *Sihwiyo*, "Willows Growing all in a Row." The stream running through the center was lined with willows. The tribe was resting there, repairing equipment and digging potatoes when the Volunteers — Willie called them soldiers — rode over the hill to the west and came on shooting. The braves, armed with old guns, gave cover as the people withdrew to the rimrock on the east. They stood off the attackers until nightfall, then the tribal council decided to shift to the water in the canyon. They left a plain trail, hoping the whites would follow into an ambush.

The braves positioned themselves so that the enemy couldn't reach the water, and prepared for a siege. In the morning, the Volunteers fell right into the trap and in the fight several were wounded and a number of horses killed. They might have killed all the whites, Willie believed, except that the Indian guns were old and the braves extremely poor shots. The Volunteers withdrew to a lava crater, but soon ran short of water. For five days and nights, the whites tried to run the gauntlet for water, but the Indians had the area under direct attack from their rimrock fortifications which Willie pointed out. The stream was kept constantly under close guard. On the final night, two "scouts" tried desperately to discover a weak spot in the Paiute defense. One of the men was wounded and the other fled to the breastwork in the lava. Had the two messengers failed to reach Silver

City, the Volunteers might have been wiped out. But with arrival of the new force, the tribe merely faded away beyond the rimrock.

It was a close call — too close for comfort — and it took something out of the Volunteers. From then on, they seemed content with limiting their Indian fighting to the confines of Silver City's saloons and letting the Army take over. It was a long campaign, but gradually by the end of 1868 the Indians were subdued, temporarily at least, and their lands opened up for grazing. And as the word spread, it brought in the cattlemen. . . .

LONGHORN TRAIL
FROM TEXAS

THE INDIAN TRIBES were no sooner subdued — it was hoped permanently — than the cattlemen moved onto the lands the Red Men had fought so long and hard to protect. The ranchers saw great potential in the rich grasslands and foliage of the high desert country for the fattening of thousands of beef cattle. There was a bonanza here, not in treasure dug from the ground, but in what the open plains and the hidden valleys would grow.

The herds driven from Texas and California, and a few from western Oregon, across thousands of miles of rugged terrain and through Indian country, ran free throughout the year. Feed was rich and plentiful in summer, but poor in winter. Yet there was little provision made for winter feed by the early cattlemen. The winters were generally mild; the cowmen gambled, and for two decades they drew lucky hands, for the winters were so open that the cattle could forage enough food to get by. There was no need for hay other than what the horses and barnyard stock required.

Then came the summer and winter of 1888/89, known as the "Great Equalizer." One of the worst droughts on record in the West struck that year. Feed was very scarce and waterholes dried up; dead cattle were strewn across the range lands. The cows that survived were weakened and in bad shape by the time the cottonwoods turned to gold. Under the mildest conditions, the winter would be tough on the cattle and many would likely never see the spring. But in mid-November, a severe Arctic storm swept down from Alaska and Canada, spreading across the entire continent from the Far West to the eastern seaboard. Entire herds — the work of lifetimes — were wiped out and cattlemen went bankrupt. By spring, ranchers who had spent twenty years growing in wealth and influence were done. Herds numbering many thousands of head were obliterated and even the big ranches went broke. They say the bigger they are, the harder they fall. There were many huge spreads in eastern Oregon at the time, and they fell mighty hard. Everything had to be built again from scratch, and some ranches never did come back.

Ellis Demitt drove in some of the early cows from western Oregon, but Con Shea, for whom Sheaville is named, and George T. Miller, a cattle buyer, brought the first herds of substantial size clear from Texas. At the time the Lone Star State had the biggest supply of cattle that could be purchased cheaply on the hoof in the West. But there were no railheads until you reached Kansas, and it meant driving them for great distances across the lonely plains and through hostile Indian country.

Photo by Bureau of Land Management

The cattle industry came to the Owyhees in the 1860s when the first herds of longhorns were driven from Texas. Cattle still graze on the region's broad rangelands where Indians once roamed and fought the federal troopers.

Shea came down from Canada to work in the Owyhee mines, first as a blacksmith. When Christopher Moore, a moneyed man in Silver City, approached Shea to trail a herd of longhorns from Texas, he took to the idea. (It's also a common legend that one of the madams of the Silver City houses put up money for Con Shea on his first drive.) Shea was one of a band of men who believed there were fortunes

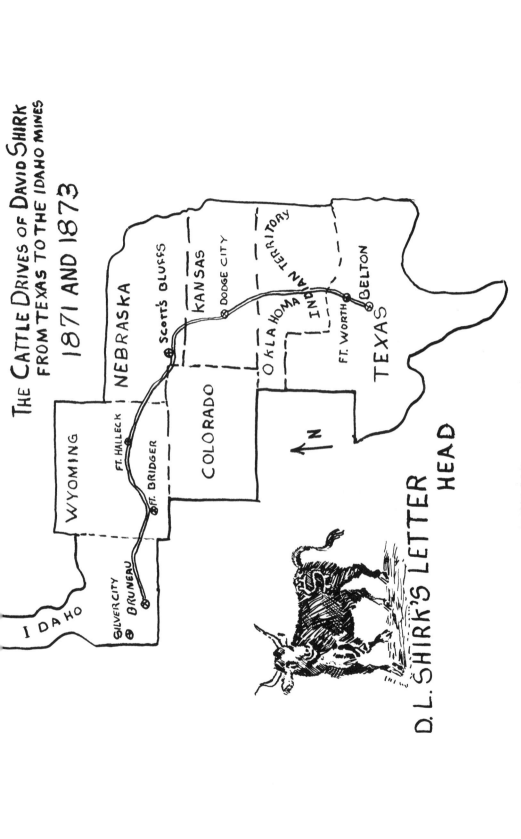

THE CATTLE DRIVES OF DAVID SHIRK
FROM TEXAS TO THE IDAHO MINES
1871 AND 1873

IDAHO
SILVER CITY
BRUNEAU

WYOMING
FT. HALLECK
FT. BRIDGER

NEBRASKA
Scott's Bluffs

COLORADO

KANSAS
DODGE CITY

OKLAHOMA TERRITORY
INDIAN TERRITORY

TEXAS
FT. WORTH
BELTON

N

D. L. SHIRK'S LETTER HEAD

to be made in the grass, and this might have attracted Moore to him. After all, the miners had to eat and would pay high prices for good beef, if you could get it to them.

Taking his brothers, Jerry and Tim, along, Con Shea headed for Texas where he put together a herd of approximately one thousand head and pointed 'em north. It sounds easy, but it wasn't. Since he was the first on the trail, Con had to move blind and blaze the trail himself. When the Sheas neared the Owyhees, they turned their herd loose near Oreana, where they spent the winter of 1867/68.

George T. Miller in the meantime had purchased other cattle from sources in California and western Oregon, and hired Dave Shirk to herd the cows in the white sage along the Snake River. By mid-winter, Shirk said later, the cattle were as fat as any of the corn-fed animals he'd seen back in Illinois. Each week he would drive fifteen to twenty head to Silver City where they were quickly sold to the butchers and soon were in the stomachs of the miners. In the spring, Miller sold the last of the bunch to Phil Kohlhire and decided to hit the trail south to drive out another herd. He asked Shirk to go along, but Kohlhire made him an attractive bargain, so Shirk decided he would stay with the herd rather than tour Texas.

Con Shea was ahead of Miller, already down in Texas negotiating for another herd. This time they profited by the experience of that first trek to the Owyhees so that the venture was better organized. They'd learned that it was impractical to bring out calvie cows, since they slowed down the drive. When a calf was born, its throat was cut so that the mother wasn't held back by her offspring. The men added a few cows of poor quality, purchased dirt-cheap for trading to the Indians whenever the Red Men halted the drive and demanded payment for crossing their lands. It was necessary to bring along only a few of

Con Shea and his wife. He came to the Owyhees to look for treasure and drove the first large herd of one thousand head of Texas longhorns to the Owyhee country.

these trading cattle, for other strays could be picked up along the trail. Mrs. Masonholder, who came with her family, the McIntyres, on the second drive, said she drove cattle on foot all the way from Texas.

Dennis Driscoll, top hand for Shea on the second drive, put up with griping from Jack Stoddard most of the way. At the big bend of the Snake, Shea turned the cattle and horses loose, for the stock had given out. It was impossible to take them any farther for the present. And for the first time, Stoddard agreed

on something — that turning the two thousand head
loose was a good idea. Then the crew walked from
the big bend to Silver City, arriving in September,
1869.

Dave Shirk was again on the receiving end. George
Miller had also come in with a herd and once more
Shirk agreed to work for the cattle buyer. Miller went
at once to Silver City for supplies. In the mining town
Con Shea picked up fresh horses and returned for his
stock. Shea and his crew were driving their cattle,
branded with the ox yoke, up the Snake, while at the
same time Miller and Shirk set out for the Bruneau
Valley. The two herds became mixed at the end of
that long drive from Texas.

"Our first duty," remembered Shirk, "after arriving
at the camp was to separate them, which was no small
undertaking as the cattle were wild longhorns, and
all the work was accomplished on horseback. Mr. Shea
wintered his herd near Silver City, while Mr. Miller
wintered his on the Bruneau and the white sage plains
between that stream and Duck Valley."

When spring arrived, Miller and Shirk drove their
herd to the headwaters of the Owyhee where Shirk
had noticed an ideal summer range, found the previous
year when he somehow got tangled with a herd of
sheep in his latch-up with Phil Kohlhire. It was an
experience he'd never forget. When they sold the last
of the beef in Silver City, Kohlhire broke the news
that he couldn't pay Shirk. He was in debt about two
thousand dollars, for he had been running an opposition meat market and had trusted too many bad customers who didn't pay their bills. However, he had
a band of sheep left.

"Dave," said Kohlhire, "I want you to take charge
of the sheep and sell them and get your money out
of them."

Shirk didn't much like the idea of becoming a
sheepherder, but he was in a trap. If he refused, he'd

never get his wages. He'd had no experience at handling the bleaters, but on June 10 he started from Big
Springs, south of Silver, with twenty-five hundred
head of sheep. He learned about sheep the hard way.
For one thing, they were sure noisy, making quite
a racket. In the mountains, every little stream and
rivulet was swollen by melting snow. It was as difficult
getting the stupid sheep across a tiny six-foot trickle
as a river fifty yards wide. Finally, Shirk broke a big
wether to lead the band, and from then on, things
went better.

"On reaching a bad place, I would take my leader
and go across, and the balance would follow or break
their necks trying," Shirk related.

The new sheepherder passed through Duck Valley,
hoping his cattle friends wouldn't see him, and on
July 31 reached Newark, a small camp six miles from
his destination of White Plains, a booming Nevada
mining camp. Next day he rode into White Plains and
contacted the principal butchers, Ulysses and Isaac
Ketchum. The sign over their door made Dave
hesitate: "U. Ketchum and I. Cheatem." But he sold
the sheep at a considerable profit for Kohlhire, plus
his own wages. Returning to Silver City, the honest
Shirk paid a very happy Phil Kohlhire thirteen
thousand dollars and was pleased with his own commission and wages which came to twenty-two hundred
dollars.

But Shirk preferred to work for George Miller,
although in time that also went bad. In the next few
seasons, others saw the potential of the cattle business,
even under the Indian threats. Among them were Ellis
Demitt, Murphy and Horn, Scott and Company,
Grayson and Company, Hardiman Brothers, Sommercamp, Jack Sands, Sparks and Harrell, and Bruce
Brothers. But young Dave Shirk was one of the true
pioneers who seemed always willing to take on a new
project, and adapted easily to new situations. In 1866,

at twenty-two, he left the family farm in Will County, Illinois, bound for Idaho and treasure. A friend, Jim Monroe, went with him. Shirk signed on as a bull-whacker with Ed and William Saguer's freighting train, headed from St. Joseph, Missouri, to Denver.

Near Julesburg the Saguer brothers joined an emi-grant train for mutual protection from the Indians. The warriors were running rampant on the central plains that summer, and there was stark evidence before reaching Julesburg in the charred wreckage of another train not much larger than their own. The wagons were burned, and the mules and muleskinners killed. It wasn't a pretty sight.

Despite the impending danger, the evenings were filled with frivolity and partying. There were some fifteen lively girls who loved to dance, and also some foot-tapping fiddle players. Life became a nightly round of partying for Dave and Jim, spinning the girls on the corners in the shadows of the circled wagons.

The Saguers looked upon the revelry as a waste of time and energy. The emigrants moved too slowly for them. They had freight to deliver in Denver and would get a better price by being there before their competitors. They decided to pull out secretly, ahead of the emigrants. Dave and Jim didn't want to leave — they were having too good a time — so during the night they stampeded the oxen, firing and yelling like Indians. The ruse worked, convincing the Saguers that the warriors were close by and that it was wiser to stay together.

Reaching Denver, Dave and Jim purchased a team, a light wagon, and some supplies, and continued west. Jim had a brother who operated a hotel at Ruby City. That gave them another good reason for going to Idaho. Reaching Ruby in August, with fifty cents between them, Dave and Jim swapped their team and wagon for a "wood ranch" and forty cords of wood located at the head of Blue Gulch, six miles from Ruby. But

Dave Shirk, who came to the Owyhee area with nothing and became a prominent enough man to win the girl desired by cattle king, Pete French.

they hadn't thought of one thing: they needed a wagon and team to haul the wood into town for sale. So they hired four mules and a wagon at five dollars a day. Feeding the animals boosted the cost to eight dollars a day, cutting into their profits. Making matters worse, there wasn't much of a road into Ruby from the wood ranch. So Jim hired out with a team and wagon to another outfit, while Dave went to work on the road which must be cut along a steep hillside.

"In just twenty-five days," Dave related, "I dug one and a quarter miles of ditch, one foot deep and two feet wide for the upper wheels of the wagon to run, and while the wood was being hauled to town,

I went to work for Overmire and Miller Sales and Feed Stables at one hundred dollars per month, boarding myself and doing my own cooking."

The work was hard and the hours long for the young partners, but they were earning money which they direly needed. Then Dave became ill from overwork and general fatigue.

"The camp doctor gave me no hopes of recovery, in fact he gave me up," Dave said. "But an old Indian doctor took hold of me and pulled me through."

While Dave was ill, Jim got into a game at Bill Wessel's gambling den and lost all their money. Then he pulled out for Camp White Horse in the southeastern part of Oregon's Grant County, obtaining a job chopping wood for the government. Dave was left penniless, but he was receiving an education in business ventures, especially partnerships, and hoped in the future he would be wiser in his dealings with others. He became a Jack-of-all-trades, working for farmers, sheepmen, trail bosses, and as a homesteader, but never having much to do directly with the mines. He worked for Con Shea and John Catlow, a Yorkshireman who ran a meat market in Silver City; and he was with Silas Skinner during the Indian outbreak when Skinner wanted someone to help him to inspect his road and they were pinned down by the Red Men at the Sheep Ranch. A willing, hard worker, Shirk seemed to be a moving-around man who often came out on the short end of things. He became best-known for two trips from Texas to the Owyhees in 1871 and 1873. His description of the cattle trail to Idaho is the only one known to exist. Later, too, he tangled with cattle baron Pete French and in the fight that followed, killed one of French's hands.

In August 1870, when Shirk had rejoined George Miller, the cattleman sold his herd to Stopher and

Dodsworth of Elko, Nevada. Dave stayed with the herd to wind up the business transaction, while Miller struck out for California where he purchased a farm. Before leaving, George told Shirk that he intended to drive out another herd next year. Would Shirk like to help? Dave said he would, so in February Miller sent word to meet him at Waxahachie, Texas, if he cared to join the drive. Shirk headed south across plains and mountains by railroad to Cheyenne and Denver, then by stage through southern Colorado. He almost didn't make it, being stranded for two weeks by the flooding Grand and Big Canadian rivers.

At Waxahachie, Shirk and Miller began purchasing horses and cattle for the long trek. There was a second junior partner, too, a Mr. Walters. They contracted for fifteen hundred head at four dollars and fifty cents for four-year-old cows and five dollars and seventy-five cents for five-year-olds. Under the arrangement, Shirk and Walters owned two hundred fifty head apiece and would furnish their own saddle horses. Miller had one thousand head and was to furnish all other supplies, including wagons, oxen, provisions, and the hired hands. Each man required three horses, two for day riding and one for night guard. I have always wondered how many men were needed to handle the big drives. Dave Shirk gave the answers. The owners calculated they required one man per hundred head of cattle, up to five hundred head, and above that, one man per two hundred head, excluding the foreman. During the first two weeks on the trail of a big drive, it required about eight men to hold the cows at night, four to a shift. When the cattle were broken to the trail routine, two men per shift were enough, except during a storm when the entire crew was needed, especially if it were hail. Then the drovers could only drift the herd with the storm, hoping to hold them and keep them from scattering.

The first night out, the Miller-Shirk herd was hit

by a howling storm, the worst on the entire trek to Idaho. The herd came close to stampeding. But then it was over; they crossed the Brazos River, skirted the Red River, and picked up the main cattle trail to Cleburne in Johnson County. There were cattle thieves along the way and the night guard had to be doubled. Before reaching Fort Worth, two oxen were stolen.

On entering Indian territory, the herd had to stand inspection for the dread hoof and mouth disease. The longhorns were found in good health, which caused the partners to draw a deep breath of relief. Now they moved 'em out, and found feed and water abundant. The cattle did well. But they hadn't gone too far when a band of Indians confronted them, demanding duty for crossing their country.

"White man must pay Indians for eating grass," the chief told Dave who was in charge while Miller was off somewhere. "My men want pay, they heap fight."

But Shirk didn't give in; he called his crew together and since they were heavily armed, the Indians backed off. It was the last they saw of the band, but the guard was doubled that night, as a precaution against the Indians sneaking back after dark. The drovers were right; the Indians did return and managed to stampede the saddle horses, but the moon was in its second quarter, it was clear, and the punchers were able to track the horses and get them back.

Reaching buffalo country, the riders found great waves of the big bison stretching by the many thousands clear to the horizon. The way was strewn with many great carcasses, stripped of their hides by the buffalo hunters.

The Miller-Shirk herd reached Coleville Station on June 9, where the herds behind were stopped for inspection by the herds ahead to seek out any strays that had been picked up. Miller and Shirk had fifty

Driscol and Lane cattle from a herd of six thousand. Since there was no DL representative around, they were ordered out, taking the DL cattle along. The trail swung left here for Utah, Montana, and Idaho, while the right fork headed for the railheads to the east in Kansas. There was more hostile Indian country before reaching the Rocky Mountains. Before sunrise one morning either Indians or whites filtered by the guard and stampeded the herd. While the men rounded up the cattle, Miller, Shirk, and Walters went after the thieves. They caught up with the rustlers who were driving a bunch of cattle. Seeing that they were being tracked, the rustlers began shooting the cows, killing two and wounding four. The light was poor in the pre-dawn, and the partners couldn't get a good look at the thieves. Their horses were played out, too, so they gave up the chase.

The herd moved by Fort Halleck and crossed the summit of the Rockies, descending to Bear River and making fifteen to twenty miles a day. Deer, antelope, elk and sage hen were all around and they ate well, the cook making good use of this wild life larder. The Mormons had a settlement at Bear River, where Miller had stopped previously for supplies. He directed Dave to buy some fresh vegetables from the farmers. Shirk got more than he was bargaining for in the negotiations. A woman had received a letter from Brigham Young, requesting her daughter for his wife. The mother pleaded with Shirk to take the girl with the cattle drive to safety. Shirk was sympathetic, although he warned the mother that a bunch of buckeroos weren't exactly the ideal companions for a young girl. He said they'd talk it over; that he would send a horse and rider at midnight if they decided that the girl could go along. But the partners concluded it was risky business, if Brigham Young had his eyes on that girl. They had fully three hundred miles of Mormon territory to cross and weren't anxious to tangle with Young's

"Destroying Angels," fully remembering the Mountain Meadows massacre of 1858. Shirk often wondered whatever happened to that girl.

On September 10, they crossed the border into Idaho and felt they were nearing home. The Raft River flowed west into the Snake. Its plains were covered with feed, game was plentiful, and so they stayed several days near the "City of Rocks" which is now an historical attraction. The partners wanted a good rest for both men and cattle before tackling the Snake River desert, one of the most dreaded parts of the Oregon Trail.

The drive down the Snake River began October 1 and was strenuous work because of short feed and alkali dust. Upon reaching the head of the Bruneau Valley, they had been on the trail five months and seventeen days. A count of the herd totaled sixteen hundred fifty head, one hundred fifty more than at the beginning of the drive. After turning over the fifty head to Driscol and Lane, they still had a hundred surplus which would help defray expenses. This was common practice among the outfits trailing that long way from Texas, if the owners never came along to part them out. It helped if the brand owner were in Texas or Oklahoma, and the cattle in Idaho.

Dave and Walters' shares came to two hundred seventy-four head apiece, now worth thirty dollars a head or more. The camp shifted midway between the Bruneau and Duck valleys before the herd was divided. Miller and Walters tried to dicker with Dave, offering twenty-four dollars a head for his share. He refused, knowing they were worth more, and saying so. His partners wanted to keep their cows together, but Dave decided to move his out. Perhaps like others, they thought Shirk an easy mark, for Dave found himself again in trouble with his partners. They tried to pawn the culls and scrubs onto him. But this time Shirk outsmarted them. He suggested parting out his cows next morning when they watered the herd, since then the bunch would be settled down. As they drove toward the water, Miller and Walters directed Dave to begin parting his cows, as this would be "fair." Then the two men began stirring up the cattle, mixing them badly. When they were still four miles from the river, they ordered Shirk to "go ahead." Suddenly the best cattle broke from the bunch, following Brigham, the lone bull. The stronger stock took the lead and Shirk quickly parted his share from these finer animals, leaving Miller and Walters with their mouths open.

Shirk drove his cows to winter quarters on the Snake, about a mile and a half from where Rabbit Creek dumps into the big river. He wintered them on white sage and bunch grass, and in the spring, moved them to his summer range on Reynolds Creek. When the calves were three months old, he marketed them to Miller and Hoffer in Silver City. Then in August, with John Catlow acting as his agent, he sold the entire herd at thirty-five dollars a head to Sam Nealy. After settling his debts, Dave realized a net profit of seven thousand, two hundred eighty dollars, not bad considering he'd arrived in the Owyhees with only fifty cents.

Shirk was now a bonafide stockman. In 1873 he brought out another herd — this time under his own steam — and sold it to Catlow who had a stake in mining ventures in the Owyhees. Catlow was also in partnership with James Gusman at the Gusman Ranch in Pleasant Valley. Later, he shifted his operations to the Steens Mountain country where the Catlow Valley on the south side is named for him. After several more years of working with Catlow and Con Shea, Shirk established his own ranch along Home Creek in Grant County, Oregon. His brother William owned a spread nearby and between the two of them, they had about fifty thousand acres under fence. This was hardly large enough to be in the same class with the

David Shirk (far right) and his wife, Frances (standing third from right). She chose
Dave over Pete French, one of the most prominent men in eastern Oregon. This
picture, taken about 1926, shows David and Frances with their family.

major spreads, but sizable enough to get in Pete
French's way, along with a certain girl.

Dave believed he and French were good friends
until they tangled over that girl during a cattle
roundup. James Rankin Crow, Dave's neighbor, was
there with his family, including his niece. Frances
Crow was an expert horsewoman who could spark the
admiration of most of the cowhands.

When the roundup was over, Dave suggested to
French that they go calling on the Crows.

"As there is a young lady there, I'm with you,"
French replied. He had a reputation of believing he
was quite a "lady's man."

Frances Crow, attracted to them both, showed off
by putting on a riding exhibition. As she rode by,
French declared, "There goes my girl."

"You will have to go some if she is," Dave replied
in something of a challenge.

There was a dance later at Diamond. French suggested Dave have the first dance with Frances, knowing full well he had already committed her for the first round. Dave declined, explaining that he came in with his buckeroos, and according to ranch protocol, felt he should move with them. Later, Shirk learned that French had asked for that first dance three days ahead; he was just trying to embarrass Dave by having Frances turn him down.

Angered, Shirk felt his friendship with French had ended, but not his relationship with Miss Crow. In March 1877 he traveled with her to the Crow home in Clover Valley, California. They were married the following month and after a wedding trip to San Francisco, returned to the Catlow Valley where Dave made filings for some land, naming the place Home Creek.

The Bannock Indians went on the rampage the following summer, and eastern Oregon and Idaho were aflame. Dave took his wife, her sister and a Miss Mary Kerby to safety at Winnemucca, secured guns and ammunition, and returned to Trout Creek. All hands went to the White Horse Ranch. After four days Dave could stand it no longer; he wanted to get to the Home Creek place to see what the warriors did to him. The previous day a war party had burned the Roaring Springs Ranch buildings and killed much livestock. One man lost sixty head of his best horses. When Shirk reached his ranch, he found about seventy horses gone. At that, he came off better than many ranchers.

When the Bannock War was over, the cattlemen set about restoring their ranch buildings and herds. By 1884, Dave Shirk needed more land to run his cattle. Being a small settler, Shirk could qualify under the Homestead, Pre-emption, Desert and Timber Culture acts to increase his holdings. But while Dave was expanding under the law set up by Congress, the big cattle barons were gathering tens of thousands of acres by fair or foul means. They had the money and the power to stretch the laws to their advantage, while the little man had to be completely legal with the government for fear of losing his holdings.

Pete French was attempting to expand his holdings in the Steens Mountain country. It meant the settlers must get out. It also brought French right up against his old friend and rival. The mounting friction over the land renewed French's hatred for Dave for having beat him out with the girl who became Shirk's wife.

In the Catlow Valley, Dave and Bill controlled much of the water. French poured on the pressure. He flawed a forty-acre strip on Shirk's west side, then fenced it, cutting Dave off from the western range and preventing a successful handling of Shirk cattle. Then he hired men to jump Shirk land. If they could make their claims stick, French would buy them out. If the Shirks went to court, the brothers would have to pay high-priced attorneys to fight the case. Either way, French would come up winners by forcing the small men out of business. If that didn't work, he and the other big cattlemen could fall back on a corps of gunfighters to browbeat, intimidate and even kill the settlers.

S. H. Crow, Dave's brother-in-law, filed on a timber claim and asked Dave to oversee the necessary work to prove it up according to government regulation. French meanwhile assigned two men to jump the claim. One day as Dave was supervising the work, two riders came toward him. Noticing they were armed and anticipating trouble, Dave shifted near a rifle he had hidden in some sagebrush.

"Good morning, gentlemen," Dave said. "What can I do for you?"

The pair began taunting him and calling him names, their hands on their six-shooters. Suddenly

Pete French, the legendary Oregon cattle king, was a good friend of Dave Shirk, until they tangled over a girl. Shirk, who was another stockman, married the girl, and French never forgave him.

James Isaacs drew, leaped to the ground and into a furrow. But Dave was equally quick to move. He grabbed the hidden rifle, took hasty aim and fired. The shot hit the ground a few feet ahead of Isaacs, ricocheted, and struck him in the forehead, killing him instantly.

Shirk was brought to trial at Canyon City and there was a hung jury. It appeared French was running true to form in that he had made a "deal" with Isaacs, and that Shirk would not go free and alive. A year later, the case was retried and by then, things had calmed down.

"After the verdict became known, there was great rejoicing among the settlers of the entire country," reported the *Harney Items* for October 31, 1889. "At the trial just had, the testimony, we are told, showed that Peter French was to pay Isaacs $1,000 for the land the trouble was over, soon as final proof was made. The testimony also showed that if Shirk had got clear at Canyon City, fifteen men from the P Ranch would have hung him. It also appeared that French was furnishing money with which to prosecute Shirk. It is understood that he was getting to be a thrifty settler and largely in the way of the cattle kings, and the job was put upon him to have him killed or to kill someone in order that he might be put out of the way. But public sentiment and the evidence was in Shirk's favor, and an intelligent jury cleared him. . . ."

Later, when Pete French was killed by another settler, Dave said about him:

"Thus ended the life of Peter French, a man of many admirable qualities of mind and heart, but whose tyrannical and overbearing temper brought about his own ruin. He lived a life of violence, and by violence he died."

No sooner was Dave freed than he and the other cattlemen were staggered by the terrible winter of 1889. The Shirk brothers lost about one thousand head of cattle and considered themselves lucky compared to some of their neighbors. It was stark disaster in contrast with the light winters of the past twenty years.

But it taught the ranchers a lesson. From then on, the stockmen put up hay and didn't rely on wintering out the cattle as they had been doing.

But in another respect, as viewed by Shirk and other cowmen, the hard winter did a service, for it cleaned out the sheepmen, especially the newcomers. Dave seemingly had little use for sheep, perhaps recalling his one experience of driving that herd to market. He picked no quarrels with existing sheepmen, but didn't like the newly-arriving "foreigners" who were at this time principally Irish. He commented:

"Cattlemen have been praying for another hard winter to clear the sheep up again. The sheep industry is an important and vital one, and one that must be maintained, but I have yet to find one sheep owner, not an American, who owned one acre of land. They are mostly foreigners, selfish and arrogant, believing that this is a free country and that they are free to do as they please. For this reason, cattlemen do not get along amicably with them, the latter believing they should be banished from the country. As a rule they come here to make money and return to their native land — come here, like the painted mistresses of King George, not for our good, but for our goods. And I predict, by reason of their presence here and methods of business, that the time is not far distant when poor people will be deprived of beef entirely, if it has not already arrived."

Six years after his acquittal, in October 1896, Dave Shirk and his family left the cattle country of Oregon, moving to Berkeley, California. It was a difficult change, but Dave realized that age was catching up with him, and he could no longer stand the hard life that the range demanded. He'd made his pile and now could take things easier. He lived a long life, however, until 1928 when he died at the age of 82. A few years earlier, Shirk began looking across his salad years in Oregon and Idaho. He set down the memories of a young man who arrived in a young country with only fifty cents, and helped tame and develop it for the future. His daughters had the manuscript published. It includes the only known account of those early Texas cattle drives into southern Idaho and eastern Oregon.

After ranchers took over in the Jordan Valley country, scenes like this were commonplace. This is a typical early cow camp, near Cow Lakes, with chuck wagon, campfire, assorted pots and pans, and all of it moving with the herds that contained thousands of head of cattle.

POOR FOOD, TOUGH HORSES

THE CATTLEMEN held full sway over the range lands of southeastern Oregon for only about ten years, from 1870 to 1880. Of course, they were a power long afterward, but by the end of that single decade, people were turning their eyes from the uncertainties of the mines to the rich grasslands which were opening for homesteading. A renewed outbreak by the Indians — the last great stand by the Red Men — badly battered the ranches and broke some of them. But it was the constant pressure of homesteading that changed the way of life forever in this sprawling range country.

The range was broken into areas of domain by the big cattle outfits. Con Shea ran cows on the Snake River. Pick Anderson and Miller and Lux wintered cattle along the Owyhee up to the Junipers. Colonel Hardin and his partner, Riley, wintered his herds on the desert, where Anderson and Miller also had cows. In the spring the three outfits met at Dry Creek with wagons for branding. Then they turned the branded

Pick Anderson, a former butcher who became an important rancher in the Jordan
Valley area. He ran a tough cow camp.

cattle loose, Pick going up the river toward the
Junipers, Hardin and Riley toward Disaster Peak, and

Miller and Lux pointing their herd toward the White Horse.

In the fall the three outfits gathered their beef, moving the cows back onto their respective winter ranges. The big ranchers under the shadow of the Steens Mountain ran their outfits in a like manner. John Devine and Peter French were the largest operators in that country, but Henry Miller and his far-flung Pacific Land and Livestock Company challenged those two powerful ranchers for dominance of the range. And Miller, unlike Dave Shirk, was a man who could deal with them on equal terms.

James Pickens Anderson was among the leading early-day ranchers in the Jordan Valley country. He was close to Henry Miller who owned one of the biggest ranching operations in all the West. A story is that Anderson was once in the butcher business with Miller in San Francisco. Pick came out from South Carolina where his people were plantation owners. When the news broke about gold in California, Pick joined the Forty-Niners swarming to the Mother Lode. He took the long sea voyage around Cape Horn rather than risking the Oregon Trail or crossing the Isthmus of Panama. Landing in San Francisco, he headed at once for the gold fields of the Sierra, going to work along the creeks and in the mines. But he saw that miners got hungry steadily and would pay top prices, so Pick bought cattle and opened a butcher shop in San Francisco.

But Pick left California because even then it was becoming too populated. Nevada's wide open spaces appealed to him; he settled at Golconda, east of Winnemucca, where he accumulated land and large herds of cattle and sheep. He had under his control all of Star Valley, Juniper Mountain and the Sheep Heads, grazing twenty thousand head of cattle and fifteen to twenty bands of sheep on his holdings.

When the Owyhee mines went broke, new cattle

ranches began springing up on all sides of the mountains, operated by people who had come originally looking for treasures in the ground. Now they wanted to run cattle, although many of them knew nothing about it. They got their start wherever they could. Anderson, Con Shea and the PLS-Wrench supplied them with stock, for most of the big outfits tried to get along with these newcomers, even though it squeezed things, rather than resorting to brute force as Pete French did. For that reason, Pick Anderson never did part out anybody's cattle when he was on the move. He figured that "they got their start from me and I have to get even."

Pick continued running cattle on Juniper Mountain until Ed Stauffer moved his operation there. That was about 1890. The Stauffers came from the Oregon Desert near where Reub Long lives today. About 1879 or 1880 Fritz (Frank) Stauffer and Frank Sweetzer located a ranch near Crane, Oregon. The ranch was operated by Ed Stauffer. They branded their stock with the Circle Bar. About 1890 they sold out and moved to Juniper Mountain where they operated under the name The Circle Bar Ranch. That is why there are two Circle Bar Ranches today. Frank Stauffer was killed by a freight wagon in the early 1900s while Ed lived till 1931.

The Stauffer invasion of the Junipers was too much for Anderson. Once again he shifted because things were getting too crowded. He left his campsite to Stauffer for headquarters of his new ranch, called the Circle Bar. For years thereafter, Fred Castro who was Pick's buckeroo boss expended much time and energy trying to gather the last of the Anderson steers. Long after Pick pulled back into Nevada, a few of his steers were running wild, nicknamed "Juniper Mountain Monkeys." Some of them (according to Frank Swisher) were more than fifteen years old when Castro was gathering them, killing some in the process.

Castro was a California Mexican who worked years for Anderson as a wagon boss. Most of Anderson's men, like those of Pete French, were vaqueros, and they were rugged hands.

"Pick paid ten dollars more, and you earned it," said Pearl Duncan who lived — or survived — many times at the Anderson camp on beans, coffee and molasses. "Either the food was poor or the horses tough."

You needed a strong stomach for the Anderson camp menu. When they butchered, they would always cut out a big jaw cow or steer. The meat would be wrapped in sacks and then thrown in the back of the wagon. About a week of hot weather and the smell got so bad you couldn't ride a bronco near camp. But Pick wasn't apologetic, nor did he believe in a fancy table on the range. He stayed at his own camp, above Golconda where his headquarters were also located. One day while Pick was away, some hoboes from the yards at Winnemucca stopped there. On their way out, they met Pick who was dressed much like the hoboes. They told him the food was good at that camp and advised him to get a meal there.

"It oughta be," Pick replied curtly. "I've been providing it for years."

Charley Loveland who worked for Anderson a long while and later cooked for our buckaroo outfit at Cliffs, Idaho, said once he and another cow puncher stopped at Pick's camp for a meal. Charley ate only biscuits and drank coffee, politely declining the boiled meat and rice. Leaving camp, the other fellow asked why Charley didn't take the full meal.

"Boiled meat and rice, hell," said Charley. "That was boiled meat and maggots."

When Charley picked up the spoon and started to dip, he noticed the rice had eyes. He didn't tip his friend off, not wanting to ruin their welcome. His companion wanted to swing on Charley right then, but he was so busy upping his meal he couldn't find the time — nor the strength.

By Charley's descriptive terms when cooking for us, you might think that some of the Anderson camp rubbed off permanently on him, but it wasn't so. The average day was launched in our camp at 4:30 A.M. with steaks, potatoes and baking powder biscuits. Usually the buckeroos came in off the ride late in the afternoon, so lunch and supper were combined. For this meal, we had biscuits, steamed potatoes and boiled meat. Dessert consisted of boiled rice and raisins which Charley called "bear shit." All this was washed down with coffee that Charley said wasn't done till it would float a horseshoe. When the food was ready, the grizzled old-timer wouldn't ring a triangle or bang on a dishpan. He'd sing out, "Come 'n git it, you SOB's, or I'll feed it to the dogs."

In the late 1800s, the "Bull's Head" became so famous in many sections of the West that checks bearing that symbol, or trade mark, were accepted readily as currency. These were probably the only checks in history that were accepted as cash at government auctions. The man behind them was a living legend. His name was Heinrick Alfred Kreiser, who took the more American name of Henry Miller.

Only once was Miller's check refused at such an auction. The event was preceded by one of the most dramatic rides in the Western saga and afterward, a reversal of the receiver's sale to another bidder.

Heinrick Kreiser was the powerful partner, and the main force, of the legendary Miller and Lux cattle and meat company, based in California. The owners boasted they could drive cattle from the Mexican to the Canadian border and sleep every night on their own land. Henry Miller and Charles Lux, another butcher, were a well balanced partnership of butchering and retailing. Miller was the field man, ranging restlessly all over the West and always striving to expand and strengthen his holdings. Lux, an Alsatian, could alway get the backing, for he mingled with San Francisco's nabobs and enjoyed city life among the wealthy.

In Malheur County, an ambitious rancher named Tom Overfelt wanted to make contact with Miller, hoping to interest him in backing Overfelt for expansion of his own holdings. Overfelt came to eastern Oregon in the late seventies and began acquiring road land and cattle. He found much of the road land in the Harney Valley had been taken up, but there was good flat meadow land, about two thousand acres, on the North Fork of the Malheur River. It was designated an Indian Reservation, where the federal government had gathered remnants of the area's tribes and was trying to turn them into peaceable farmers, even working them at digging ditches and building levies. When the tribes revolted, the Indians broke off the reservation and went rampaging over the countryside, killing settlers and livestock, burning buildings and running off the horses. They refused to surrender and were hunted down until most of the tribes were killed. That left the Malheur Indian agent with an agency and no Indians, since those still alive were moved to the reservation at Duck Valley.

One day down in California, Henry Miller was surveying his corrals when he noticed a good-looking bunch of steers with the LF brand on their hips.

"Those are the finest looking steers I have ever seen," Miller remarked. "Where did they come from?"

The foreman said they were from Malheur County in Oregon, and that a fellow named Overfelt brought them down personally.

"Let me see him," Miller said.

Overfelt confessed later that he had brought down those cattle for a purpose. He knew Miller would spot them. Describing Malheur County in glowing terms, Overfelt said that he needed money to buy more land and that the rich Agency area would likely soon come up for public sale. If he didn't have the funds to buy it, that fine cattle valley would be broken up for settlement.

"The settlers will not make it because of the long distance to market," Overfelt added.

"How do you drive your cattle to market, Mr. Overfelt?" asked Miller.

"I drive them right down by your Quinn River Ranch in Nevada," replied Tom, quickly seizing the opportunity to bait Miller.

Miller said he was leaving next day for Nevada and suggested Overfelt travel along to show him that Oregon country. The invitation was almost more than Overfelt could have dreamed possible.

"If it's as good as you say it is, maybe I can help you," Miller added.

They swung north through Fort McDermitt to the town of Vale on the Malheur River. Thus far, Henry hadn't been too impressed by what he saw. The land was rough and broken, and there was considerable alkali. There was some good land in the valleys, but the dusty roads curbed his optimism. But as they went through the mountains of the Malheur country, Miller became alert. His excitement swelled. There were many rich valleys nestled in the hills and along the streams, over which water could be spread. *And there was plenty of water.* He was pleasantly surprised upon seeing the ranches that Overfelt had acquired and developed. In this arid country, good crops of alfalfa and hay were growing, surrounded by dry hills. Miller had never seen anything quite like it.

The Agency Valley was the epitome. Miller saw at once what made Overfelt so enthusiastic, and why this man would travel so far on a gamble to interest one of the West's great cattle kings in such a remote

Photo by Bureau of Land Management
The Agency Valley as it appears today, now the Beulah Reservoir. This was the area which Miller felt he must have for his empire.

operation. There was water running in the ditches the Indians had dug across two thousand acres of meadow land. Miller didn't hesitate; he agreed to a partnership with Overfelt.

"You put in everything you have at what it cost you," Miller said. "I'll advance the money as fast as it is needed to acquire land and cattle. I'll take the cattle at the market as fast as they are produced. You will manage the property up here and we will divide the profits in proportion to the money we put in." Thus, Henry Miller became a "silent partner" in the firm of Overfelt and Company.

Before returning to California, Henry Miller issued a warning:

"I can never forget the Agency Valley. It is beautiful and will make a wonderful headquarters. Keep your eyes open and as soon as it is offered for sale, buy it at any price. I will never forgive you if you fail to get Agency Valley."

Overfelt's growing operation became known as simply The Company. It soon embraced Silvies Valley, Drewsey, Warm Springs, Big Stinking Water, Little Stinking Water, Indian Creek, Miller Field, Moffat Ranch, Pine Creek, Otis Creek, Lamb Ranch, Harper Ranch, and many others. Tom continued biding his time, waiting for Agency Valley to come up for bid. It would be the crown jewel of The Company's holdings.

Tom was working one day in the headquarters office at Trout Creek, in Silvies Valley, when a horse and rider thundered to the door. Moving to the window, Tom saw that the horse was covered with lather. He would give that buckeroo hell.

But the rider cut him short: "Mr. Overfelt, I was over to Agency Valley looking for stray cattle and saw a posted notice that the Agency Ranch is to be sold by the receiver at Lakeview, noon tomorrow."

Lakeview was two hundred miles away and for a moment, remembering Henry Miller's words, there was a sinking feeling in Tom Overfelt's mid-section. Then he was leaping to his roan and shouting to the buckeroos, "Lakeview!" He spurred the mount into what became the greatest long-distance ride this country has ever known.

Tom had but one day to cover the expanse to Lakeview. He galloped to Burns, through the springs of the Double O Ranch, past Iron Mountain and Skull Springs, through Buzzard Canyon, over rimrock passes, and finally into the timber east of Lake Abert. When he met a rider, he exchanged horses with him. When he saw horses in a corral, he lassoed one, threw saddle and bridle on him, and was off like the wind before the astonished owners could find their voices. But they could tell that this was a man in a hurry, not a thief, and in the tradition of the country, let him go on, knowing their horse would get back one of these days.

All night Tom rode; farmers and their wives could hear him coming from a long distance, shouting for a horse, the hooves of the mount pounding a staccato rhythm along the floor of the desert, under the starry sky. Children leaped from their beds, as occupants of the farms obliged him, getting a mount ready and then trying to give him some food. But Overfelt couldn't stop. Time was running out, and now the sky was growing light behind him on the eastern rim.

The final leg of the trip was down a precipitous grade into the village of Lakeview. Tom dared not press the horse too hard. A fall . . . an injury . . . and the pony might not get him there in time. The gap was closing, but so was the time, pushing hard on twelve o'clock. He was worried that his watch might not jibe with that of the land office. In a final spurt for the finish line, Overfelt spurred the tiring horse into Lakeview at a pace that brought people popping from the buildings.

Overfelt hauled up before the land office, the horse still in fair shape but breathing hard. He leaped to the ground and smashed through the door. It was high noon. The receiver was holding up the notice of the sale and puffing on a cigar with the prospective bidders. The men couldn't have been more surprised at a band of attacking redskins.

"Clear from Trout Creek?" they declared. "Don't believe it."

Overfelt outbid all the speculators, for he had his orders. Then he pulled out his book for a draft on Miller and Lux for the full price of Agency Valley. The draft carried the familiar Bull's Head. In eastern Oregon, where currency and coin were sometimes scarce, and where people like Bill Brown, the horse king, wrote checks on shingles and chunks of leather, the Bull's Head was used as a medium of exchange right along with federal money. It was coveted and never refused.

But there is always a first time, an exception that proves the rule, and this was it. The defeated bidders challenged the Bull's Head, and the receiver, obviously in cahoots with them, echoed their protest.

"This is a cash sale," the land agent declared. "You will have to pay in cash."

Overfelt was shocked — and desperate. He didn't have that kind of currency with him. The other top bidder produced the cash of his final bid and the land was sold to him.

Tom wired Henry Miller immediately. Miller acted promptly, appealing to the commissioner of the General Land Office in Washington, D.C. Miller had the power to demand a quick decision. The commissioner held that "these Bull's Head drafts passed as currency in that particular part of the country, under the conditions that there existed, that the draft was no doubt good and should have been accepted by the receiver, and therefore, the sale to the company was confirmed and a patent for the land issued to it."

Overfelt could breathe easier. But Tom Overfelt didn't live long to enjoy the fruits of Agency Valley. He was riding a spirited horse one day in 1886 when the saddle turned and he was dragged to death. That ended the partnership, for in settling the estate by Tom's widow, the LF brand and the holdings of Overfelt and Company merged into Henry Miller's vast domain.

John Devine was the opposite of Henry Miller in both temperament and style. The owner of the White

Horse Ranch liked to live high on the hog. He was a showman, who wore Spanish-style clothes of the grandees and lavished huge sums on his personal pleasures and in the entertainment of guests. He tried to impress people with his wealth and power. Devine maintained a game farm which was stocked with wildlife for hunting. He had stables of top-grade race horses capable of winning anywhere in the land. People boasted that they knew him personally, and Devine liked that citation of his importance. When they came to visit, he made them warmly welcome and encouraged them to stay on for long periods of time. Devine was a true cattle baron, as portrayed on the Hollywood screen.

But like many kings, Devine was riding for a fall. The combination of hard winters and dry summers broke him and Henry Miller, who had often enviously eyed the Devine spread, moved in quickly as the only bidder at the bankruptcy sale. This time, there was no question about the Bull's Head, for Miller got the ranch. Feeling sorry for the defeated rancher, Miller hired Devine to run the outfit. That was a come-down, almost an insult, for the proud cattleman. And it didn't work; the two men were miles apart in personalities and the way they operated.

Miller's subordinates were required to check with him on what they were doing. Devine had been used to operating independently, making his own decisions. He ran afoul of Miller's policy of being the top hand, who gave the orders and had superintendents notify him before going ahead on anything. It was the way Miller kept track of his holdings; it had made him a success in the cattle business. Unable to live by this rule, Devine resigned. Then Henry Miller did something strange, completely out of character for him. He deeded the big Alvord Ranch to Devine, giving him a lifetime non-transferable ownership — complete with cattle. Henry must have had a strong admiration

John Devine, early cattleman.

for Devine, for he was never again known to do such a thing.

When Miller took over the Devine operation, he organized the Pacific Land and Livestock Company, bearing the S-Wrench brand. It became among the most famous in the West, carried on the left hip of cattle in Oregon, California, and Nevada. The PLS Company branded its horses on the left stifle. Miller

grew to be one of the largest and most powerful cattlemen of his time, although he was almost an illiterate
and at times was difficult to understand, speaking with
a deep German accent. Still he was a good judge of
men. He could size up a man instantly, was a shrewd
dealer, was able to view the future with amazing
accuracy, and possessed great physical strength to
keep him on the move.

Henry Miller was more butcher than cattleman,
some historians believe. He was sometimes called
"The Butcher" and the reference was wrongfully taken

California Historical Society

Henry Miller, of the great Miller and Lux cattle empire, was attracted to Oregon
when he saw fat cows from the Agency Valley area. Based in California, the
celebrated cattle king extended his holdings into the Pacific Northwest by teaming
with Tom Overfelt. Miller's famous mark was the Bull's Head.

by those of later generations to mean that he was a killer. Not at all! Miller migrated before the Gold Rush in California from his native Germany to New York, where he worked at his trade of butchering. Heinrick Kreiser acquired the name Miller by accident. A friend by that name had booked passage on a crowded ship bound for California. At the last minute, he decided not to go. Henry took the name to keep the passage space and held onto it the remainder of his life.

In California, rather than dig for gold, Henry pursued his butchering trade, for there was good opportunity supplying beef for the mining camps. He was only twenty-three, but so efficient at his trade that customers said he marketed everything but the squeal. Prices were high, and the demand for cattle was critical as more and more boats arrived, disgorging thousands of hopeful miners. There were fortunes to be made in cattle, if you could get the stock. Ben Holladay, for one, was driving Mormon cattle across the plains for sale in California, and parlayed his funds into the greatest transportation system in the world. Henry Miller couldn't fill the demands of his customers. He needed beef and beef needed range land. He began buying land and stock, and he never quit until his death at eighty-nine in 1916.

Miller built an empire of more than a million acres spread over five states, making him the biggest cattleman in the West. His holdings were not only vast but varied. He and Lux invested wisely. Miller and Lux owned a million head of cattle, two banks plus innumerable branches, canals and reservoirs, and many other properties, appraised at fifty million dollars. He tamed the country with networks of mighty canals, built big dams, reclaimed barren land, and developed water power. He was a shrewd and ruthless businessman, but he didn't resort to the gun or a private army as did Pete French. He ruled his crews with an iron fist. They learned that Miller's orders were to be obeyed. Many became irritated with his continued criticism of small details in running the ranches. Miller had his own special methods. He was all business; there was nothing fancy about him. He never relaxed or "played." He was patient, but greedy and tough to dislodge from his point of view. In the end, he always got his way. What Henry did was good for Henry, but what Henry did was also good for the country.

Miller's make-up was one of strange and conflicting contrasts. He would never hound an enemy. Once an incident was behind him, he didn't linger nor allow it to slow him down, because he was forever busy on some new venture up ahead. Many people tried to rob or trick Miller. He was forever in the courts over land or water rights. But not for long, for he always won. There are many stories of his generosity and kindness, such as with John Devine. Former enemies would come to him, defeated, asking his help and he would give it to them. Yet you get the impression that these acts of goodness — there were hundreds, maybe even thousands — were a matter of policy and investment, and that Henry Miller always was on top in the end. He was a practical man, who looked down the years at the long range of things in deciding a course of action.

Once when riding in California, Miller came upon the famed outlaw Garcia and his band of renegades skinning a beef.

"Whose animal are you skinning?" Henry asked, as if he didnt know.

"Miller's," thay answered in chorus.

"All right, boys," Miller replied, having no desire to take on these cutthroats. "Whenever you need an animal of mine to eat, take it but be sure to hang the hide on the limb of a tree, and tell my men where they can find it. And if you don't need all the meat, but only want the best juicy steaks, tell some of the

Mexicans around the country where they can find it, so the beef won't be wasted."

Miller rode off, leaving the outlaws gaping after him. Miller knew he would profit by this arrangement, for there was no use bucking the outlaw gang. Besides, it would take a lot of time and energy that could be better devoted to constructive matters.

Another time, Miller found his water at Trout Creek down to a trickle and rode out personally to seek the cause of the trouble. He came upon his homesteading neighbor.

"Good morning, Mr. Byers," greeted Miller. "That's a fine dam you put in the river, but if you don't mind, please let a little water come down for the cattle at Trout Creek."

Byers spat in defiance. "Well, I was here first."

"Well, I'll be here long after you're gone," replied Henry, remaining calm.

"Does that mean you want to buy me out?"

"You already owe me more than your place is worth," declared Miller. "But the two places are better together, so I'll give you two thousand dollars for what you have left."

"Sold," said Byers quickly. He realized he better get out while he had the chance, for you couldn't take on Miller and expect to win.

Yet the cowman-butcher overlooked things conveniently when it didn't appear profitable to oppose them. His wealth was so great that he wasn't hurt by losses to down-and-outers and small operators. Miller weighed everything in terms of the over-all picture. Many settlers of eastern Oregon, Nevada, California and Idaho got their start from Henry's herds. The settlers of Harney County, in the first years of their farms, might have starved were it not for Company beef which they butchered. The Owyhee mining camps consumed huge quantities of beef, mostly from Texas, but there were times when the supply ran low. Then some Silver City butchers would team with Jordan Valley buckeroos. They thought nothing of dropping down toward the White Horse and driving up a herd of Wrench cattle.

Miller was a strange enigma. He could be shrewd and penny-pinching in the operation of his ranches, and sometimes as fussy as an old maid. Like many of the nineteenth century nabobs, the little things counted up with Miller. Whenever he arrived at a ranch, the first place he inspected was the kitchen, looking for waste. The cooks were ordered never to peel potatoes for boiling.

"The peels carry wit dem some goot," Miller said.

His eyes rubbered around the room, looking for other signs of wastefulness. He would always inspect the garbage barrel to see if the cooks were carelessly throwing out good food. If in doubt, he'd roll up his sleeve, plunging to the bottom of the barrel to learn what was there. If it was something good, the cook could count on a chewing out, for there were chickens and hogs that could take the leavings as slop.

The cooks broke out in a sweat when hearing Miller was on the way. He liked fried chicken, demanding it wherever he went. A cook at Drewsey was down to a tough old hen. Luckily she had advance notice that Miller was in the vicinity. She killed the hen and boiled it all night, then fried it for the boss, holding her breath while he ate. Henry declared it was the best fried chicken he ever had.

When Miller had checked out the kitchen, he headed across the barnyard, mentally noting the number of dogs and cats that were about. These had to be fed, too. The place must be kept neat, clean and orderly at all times. Everything had its proper place. He went over the barn from end to end. If he found a pitchfork with the tines down, he would flip them around "mit der tines oop." He didn't want the tines to rust.

If he saw any hoboes, he ordered the cooks to feed them. They were told never to turn away a hungry man. Here again, Miller had his own unique system. The cooks must make the visitor wait until the hands were fed, then give him a *used plate* heaped with food. His string of ranches was known among the vagabonds as "the dirty plate route." But it was a practical means to an end. A happy hobo wasn't likely to burn Miller's haystacks.

Miller never missed a bet. On an Oregon visit, he noticed that the Island Ranch kitchen lacked a meat grinder. Returning to his headquarters at Los Banos, California, Miller purchased a grinder. He discovered (he wrote the Island superintendent) in checking the boat freight rates to The Dalles, that shipping the grinder would cost as much as a hundredweight. Miller therefore took a hundred pound keg of staples, removed enough to accommodate the grinder, and shipped it that way to get his money's worth. He also supplied the super with specific directions on how to divide up the staples with the other ranches, to avoid waste.

Fence posts were another matter on which Miller saved by his own inventive system. As baron of so much land, replacing fence could be a very costly item. Miller insisted that the posts, cut or purchased, be long enough for several resets. Many were nine feet long, burned at the end to reduce the rotting. Still standing on ranches that belonged to The Company are posts that haven't rotted, and which have two resets left in them.

This tough cattle king observed things cryptically, and with a steady calculating eye, made his observations and gave his orders:

"*It is not work that ruins so many horses, but incompetent men handling them. . . .*"

"*Unbranded calves on the ranges is bad business,*

as it might induce some of our neighbors to be dishonest. . . ."

"A friendly neighbor is a great asset. . . ."

"A man can't do justice to his employer on an empty stomach. . . ."

"It is no disgrace to ask advice from one holding a position beneath you. . . ."

"There is a class of people not made to be prosperous. The minute they have a jingle in their pocket or a dollar's credit, they are ruined and lose their bearings. . . ."

"If a man is sensible, he will not run his horse to death to get back a calf that runs away, but will let it come back of its own accord. Knowing these things is what makes a good cattleman. . . ."

"It is nonsense to keep up stock in summer and let them starve in winter. . . ."

"I hear that our supervisor has been defeated, and his successor will probably give us a fair deal. I hope nothing has been said to cause him to feel that we have been working against his election. I am told your foreman voted against our supervisor. I can hardly believe that, but I shall find out. I wrote him explicitly that we not only wanted his assistance, but also that of his men who were registered, and have them vote for our man. . . ."

"I have seen men trimming trees that were dead. They did not take pains enough to notice. . . ."

"Explain to the editor of the paper our standing with the people, and once in a while give him some advertising so that he will have a chance to make something which will have its good effect. . . ."

"I thought that man was getting fifty dollars a month, and now I find that we are paying him sixty-five. We want to get rid of him as soon as possible."

John Gilchrist was for many years the superintendent for Miller and Lux on the Oregon and Nevada
ranches. He was a loyal, trusted employee, one of the
very few given free rein in handling company
business. He was well liked by the men and by the
neighbors. When age forced Henry Miller out of the
driver's seat, a nephew took over management of the
big cattle empire. He and Gilchrist didn't hit it off,
and the superintendent resigned. Arthur Olsen, a
Miller and Lux man from California, was selected to
replace Gilchrist. From the beginning, he had trouble.
Many of the hands and former employees still in the
area refused to accept the new man, for they were
loyal to Gilchrist. There was a generation gap, too,
in those days, since Olsen was in his early twenties,
had only limited ranching experience, and was considered a greenhorn. Yet if he were to succeed, he
needed to win the respect of the men under him.

Riding the stage from Bend to Burns, Olsen chatted
with a man from Harney County. He told the fellow
his problem. The weathered eastern Oregonian
advised him to call upon Gilchrist who was living in
Burns and give him the full story. Gilchrist listened
intently, then promised Olsen he would see Charlie
Miller, the cattle superintendent, in a few days. He
assured his successor that "everything will be all
right." It was the beginning of a strange relationship.
As long as Gilchrist lived in Burns, Olsen sought him
out for advice on company business, and Gilchrist
never hesitated in giving it. This was the kind of loyalty
Henry Miller drew from his longtime top hands.

Nevertheless, Olsen continued to have his problems. Hands gave him cool treatment for a long while
before finally accepting him and his authority. The
Chinese cooks were especially rough and
uncooperative. When Olsen arrived late for a meal,
the cook would set out anything handy, making no
effort to give him something fresh and piping hot. But

gradually he broke them down. One afternoon he rode up late to the ranch house, seeking a meal.

"Mista Olsen likee steak?" the cook asked.

Olsen knew then that he was finally "in."

Gradually, too, Olsen gained the respect of the other ranchers, except for one at the Harper Ranch. One day Olsen had been into Vale on business and decided to drive out to the Harper Ranch for the night. He became lost, spending most of the night beside an irrigation ditch. Long before daylight, Olsen froze out, so began driving again and reached Harper's in time to catch the foreman still in bed. The foreman was obviously embarrassed, caught without his pants. Olsen told him he'd just come from Vale, but omitted the fact that he'd been lost all night. It was a stupid thing; the foreman would hold it against him. A few days later, Olsen ran onto Charlie Miller who gave him some good news, repeating what the foreman said:

"Any son-of-a-bitch that could come from Vale and catch me in bed in the morning just has to be a good man!"

By the time of his death in 1916, Henry Miller had fulfilled his ambition of becoming the largest cattleman in the world. He owed no one, and there wasn't a mortgage on any of his holdings. But his personal life, like that of many men of wealth, ambition and constant drive, had been a failure. His son was crippled, his daughter had been killed years before in an accident with a horse, and his wife was also dead. There was no one to carry on the business of that great empire. It was only a short time before it fell apart.

LAST INDIAN UPRISING

WHEN THE INDIANS were herded onto government reservations in the late 1860s, the settlers and cattlemen felt reasonably safe from attack as they spread out over the eastern Oregon-Idaho grasslands, and those of northern Nevada. The Indian had been tamed, subdued, or annihilated, and now it was hoped the reservation system would secure the peace.

The Indians didn't like being turned into farmers and oftentimes moved from their traditional homelands which were closely interwoven with their culture and religion. Wise old chiefs knew that the ways of yesteryear were gone and that to survive at all, they must adjust to the patterns of the white man. But the young bucks, filled with wild energy and stubborn pride, believed it was beneath their dignity to work at tilling the soil and accepting government allotments. They longed for the freedoms of the past; death was more honorable than accepting the white man's charity.

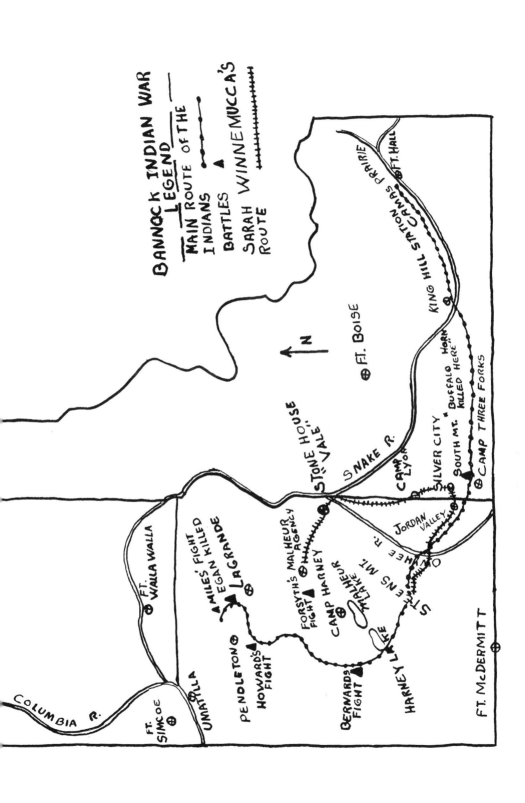

BANNOCK INDIAN WAR
LEGEND
———— MAIN ROUTE OF THE INDIANS
▲ BATTLES
•••••• SARAH WINNEMUCCA'S ROUTE

COLUMBIA R.
FT. SIMCOE ⊕
UMATILLA
FT. WALLA WALLA ⊕
PENDLETON ⊕
HOWARD'S FIGHT ▲
MILES' FIGHT ▲
EGAN KILLED ▲
LA GRANDE ⊕
N ↑
FT. BOISE ⊕
KING HILL STATION
CAMAS PRAIRIE
FT. HALL ⊕
STONE HOUSE VALE
SNAKE R.
SILVER CITY
SOUTH MT. "BUFFALO HORN KILLED HERE"
CAMP LYON
CAMP THREE FORKS
JORDAN VALLEY
OWYHEE R.
STEENS MT.
FORSYTH'S MALHEUR AGENCY
FIGHT ▲
CAMP HARNEY ⊕
MALHEUR LAKE
HARNEY LAKE
BERNARD'S FIGHT ▲
FT. McDERMITT ⊕

The reservation system, begun before the Civil War, bogged down during that conflict. But I believe the U.S. government meant well when it promised the Indians reservations and "just compensation" for the lands that the whites now occupied. During the War Between the States, funds for the reservation system were funneled into the Union's effort to subdue the South. After Appomattox came Reconstruction and the Great Migration. The United States was suffering from growing pains, and no one felt them more directly than the Red Men who were starving on their designated reservations.

The first revolt was by the Sioux in 1862, brought about by near-starvation conditions when the annuity payments didn't arrive on schedule. While the basic idea of reservations may have been sound, the administration of the system caused much grief. The Sioux revolt spread through western Minnesota, northwestern Iowa and eastern Dakota. It lasted a month, thousands of acres of fine crops were burned, two hundred women and girls were taken captive and subjected to brutal forms of rape, and seven hundred thirty-seven whites and forty-two Indians lost their lives. There was an ironic twist. Only a few hours after all hell broke loose, the seventy-one thousand dollars arrived which would have purchased the needed food and probably would have quelled the New Ulm Massacre, as it was called. But from then on until the Little Bighorn — the high water mark for the Indians — and the flight of Chief Joseph's Nez Perce, the West was on fire.

By the summer of 1877, the fighting was about over and many of the Indians were back on their agencies. Only Sitting Bull with a small core of diehards refused to surrender, and had fled to Canada. Before his final surrender, Sitting Bull stirred up the hopes of Indian tribes everywhere. His influence was felt with great impact among the people of Chief

Oregon Historical Society
Indian braves, probably Bannocks and typical of the warriors who roamed the land of the Owyhees during the uprisings of the 1870s.

Joseph, and with the Bannocks, Paiutes, and Snakes. The Bannocks under Chief Buffalo Horn were champing at the bit, eager to go on the warpath from their reservation at Fort Hall, Idaho, through which thousands of wagon trains had passed on their way to Oregon and California. And Buffalo Horn was a far more reckless and vengeful leader than Chief Pocatello who led the aggressive Bannocks a decade earlier.

Camas Prairie in Idaho provided the impetus to reopen hostilities. A clerk's error in writing "Kansas Prairie" and the bullheaded stubbornness of officials in refusing to correct it opened the Camas Prairie Reservation for settlement. It was treasured land to the Indians, a primary source for the gathering of camas roots. Before long, hogs and cattle were ravishing the camas. This was too much for the Bannocks who only the previous year had served the U.S. Army during the Nez Perce retreat. Chief Tendoy opposed the war, so pulled back to his reservation on the Lemhi River. Buffalo Horn felt he had ample cause for taking action. His people were starving and the reservation agent was being investigated for shipping supplies destined for the Indians to his eastern relatives for personal profit.

The restlessness spread to the other tribes. Eagle Eye of the Weiser tribe took his rations from the Malheur Agency supply point and headed east with his braves. Chief Egan of the Malheur Paiutes rode southeast. On Malheur Bench the Indians accused Agent William V. Rinehart of harsh and inhuman treatment, and of issuing starvation rations. Egan didn't wish to go to war, despite the terrible conditions on the reservation. But the pressure was put hard on him; he gave in and promised to lead the hostilities only after threats by the hotheads against him and his people, if he refused.

General George Crook who was aware of the agency conditions made an inspection of Fort Hall just prior to the outbreak of fighting in April 1878. But nothing was done in time. Crook reported: *"The apportionment of rations for the supply of this agency was ridiculously inadequate; the Indians complained that three days out of seven they had nothing to eat, and the agent told me the allowance had never been adequate."* A short time later, Crook added: *". . . It was no surprise . . . that some of the Indians soon afterward broke out into open hostility, and the great wonder is that so many remained on the reservation. With the Bannocks and Shoshones, our Indian policy has resolved itself into a question of warpath or starvation, and being merely human, many of them will always choose the former alternative, where death will at least be more glorious."*

Buffalo Horn, wanting to avoid the mistakes of the past, tried to keep out of contact with the whites until he could whip them in a decisive battle. The word was spread among the tribes so that an uprising could be timed simultaneously in all the sections. It has never been determined just how word was spread quickly among the tribes, widely scattered for hundreds of miles across rough country, but the Indians had their ways. The plan was to gather supplies and horses for a huge force under the general command of Sitting Bull. Chief Egan and his braves were assigned to gather "broke" horses by whatever means it took.

Idaho Historical Society

Chief Buffalo Horn of the Bannocks took his warriors to war and broke out of the reservation at Fort Hall to join other tribes in a widespread uprising.

Now Buffalo Horn attacked the invaders of Camas Prairie. On June 2, Captain Reuben F. Bernard drove Buffalo Horn and his braves from the prairie into the lava beds at the head of Clover Creek. He soon escaped, starting down the Overland Road on the Snake. Near King Hill, Buffalo Horn plundered some freight wagons, adding much ammunition to his supply. Then he crossed the Snake at Glenns Ferry, and cut the ferry adrift.

Meanwhile, John P. Hoyt, territorial governor of Idaho, and Generals Crook and Howard were rushing troops and volunteers to the field, hoping to prevent the Buffalo Horn hostiles from joining their Oregon allies. Some of the Indian bands didn't want to join up, but like Egan, were forced to do so under threat of death. Sarah Winnemucca, daughter of the celebrated Chief Winnemucca and granddaughter of Chief Truckee, was using all her diplomatic skills to keep as many of her people as possible from the conflict.

Sarah was ahead of her time. *Thoc-me-to-ny* meaning "Shell Flower" and one of her sisters had for a short duration attended a Catholic mission school at San Jose, California. When she returned to Nevada, for the first time she saw clearly the plight of her people. Things were now in better perspective for her. She continued acquiring education from the whites and then teaching her own people. The old times were gone forever, she stressed. There were advantages to the white man's ways, and the only way to survive in this new world was through education. Ignorance was the Indian's greatest enemy, not the whites.

During the decade of 1868 to 1878, Sarah served as a go-between for the Indians and the soldiers on the McDermitt and Malheur reservations. Her education and inborn intelligence allowed her to talk with clarity to high government officials. She gained the respect of both the whites and her own people. While living at Fort McDermitt, Sarah married a dashing white officer, a Lieutenant Bartlett. He was a heavy drinker and the marriage didn't last, for they became permanently separated when he was transferred. Sarah moved to the Malheur Agency where she worked for Agent Rinehart as an interpreter. But Sarah was fired when she reported his shortcomings to the military. Agent Rinehart was trying to force the Indians to work at digging irrigation ditches by refusing them food. The Red Men didn't take kindly to it. Relations deteriorated and a rebellion appeared in the making. Egan, Oytes and their tribesmen and some Bannocks asked Sarah to join them in a parley and to list their grievances for a powwow with the Great Father in Washington. Oytes argued for the use of force. When the parley was finished, Egan passed the hat and collected $29.25 to pay her fare to Washington.

Sarah promised to go at once to Elko, Nevada, where she might get additional funds from influential citizens and officials who weren't anxious for an all-out Indian war. She departed next morning for Silver City, on the route to Elko, with a Mr. Horton and his child. He wished to go as far as the mining camp and would pay Sarah fifty dollars — half at the start of the trip — for using her team and hack. Three days later, as they neared Camp Lyon, a traveler told them that the Bannocks had launched the war. Sarah turned her team south toward Jordan Valley, stopping at the Stone House where excited settlers were gathered. They had many stories to tell of events of the past three days, but to Sarah Winnemucca, it meant only one thing — disaster for her people.

The hostiles under Buffalo Horn passed up the Bruneau River, killing all settlers they found along the way. A band of volunteers was organized at once to protect the settlements. The original members of this volunteer company were Captain J. B. Harper, O. H. Purdy, Chris Steuder, Tom Jones, Guy Newcomb, Frank Martin, Ole Anderson, John Davidson, Ben White, William Nichols, Peter Donnelly, Mark Leonard, John Posey, W. Cooper, George Graham, J. M. Brunzell, Sr., John Anderson, Nick Maher, William Manning, W. W. Hastings, Al Myers, M. M. Rogers, Joe Rupert, J. J. Outhouse, J. M. Dillenger, Alex Wellman, Frank Armstrong and Paiute Joe and his brother. More than thirty others from the area joined up a bit later.

The volunteers left Silver City on Friday, June 2 for the "front," wherever it might be. That night they camped at O'Keefe's Ranch, seven miles from South Mountain. At the same time, a few miles away, the Indians they sought visited another rancher. Norman MacKenzie, who heard the story from Pete Disenroff himself, says, "The evening before the battle at South Mountain, Buffalo Horn and several of his subchiefs paid a social call to their old friend, Pete Disenroff, who lived on the present MacKenzie Ranch, just below where the main body of warriors was camped. In the past Pete had hired some of the Bannocks to help put up his hay, and since they were passing through, he invited the chiefs to have supper with him. Halfway through the meal a scout galloped up and exchanged a few hurried words with the chiefs, then they all left. Pete later realized that the scout had brought word of the volunteers approach." Despite the feeling of Owyhee settlers, the Indians were not unfriendly to all whites, nor were they inhuman, as sometimes seemed.

Early next morning the volunteers were in the saddle again and about noon they ran head-on into Buffalo Horn's braves. Seeing they were outnumbered, the volunteers broke and fled, barely escaping annihilation. In the running battle volunteers were unhorsed and Chris Steuder was wounded fatally, dead as he fell. O. H. Purdy was also killed. But the day was saved, for someone — it was believed to be

Paiute Joe, according to Sarah Winnemucca — got off a shot at close range that killed Buffalo Horn. The Indians, suddenly leaderless, were split apart. Some of them quit the war, but the majority fled to join Egan's Malheurs, the Northern Paiutes, Eagle Eye's Weisers, and some to the Shoshones and probably the Umatillas. Reports were rampant of ranch raiding and killing in the Steens Mountain country. Pete French's operation was hit, causing French and his men to flee many miles back to make a stand in the great house at Frenchglen, with the warriors on their flying heels. Egan took command of the hostiles who had gathered some three thousand horses, trailing them north through the vast eastern Oregon country. They crossed the Blitzen River near the Rocky Ford, headed toward the Double-O territory, and along the way burned all the settlers' homes and drove off their horses and other livestock.

Captain Bernard was trailing the hostiles, who now numbered three hundred, toward the headwaters of the Owyhee. On June 8 Colonel Orlando "Rube" Robbins' scouts up ahead located the Indian encampment on Battle Creek. But Bernard didn't take them on; he needed to replenish his supplies at Silver City and planned instead to march to the Steens Mountain country where the main body of the hostiles was reportedly located. Meanwhile, General Howard arrived at Fort Walla Walla and by June 18, he had almost nine hundred troops in the field.

As Bernard made ready for the Steens, he gained an unexpected ally in Sarah Winnemucca, who had just arrived in Silver City from the Stone House with her two traveling companions. Coming into town, too, from the south were two Indians Sarah recognized as friends. They were carrying a dispatch from the commander at Fort McDermitt to "the cavalry leader in the field." Sarah was quick to seize upon the opportunity. With her boldness and quickness of mind,

Nevada Historical Society
Sarah Winnemucca, who understood the plight of her people and fought gallantly
to help them.

she left her team to accompany the messengers to Captain Bernard's camp. On the way, the Paiutes informed her that her father, like her grandfather, was risking his life and also members of his band by refusing to join the hostiles. Sarah decided she must help her people, and other tribesmen, to flee the Bannocks.

Bernard, knowing her reputation, scribbled a note for use as identification:

To all good citizens of the country: – Sarah Winnemucca, with two of her people, goes with a dispatch to her father. If her horses should give out, help her all you can and oblige. CAPTAIN BERNARD

Sarah and her two Indian bodyguards left next morning for the Steens Mountain. It was a good thing they carried the note. At the Owyhee Crossing, they met some white scouts. Shown the note, the scouts gave them fresh horses.

The Crowley Ranch was still burning as they passed. Another ranch in Barren Valley was also burned and dead livestock littered the barnyard. Following the Steens Mountain trail, they made contact with Sarah's brother, Lee Winnemucca. The Bannocks had caught up with his band and taken their guns, blankets and horses. They were virtually captives. At the moment they were camped near the Bannocks in a little valley not far away. They had posted guards, fearing the pent-up Bannocks might attack.

Hurriedly, Sarah disguised herself by wrapping up in a blanket, unbraiding her hair, and dabbing on war-paint. As they came upon the camp, she estimated there were three hundred lodges. Things were in turmoil, as the braves prepared for war. Some were working on equipment, others catching horses, and still others were butchering the captured cattle. After dark, Sarah slipped into her father's lodge. He was expecting her, for Lee had told him of his daughter's arrival in the camp. The troopers were approaching, she said, and their only chance to survive was to escape during the night while the Bannocks slept and go with her to the soldiers for protection. Under cover of darkness some seventy Paiutes fled, but next morning a courier brought the warning that the Bannocks intended to pursue them. Sarah and another Paiute rode ahead to notify Bernard of her people's whereabouts. It was June 15 and she had traveled a good four hundred miles since leaving the Malheur Agency two weeks before.

General Howard turned over the rescue of Winnemucca's band to Robbins' scouts. Winnemucca's people were able to return to Fort McDermitt, but Sarah remained with Howard's command to be handy if she were needed again.

Rumors spread unbridled among the settlers as the Army advanced over the range lands. There were tales of mass murders, of entire families being wiped out. The roads were unsafe — in fact it was unsafe anywhere — and there were reports of Indians all around, killing and plundering at will. There were unconfirmed stories of stage drivers being killed between McDermitt and Jordan Valley. Settlers to the east, from Fort Hall into Wyoming, were on the alert to mounting danger from the tribes.

Dugouts and stone buildings made ideal forts, but most of the settlers from the Bruneau River to Jordan Valley headed for Silver City. When the Indians crossed the Bruneau Valley, they went through John Turner's ranch. Fortunately he and his family were absent. Other ranchers and their wives and children were hidden in a cave on Uncle Abe Robertson's ranch which was being defended by a group of volunteers, organized for protection. In Jordan Valley the Stone House that stood a mile above the Gusman Ranch at the Jordan Creek crossing became a sanctuary, but

Stone buildings of the old Ruby Ranch, near Danner, proved excellent fortifications during Indian raids. These remains are visible today. Note slot for rifle at right.

was soon jammed with people. Other families went on to the State Line Ranch, which had a stone house on it, or to the Sheep Ranch.

Lavern Anawalt described the uprising as told him by his grandmother:

"My father was tending stage horses at the Ruby Ranch for Wells Fargo. He was fifteen at the time. When word came that the Indians were coming, he had instructions to take the horses across Jordan Creek to the Sheep Ranch. There was a Chinaman cook working for the company and father was ordered to take him along. The Chinaman was going to ride a mule. As they started across Jordan Creek, the Chinaman lost his mule, so father had to take the mule back the second time for the Chinaman. This time he held the mule and the Chinaman got on. The mule took off so fast that the Chinaman's cue was flying straight out behind. They were going down the south side of Jordan Creek when father saw a man afoot on the hill parallel to the creek. The sun reflected off his rifle, and he thought it was an Indian, but it turned out to be another white man heading for the Sheep Ranch."

Sister Mary Frances Claire (Aunt Esther Maher) reported:

"My mother was all alone on the ranch. Father was in Silver City. She saw twenty-eight Bannock Indians and since there were no squaws with them, she knew they were on the warpath. The day before, they cut a man's head open with their weapons. They entered a home and the husband hid, letting his wife face them. They were so disgusted at the cowardice that they would have killed him when he did appear, if the neighbors did not prevent it. Charles and I were two years old and were playing on the floor. When the older children — nine, eight and six — saw the Indians coming, they rushed to lock the doors. Our mother motioned to step aside and leave the doors open. The Indians came; the chief entered first, followed by the others.

"Mother handed out whatever they asked for in the line of eats. The chief then told mother that they had some horses with our brand. He asked where they could put them. Mother told him and he ordered two Indians to drive them into the corral. Bill was looking out of a window and saw an Indian riding a pinto horse that belonged to him. The chief ordered the Indian to put the horse in the corral with the others."

The family wasn't harmed by the braves. Since the Army ordered people living in the rural districts to leave, they went to Silver City.

Many of the old families in the Jordan Valley country remember the Indian outbreak, or recall hearing their elders tell about it. Frank Swisher who worked for us told about two hunters:

"John Batchelor and Jep Osborn were hunting deer two miles above the Swisher Place on Swisher Mountain. They saw a group of Indians and, not knowing they were on the warpath, paid them no attention. The Indians fired on them and hit Batchelor, giving him palsy for the rest of his life. Batchelor told Osborn to save himself, but Osborn hid them both in a bunch of quaking aspen."

"My grandfather, Silas Skinner, and his hired men were at Parsnip looking for horses," relates Kirt Skinner. "He had a Paiute Indian working for him, too, but he left him at the Trout Creek station. The Indian told my grandmother that he had seen signal fires from the top of Trout Creek Hill and that he could tell from them that the Indians were on the warpath. My grandmother went to Parsnip and warned my grandfather of the danger. Then they went to the Stone House, but moved on to Silver City when it got too crowded. Purdy and the volunteers commandeered horses and guns from my grandfather, and it was my grandfather's horse Purdy was riding when he was killed. My father, Bill Skinner, remembered

Fleeing families during the outbreak of Indians in the 1860s and 1870s took refuge in various strongholds throughout the Jordan Valley country. One was the State Line ranch house which was built of stone. Many sought safety there; later some went on to the safety of Silver City.

the soldiers that stopped at Trout Creek, and their leader, General Howard."

"One day before the scare of '78, father was up by Sheep Springs near Jaca's ranch in Jordan Valley looking for his work horses and saw a lot of Indians there on the move," recalls Blanche Miller. "He rode up and talked to them. They were all squaws and children. He said hello and tried to find out where they were going. All a squaw said was, 'How about match?' He gave them matches. He could see two riders coming their way at a fast pace. They turned out to be two bucks who said they were taking the squaws and children to the Salmon River. . . . At Dry Creek during the scare, people were panicky. During the night a face appeared at the window and they thought the Indians had come. It was an old Chinaman and he said, 'Stay all night and go in the morning.' Father said he could have hugged the old S.O.B."

And over in the Mahogany Mountains, John Strode met a Paiute chief who told him that the Indians were about to go on the warpath. He couldn't control some of his young men, he said, and advised Strode that it would be best for him to leave his ranch until the thing had blown over. Strode took his family and went to Silver City.

Even in war the Indians tried to help individual whites and their families, and not every white met along the trail or on his ranch was immediately shot and scalped, as some historians would have you believe. . . .

The settlers fled to Fort Harney from the Steens Mountain country and the Harney Valley. Learning that the troops were closing in on them, the hostiles broke camp and fanned out. Egan knew they couldn't withstand heavily armed, swift-moving troops. He wanted, if possible, to avoid a fight with the Army;

if he had to meet them, he wanted to do so near the Blue Mountains where he could retreat if necessary. The main body passed north of Happy Valley to cross the Blitzen River at Rock Ford. They skirted the south shore of Harney Lake, then headed north to Silver Creek. Small parties went out to kill and plunder, their main purpose to gather horses.

At Fort Harney, the settlers were growing impatient, wanting to find out what was going on. They felt reports reaching them were distorted; they wanted to return to their ranches, risky though it was, to save all they could if the Indians did attack, or to go down fighting. "Doc" Kiger who had joined his Happy Valley neighbors, the Smyths, in the flight to Fort Harney remembered:

"Went to the barracks and . . . they were all gone but thirteen soldiers. So they issued us guns, carbines to protect the family, said, 'You men will have to protect the families now.' So we went out and tried them guns, didn't like the looks of them. It was an old linen cartridge with a lead bullet or slug, one of these old carbines, you know. You would have to pull up and put in your cartridge, pull up this lever and that would cut the cartridge and then the powder would run out on the pan there and a thing you pulled back and whis-s-s-s-boom she went. Well, we shot at marks and I couldn't hit any. . . .

"We said we couldn't hit the damned cavalry barn down there. You've got better guns and we want them. He says, 'Yes, we got better guns.' He issued us Springfield rifles with a long copper cartridge, 50 caliber. We took them out and we could shoot pretty good. John Smyth, hearing from over there (toward Happy Valley) men coming in, nobody had seen any Indians. We thought we had better just go back there and get the best of things out of the house and bring in our horses, back to camp. So we started back. . . ."

Doc and his brother accompanied John Smyth and

his father to Happy Valley. Fortunately they didn't stay, but went on to Diamond Valley. Smyth and his father were burned to death when the Indians fired their ranch house. At Diamond the Kigers ran onto Pete French and his buckeroos, working cattle. French said they hadn't seen any Indians. They started back toward Happy Valley and met Sylvester "Coon" Smith with a span of horses hitched to a wagon's running gear. He would go with them. On the grade leading to the valley, they overtook Sam Miller. At the top was a gap in the rimrock and a gate. Miller rode ahead to open the gate and rushed back. The hostiles were coming up the other side. At that moment they were opening the gate. Miller and Smith cut the team loose from the wagon, mounted the horses and rushed back to Diamond. By this time the Indians had the gate open, spotted them and opened fire, but missed.

Miller didn't think so. Pulling up his horse, he said, "Boys, I'm shot."

"I guess not," answered Doc.

Miller felt the back of his head. When he looked, he saw no blood on his hand.

"I guess it must have been that tug that hit me," he concluded.

The four men overtook John Witzen and George Bollenbaugh who were working horses. By the time they reached the ranch, the Indians were right on their tails. French's men were saddling up. French ordered them to pick a good horse apiece and turn the others loose. Pete then climbed to the top of the corral and began shooting at the oncoming Indians. This discouraged the hostiles just long enough for the crew to get saddled. They all hit for the P Ranch sixteen miles distant. In the flight the Chinese cook was killed and Coon Smith's horse shot from under him. Luckily he was able to grab the rein of the cook's horse, throw himself aboard and catch the crew. They made it to the P, then decided they'd be better off at Fort Harney, so rode over rugged terrain west of the Jackass Mountains and finally reached the fort with one wounded boy, John Witzel, who took a bad shot in the hip.

At Sheep Ranch on June 16, General Howard announced his first major campaign plan. His strategy was to allow the Indians to move on, trailing but not agitating them, until they shifted into a position where he could defeat them with hopefully little loss of life on either side. Howard was sympathetic, not a butcher or destroyer. But Captain Bernard was angry, for he wanted to crush the hostiles at once, no matter the cost. The settlers were also opposed to Howard's strategy, but Howard felt that as long as the ranchers and homesteaders were finding their way to safety, his plan was practical. Only on some occasions, it didn't prove out, as with the Smyths and the stage drivers.

Now there was a new worry. Reports reached Howard of Egan's plan to move east to join forces with the other tribes. Friendly Indians reported that when Egan left the Steens, he split into two bands. These would come together again at a rendezvous place in the Blue Mountains and then attempt to join the other warring tribes. Howard wished to cut them off. Marching toward the Malheur Agency on June 20, Howard sent Sarah Winnemucca and her sister, Mattie, to Fort Harney to learn if Bernard had received reinforcements from that post. Bernard was moving through Barren Valley at this time, arriving at the fort a day or two after the skirmish in Happy and Diamond valleys. From here, the noose would be drawn on the Red Men.

Bernard secured reinforcements at Fort Harney — volunteers under the loose command of Pete French. Meanwhile, Robbins and his scouts picked up fresh Indian trail along Silver Creek, forty-five miles west of Harney. Bernard and his men arrived late that night, June 22, and as he planned for the attack, Robbins and his men reconnoitered the Indian camp.

W. A. Goulder, reporter for the *Idaho Statesman*, wrote: "When a shelter near the redmen had been gained, Robbins ventured alone to a shadowed spot near the natural stronghold. The camp of the Indians, screened by black lava walls and dense willows, was calm. Unguarded stock grazed at will. Surprisingly strong, the enemy numbered between 1,200 and 2,000 persons, 700 of them capable of fighting."

Next morning beyond eight o'clock, Bernard attacked the camp, warning his men that they would be shot if they retreated and they might as well be killed by the Indians as their friends. Twice the troops were repulsed in the initial charge, three cavalrymen being killed and three others wounded. During the height of the battle, Robbins and Egan charged each other. Robbins blasted Egan from his horse, then shot him again in the chest. The Indians carried him off, still breathing, and resumed the fighting with such frenzy that Bernard ordered recall sounded.

The battle on Silver Creek which lasted through the day took place at a point forty-five miles west of Fort Harney and a few miles south of old Camp Currey. Darkness was coming on when Bernard sent a dispatch to General Howard:

"Conduct of officers and men deserves commendation; all behaved splendidly . . . Indian losses unknown . . . Shall locate their camp again tonight. They are moving leisurely, burdened with stock and many wounded."

Howard was well aware of Bernard's feelings about his overall battle strategy, and he knew that the captain was spoiling for a fight. He also hadn't been very specific on how the battle was going. Reaching Fort Harney June 24, Howard left at once for the scene.

Meanwhile, the Indians were eluding Bernard.

Although badly wounded, Egan directed a retrograde movement, assisted by his subchiefs. They piled sagebrush high and set it afire, making the troops believe they were standing their ground. Thus they escaped the trap that Bernard was to spring in the morning.

On the way to the battleground, Sarah Winnemucca talked to an old Bannock woman who told her the hostiles were attempting to reach the Umatilla Reservation. Howard wanted them cut off from joining the eastern tribes, and now they were on the rampage.

The Indians crossed the John Day, killing, burning, and driving off large herds of cattle and horses. They caused near-panic at Canyon City, but then bypassed the alarmed and barricaded town. Their numbers swelled as other malcontents joined from the Columbia, Shoshone and Lemhi tribes. The tension grew as the hostiles neared the Columbia River.

Bernard's scouts tracked the main body, now nearly two thousand strong, into the high country between the John Day and Grande Ronde rivers. Bernard had to wait for Howard's reinforcements, slowed down by the lumbering wagons and infantry, much to the captain's frustration. He was eager to get on with it. The Indians had now moved onto the north slope of the Blue Mountains between Butter and Birch creeks. Howard's attack scattered the natives, pushing them by retreat deeper into the mountains east toward the Grande Ronde Valley, with the women and children moving ahead of the braves.

Upon posting troops on the trails leading to the Snake and Salmon rivers, Howard headed for Lewiston and the mouth of the Grande Ronde, hoping to keep the renegades from going any farther north.

Meanwhile, Egan's band was reported moving across the Columbia, below Umatilla. The Bannocks and Paiutes offered the Umatillas two thousand horses to help get them across, adding the assurance that they

A Bannock brave, displaying arrogance, was photographed at the Snake River Agency. He may have participated in the Indian wars, when the Red Men tried to drive the whites from their ancient lands.

would need no support once they gained the north bank. But the Umatillas refused and in retaliation, several were shot by the pent-up hostiles. Only small parties of Indians got across the Columbia, however, for Army gunboats patrolling the river drove them off. This was reason enough why the Umatillas backed away. Along the banks, the troops found tons of equipment abandoned by the fleeing Indians.

Fifty white volunteers were attacked near Willow Springs, and five were killed. The warriors hit the Cayuse stage station between La Grande and Pendleton, wiping it out before Captain Evan Miles, commanding a mixed force of artillery, infantry and volunteers, drove them back. Some of the less reluctant Umatillas had now joined the Bannocks, but surrendered that evening. The fighting went on the next day, but Miles was frustrated by thickly wooded mountains near the station, making it difficult to deploy his troops.

The Umatillas came to Miles and said they wanted to help, but the parley was interrupted when Colonel Frank Wheaton took command. So the Umatillas went off on their own. When they caught up with Egan, they told him they wanted to join up. Egan was a Umatilla and had no reason to suspect a doublecross. But Chief Umapine of the Umatillas arranged with another chief, Walsac, to murder Egan. Umapine wouldn't do it himself, for he and Egan were of the same tribe. As the two bands talked, the Umatillas opened fire, killing Egan and some of his men. Then they cut off Egan's head as proof and returned to the soldiers. Near Emigrant Springs on July 15, they brought the head into camp, where Dr. J. A. Fitzgerald, an Army surgeon, identified it.

Egan's death broke the back of the Indian offensive. Both war chiefs were dead, and the hostiles scattered in small bands. There were more depradations and killings, but the spirit was gone from the drive. By October the largest of the Indian wars in terms of area and men was over.

THE LEGEND OF BIGFOOT

WHAT THIS LAST great Indian uprising in the Pacific Northwest cost in lives is difficult to determine. Estimates were that about thirty-three whites and one hundred fifty Indians were killed or wounded. It may have run as low as seventy-eight among the hostiles. In any case, now that the fighting was over, the Paiutes drifted back toward the Malheur Reservation, the Shoshone to Duck Valley, and the Bannocks to Fort Hall. However, it would be years before some of them returned to their allotted homes. Others never did. . . .

Agent Rinehart of the Malheur found he had a reservation, but few Indians. The numbers were so reduced that they were moved in the 1878/79 winter to Duck Valley and then to Yakima, Washington. The agency was put up for sale, the beautiful valley coveted by Henry Miller. It is now the site of the Agency Valley reservoir.

Sarah Winnemucca continued her battle for rights

for her people. She was the first of her race to publish a book. Although no literary prize, *Life Among the Paiutes; Their Wrongs and Claims* had an impact on the federal government which brought about an improvement in Indian policy in later years.

Uncle Bill Hanley was a great admirer of Sarah Winnemucca. In *Feelin' Fine,* he wrote:

"The Paiutes in Nevada that stayed out of the war were left in their own country in good shape. Old Chief Winnemucca lived in security on his homelands till he died. His daughter Sally was mostly responsible for his good fortune, a little black Indian, but most important as a chief's daughter. She was against the war — was perhaps the first American woman to stand out against her tribe for peace . . . never gave up till she got a good part of them with her. . . . Always loyal, faithful to the white men like all those Indian women that married them. But she was a modern girl to the end, not very good at staying married — married four or five times, but kept her name through it all. After the war she was frank to say what she thought about Indian agents — wasn't very flattering. But she was never against the government, just against some of the men acting for it . . . pretty fine distinction for a native girl to make."

Uncle Bill, who got around this eastern Oregon country, knew most of the folks and was a keen observer. He sought out the Indian chief credited with killing Egan. He had doublecrossed his own people and was now the fallen hero.

"There was that Umatilla chief that shot Egan for money," Uncle Bill wrote in his book. "Lived alone at last in a dirty little tepee, bitter, resentful, sick with old age and loneliness, all crippled up. No son, no squaw, no tribe. All he had left from his life of glory was his scalps, white and Indian, that he'd slipped off heads, tied to his saddle, and galloped away with.

"Would go see him sometimes . . . peer in. There

he would be, all drawn up back in his smoky tepee, his sunk eyes red and shining out like a trapped rat's . . . muttering and mumbling: Me big chief — brave man — kill Egan. Now die like squaw. No one to care for my scalps — bugs, moths eat 'em. Put 'em out to sun and air and white man come along and steal 'em. What you think of that kind of white man, uh?

"What an awful world it was, even bugs and moths taking his scalps. . . . Just a hero reduced."

During the 1890s there were still quite a few Indians living in the Jordan Valley area. Frank Swisher remembered as a small boy when the Indians in numbers passed their place on Cow Creek to their meets in the mountains. There were several popular gathering places, among them Indian Meadow on South Mountain, the head of Slaughter House Gulch, and the big springs at the head of Trout Creek. Umatillas, Paiutes, Bannocks and Shoshone gathered to take part in the big powwows, the gambling, horse racing, dancing, and feasts. These were large, festive occasions in the traditional ways passed down from generation to generation for many centuries, and now finally beginning to fade.

Jess Winnemucca, John Camas, Little John and Pretty Jhonnie were among the leaders of the later-day Paiutes around Jordan Valley. They worked at clearing sagebrush and doing odd jobs. Jess Winnemucca, who was son of the old chief and brother of Sarah, took contracts to grub sagebrush. One bunch of Indians camped near town at the spring bordering the race track. Another group was just below Jones' place on Baxter Creek and still another east of town on Willow Creek. When the racing season opened in the spring and fall, the Indians — who loved to race — came from all over the Owyhee country, just to be on hand.

But in the off-season and during the winter, they went back to their reservations.

The Indians had a tough time of it, living in a state of poverty as they grubbed brush and chopped wood for their white neighbors. The pickings were meager. Women earned a little cash-money making buckskin gloves for sale. When Dr. Walter W. Jones, the much-beloved valley practitioner, delivered one Indian woman's baby, she paid him by hauling wood to his drug store.

Another Indian war, on a small scale, was almost started in the 1890s when Billy Beers shot Pretty Jhonnie. Beers and several others were drinking and Jhonnie was peeking through a window watching the action.

"Let me see how close I can come to the s.o.b. without hitting him," Billy said.

The shot hit poor Jhonnie in the eye. The Indians took him to their camp. Beers and his friends were fearful they might have provoked an Indian uprising. But Jhonnie lived, although he wore a patch over the eye the rest of his life, and the Indians didn't press to even the score. It was recognized as an accident, for Beers had always been good to the Indians. They knew it, and didn't let the shooting spoil that relationship.

Pretty Jhonnie, sometimes called Patch-Eye Jhonnie after the accident, was a familiar figure around Jordan Valley for years. Then on December 9, 1909, the *Jordan Valley Express* carried the following notice:

"The spirit of Patch-Eye Jhonnie, one of the oldest and best-known Indians in this section, passed to the happy hunting grounds Monday last. His remains were laid to rest in the Indian cemetery."

There was a crisis also when Jess Winnemucca's son, Willie, broke from the reservation. He was twelve years old and didn't want to go to school, so ran away from McDermitt and came to Jordan Valley. The authorities arrived and took the unhappy boy back home. Then he committed suicide.

Around 1915-20 the Indians faded from the valley because the work played out. From then on, the only times they showed up were during the haying seasons and to hunt groundhogs in the spring. It was indeed the end of an era. . . .

For many decades, the fear of one Indian would not die. Despite reports of his death, people believed they saw this legendary giant on the ridges, along the streams, and in the shadows of the Owyhees. The legend of Bigfoot, who was blamed for countless depredations against the whites, has become the most retold story in this part of the West, and even a town carries his Indian name in memory.

For years Bigfoot terrorized the country around Silver City, killing and plundering at will. There was a mysterious aura about him and the way he got around, seemingly at the speed of a ghost, because he was so huge and could cover the desert and mountains in long strides and with powerful stamina. Bigfoot was a giant among men. He might bob up in one area and a day later be many miles away. Fresh tracks were found one day near Weiser and the following day on the Owyhee, eighty miles distant. He was elusive and knew the country like the palm of his hand. Some people felt he possessed ethereal qualities; others believed that perhaps he was only a figure of vivid imaginations from mining camp legends and campfire yarn-spinning. But there is little doubt of his existence, from the accounts of those who said they actually saw him, and from the man who claimed that he witnessed

Bigfoot on a rampage. The giant Indian terrified the Owyhee country and became
a legend.

the killing of Bigfoot and helped bury him. His story, when finally pieced together, proved to be a pathetic one.

Bigfoot was called "Oulux" by his Indian compatriots. They also called him "Nampuh," from which the city of Nampa, Idaho, gets its name. He was indeed a giant, for his tracks were of unbelievable size. Many pioneers found them, and were frightened by the knowledge that he might be lurking close at hand. William T. Anderson who saw the end of Bigfoot near Silver City measured the corpse. Bigfoot stood 6 feet 8½ inches in height, measured 59 inches around the chest, weighed an estimated three hundred pounds of bone and muscle, had hands eighteen inches around at the widest place, and feet seventeen and one-half inches in length and eighteen inches circumference around the ball. He also noticed that the giant was light-skinned.

The big fellow had a price on his head of one thousand dollars for the many murders and other crimes blamed on him, including the attacking and burning of wagon trains along the Oregon Trail. Nampuh and his raiders struck hard and often. To the giant Indian who really wasn't a fullblood at all, it was often revenge against people who had mistreated him. It began because another man stole his girl, who had rejected him, and both had ridiculed him and his monstrous size and his race. Bigfoot was part Cherokee Indian, part white, and part black. His real name, he revealed as he was dying, was Starr Wilkinson, for an early-day desperado. He was born on the Cherokee Nation. His father was a white, Archer Wilkinson, and his mother part-Cherokee and part-Negro. His size haunted him. He gained the name "Bigfoot" at an early age from other boys. He had a hot temper and a low boiling point, and several times nearly killed others over the hateful nickname.

Wilkinson realized he must leave the reservation or be killed by his enemies. He went to the capital of the Cherokee Nation and in 1856 put in with a wagon train, bound for Oregon. He drove a team for his board and fell in love with a young woman who encouraged the relationship. They merged with a train of New Yorkers, and among the newcomers was a handsome young artist named Hart, who quickly won the girl's affections. She would have little to do with Wilkinson now. Being very sensitive, Starr was certain that Hart had maligned him with the girl, since the fellow had boldly ridiculed him to his face about his huge size.

Things built up inside Wilkinson as the train continued west. While camped near Goose Creek Mountains, near the Snake River, Bigfoot and the artist went out one morning looking for livestock. On the bank of the Snake, Hart told Wilkinson he intended to marry the girl and take her to Oregon. Starr warned him not to try, that he had prior rights to her.

"Do you suppose she would marry a big-footed nigger like you, and throw off a good-looking fellow like me?" the artist retorted.

Wilkinson grew angry; he denied being a Negro. If Hart called him that again, he would kill him. The artist drew his gun and repeated the words. Starr went for him. Hart fired, wounding Starr in the side. But Wilkinson grabbed Hart, choked him to death with those powerful hands, and threw the body into the Snake. Taking Hart's gun, pistol and knife, he ran off into the hills.

Near the Boise River, Starr came upon a French trapper and trader named Joe Lewis. The Frenchman claimed he'd lived for many years with the Indians and had helped them massacre the Whitmans at Waiilatpu. Starr joined the Indians and spent the remainder of his life as one of them, hating the whites and staging raids on settlers, miners and wagon trains.

In 1857 Nampuh went with a band of warriors to the emigrant trail, hoping to steal stock from the pioneers. During a raid, Bigfoot recognized cattle belonging to the family with whom he'd crossed the plains. They had apparently wintered at Boise, but were now on the move again. He was determined to find his girl, even though the risk was great, so went to the train. The girl was there, but she and the others turned upon him in anger. They believed, seeing him alive, that he had murdered the artist. He was ordered from the camp. Starr warned the girl if she wouldn't have him, she would regret it before reaching Oregon. Again she refused. He left the camp in a rage, determined to have revenge against these people who had befriended him on the trek West, and especially the girl.

Bigfoot organized a band of thirty warriors and taking Joe Lewis along, attacked the wagons where the Boise River dumps into the Snake. All who were with the train were killed, including the girl. Later, Bigfoot regretted his action, admitting that "I was mad and foolish."

From then on, Wilkinson took part in many massacres and killed many times. He said that he lost count. The whites put a price on his head and travelers feared taking lonely routes through the Owyhees. His hatred for the whites increased after he married an Indian woman and they had a son. She was killed and the boy carried off.

"Since that time," he said, "I have done all the mischief I could, and glad of it."

The way he could cover the ground, even outdis-
tancing good horses, amazed the whites who tried
tracking him down. Once John W. Wheeler, Frank
Johnson, and Ben Cook spotted his fresh prints and
gave chase, hoping to claim the reward. They shot
two average-size Indians with him, but Bigfoot swam
the swift Snake River and got away, for their horses
were played out. Later, the trio found his camp. He
had consumed two huge salmon, leaving only the bare
bones. His trail doubled back to the river, which he
swam a second time, while the men and their beaten
mounts had to go five miles roundabout to the nearest
ferry.

Oregon State Highway Photo

Near this point, Farewell Bend of the Snake River, Bigfoot escaped by swimming
the swift river not once but twice. His pursuers, riding tired mounts, had to
travel five miles around via the nearest ferry.

I have heard many stories about Bigfoot, but the
thing that always bothered me was that this same man,
John Wheeler, who said he killed Chief Nampuh,
never tried to collect the reward. I felt there must
have been some good reason, for one thousand dollars
was a sizable chunk of cash in those days. Wheeler
first came to Silver City from the Boise Basin in 1868
as part of a special force of lawmen dispatched by
Governor David M. Ballard to restore order between
the fighting mining companies called the Golden
Chariot and the Ida Elmore. The feud put the entire
town into an uproar. There were pitched battles and
lives were lost, among them the two owners. Wheeler
was well chosen as one of the special band of lawmen,
for he was rated as an expert pistol and rifle shot.
But he had his weaknesses. He haunted Silver City's
gambling tables and always seemed to have money
to blow. Suspicions were that Wheeler was involved
in a rash of stagecoach robberies on the roads from
Silver City to the Boise Basin and down on the Burnt
River.

Late in July 1868, William T. Anderson was traveling from Silver City to Boise City with a two-horse
wagon. Reaching Reynolds Creek, he pulled off the
road to wait for other travelers to come along. This
was a dangerous section; Anderson had no desire to
go down that canyon alone, for in that dark slot Bigfoot
had murdered many people. Unthinking, he turned
the horses loose and they broke away from him.

Now Anderson was in a fix. The horses went down
Reynolds Creek toward the massacre grounds. Anderson followed reluctantly. Suddenly he saw three
Indians coming his direction. One was a huge fellow;
he was certain it was Bigfoot. By their pace, he felt
they hadn't yet spotted him. Anderson hid behind

some rocks as the Indians passed by him. Anderson realized what had drawn their attention. A stagecoach with a load of passengers was coming into sight along the road.

There was the crack of a rifle from a tree near the creek. One Indian dropped and Bigfoot abandoned his plan to attack the stagecoach, realizing he was being bushwhacked. The rifleman, who turned out to be Wheeler, had Bigfoot in his Henry rifle sights, putting shot after shot into him, sixteen in all before he was downed. The third Indian took off over the hill. Anderson witnessed the ambush from his hiding place, then cautiously went forward to join Wheeler beside the dying giant. Bigfoot was able to talk and using plain English, told about himself and his life. He solved the mystery as to his identity in exchange for a last request. Starr asked Wheeler not to take his body or any part of it back to the fort to claim the reward, but to bury him along the creek with his old rifle. Wheeler, who claimed to be part-Cherokee, and therefore a blood-brother, made the promise. Anderson was pledged to secrecy as to the exact location of the body.

Wheeler had good reason, it seems, to go along with Bigfoot's request and not try claiming the reward. He had come to Reynolds Creek to rob the stage. He was already under suspicion as a road agent. If it became known that he was in the area that day and hour, when the stagecoach was due, the suspicions about his activities would no doubt increase several-fold, and there would be questions asked. As it turned out, Wheeler and several others attempted to rob a Blue Mountain stage a short while later. A posse tracked him down and he drew a ten-year sentence in the Oregon Penitentiary. He was released short of the ten years on "good behavior" and went to California, where he later committed suicide.

Ten years after the killing of Bigfoot, Anderson, who was also living in California, sent a detailed account of the day on Reynolds Creek to the *Idaho Statesman*. By then Anderson had lost track of Wheeler and didn't know he was out of prison, and in California. Possibly if he had, the witness to the end of Bigfoot might not have released his story. But he swore that the account was true and tried to explain why he had kept his pledge for so long. Some believed him, others didn't. People continued to say that they had seen the monster, that he was still alive. He was blamed for unexplained killings, and the legends about him persisted for many years in the Owyhee Country.

MUTTON FOR THE HUNGRY MINERS

NO SOONER HAD the miners swarmed into the Owyhees than the sheepmen were on their trails, knowing that the gold-seekers would pay high prices for mutton, especially when beef was scarce. It set the stage for a thriving industry which came down to the present. The Jordan Valley country was known to many outsiders more for its sheep than for its cattle, largely because of the association with the colorful Basques who actually were latecomers in the Owyhee saga.

Sheep were plentiful in the Far West. In three decades following the Civil War, approximately fifteen million sheep were trailed from the Pacific States to the Rocky Mountain region and the Great Plains. The West has been tied romantically to the cattle industry. But the sheep were also there, although the cattlemen often took a dim view of them which resulted sometimes in sheep and cattle "wars." Yet despite the image built by Western novelists, the cattlemen often ran sheep, too, because it was profitable. Yarns that cows wouldn't graze where sheep had trod were simply untrue.

The sheepmen were an enterprising lot. You had to have grit to put up with the nervous bleaters. Many a buckeroo like Dave Shirk found handling the sheep an exasperating experience. Nevertheless, the mining camps of the Idaho Territory offered opportunity for enormous profits, despite the hazards from Indians and terrain. The bold sheepmen were willing to accept the challenge, and the gamble.

The trails from California across Nevada were sufficiently hazardous for travelers bound for the mines, but when driving a band of sheep, the risks were increased many fold. First to test this venture were two Californians who left the Golden State with a thousand wethers — mutton on the hoof for Ruby City. They made it across the arid rolling lands of Nevada without apparent incident, finally reaching the Owyhee Crossing. The first night beyond the crossing, they camped at what became known as the Sheep Ranch, presently owned by Fred Eiguren. Early next morning the Indians hit, killing them both. The warriors herded the bawling sheep back to Owyhee Crossing, then up a side canyon where they slaughtered the animals. Next spring, the Indians were seen with sheepskins for saddle blankets.

The incident might have discouraged the sheepmen, but far from it. In 1865 Major Gorham Gates Kimball and his partners, George Hoag and John W. Burgess, pooled their resources to purchase thirty-seven hundred sheep in California. The plan was to drive the herd from Red Bluff through the Steens Mountain and Owyhee country to Boise City. The trek proved a miserable one; Kimball and his party found their progress slowed and sometimes halted by Indians, bad water, hot weather, short feed, and rocky

Photo by Bureau of Land Management

Sheep by the thousands were brought into the Owyhee country to feed the hungry miners. Later came the picturesque Basques, who for many years tended the flocks on the plains and in the mountains. Sheep are still grazed thoughout the region. This flock is near the famed Owyhee Crossing.

trails. While camped July 28 on Crooked Creek near where it passes today beneath U.S. 95, south of Jordan Valley, Kimball met Lieutenant Gates from Camp Lyon and his command who were looking for Indians. Kimball asked Gates if the trail grew any better as they moved north. Gates shook his head. He could expect nothing but more of the same — sand, sage, alkali and rocks.

But Kimball was determined, and he was too far out now to turn around. Bypassing Silver City, he reached the vicinity of Boise where he halted to fatten up the tired herd on lush feed along the Boise River. The sheep were sheared, but the market at Boise City wasn't as good as it should have been, so Kimball

drove the bunch on east the following spring to the
Missouri River. But he never forgot the drive to Boise.

"I was brought up and educated to believe there
is a hell where all had to suffer for their sins," Kimball
wrote in his journal. "I now think there was one once
and the country over which I have just passed must
have been the place where it was located. I have seen
no boundary lines, but the marks of the heat are still
there — and I guess all the rocks that were not used
were thrown into the devil's half acre."

After the Indians were subdued in 1868, the cattlemen moved into the valleys and soon steers outnumbered the sheep. The cows continued to dominate the
Owyhee country until the death-dealing winter of
1888/89 which wiped out both cattle and sheep herds,
and broke many a rancher. The sheepmen were
opportunists; the following spring they were swarming
over the ranges formerly grazed by cattle. Henry Long,
a cattleman who homesteaded near Riverside, got out
of bed one morning to strange sounds. Rubbing his
eyes in disbelief, he saw a band of sheep swarming
over the hill adjacent to his place.

Long turned to his hired man. "We're going to have
to pull out. The damned sheep are taking the country."

Sheepmen didn't need the investment required by
the cattlemen and therefore could recover quicker and
easier. Among the first permanent sheepmen to survive the winter of '88 was a Scotsman, Thomas
Turnbull, who immigrated to the United States in 1883
at the age of 26. He didn't stay long in New York,
but boarded another ship for San Francisco and then
came up the West Coast to Astoria. Arriving in Oregon,
he spent a brief time around Shaniko, which later
became a sheep shipping center after arrival of the
central Oregon railroad. Then "Uncle Tom," as he

would come to be called, went east to Malheur country, spending a full year at McDermitt. In 1888 he entered a partnership with John Wood.

"We leased a band of ewes for six bits a head and got the wool and the lambs," Turnbull told the *Eastern Oregon Observer*. "We trailed them to Barren Valley where the other sheepmen said we would go broke. But we did not. That was a good time to make money, even though we suffered losses in the hard winter of 1888. During the hard times of the early nineties, we sold wool at six cents a pound, but we bought lambs at seventy-three cents a head.

"We did not farm much, but put up enough hay at the Duck Ponds for our horses. We wintered our ewes on the desert and bought hay from Phen Venator for our lambs. In a tough winter, we fed sixteen hundred head on twenty tons of hay, but they got by."

James L. Turnbull, Uncle Tom's nephew, disclosed how they "got by:"

"Every morning they had to help a lot of the old ewes to their feet on the bed ground because they were so weak. If they kicked, they went on with the load. If they were too weak to kick, they got a little hay. I think this conservation of hay stayed with him, because one thing he would eat you out on was to leave hay scattered about a haystack when you were feeding the stock. The yard had to be raked up clean."

The Folly Farm country was the base for Turnbull's operations. His headquarters in Barren Valley became known as Burnt Ranch, having been burned in the Bannock War. Turnbull ran his sheep in the Steens and Blue mountains, and wintered them on the Sheep's Head of Barren Valley. Characteristic of his ancestry, Turnbull was able to compile a modest fortune. He told his nephew that he made his money "when wool was five cents a pound and ewes were a dollar a head." Active in his own community, he was known by his nickname with fond affection for

Tom Turnbull, who came to Oregon from Scotland as a young man, pioneered sheep herds in Barren Valley and the Steens and Blue Mountains. He became a leading citizen of Ontario.

his charitable benevolences to organizations and people needing help. He was a director of the First National Bank of Ontario and long a trustee of the Acacia Masonic Lodge.

After being injured in 1926 when a wagon overturned, Turnbull retired and moved to Ontario. He took up traveling, visiting not only many points of interest in the United States but returning to his native Scotland. When he died in October 1942, nothing summed up his life better than the bequests left behind: seven thousand dollars to the city of Ontario for the Malheur County Library; twenty-two thousand five hundred dollars to Acacia Masonic Lodge to be apportioned at ten thousand dollars to the lodge's building fund, twenty-five hundred dollars in trust to the lodge for the Ontario cemetery, and ten thousand dollars in trust to the lodge, the income to be used to provide medical care, food and clothing for the poor and needy of Ontario, without regard of race, color, creed, or lodge affiliation.

Uncle Tom never married, but he had one of the largest families in Malheur County — his many friends.

James McEwen was among those who saw the full promise of the sheep industry in this eastern Oregon-Idaho country. He is typical of thousands of young men who pulled up their roots to follow Horace Greeley's advice by going West. More often than not, they were the younger sons of large families. The farm went to the oldest son and the younger ones had little choice but to strike out on their own. Jim McEwen was one of these, for he had ten brothers and sisters.

Jim's parents had stark memories of the War Between the States. They were youngsters while the war was going on. The farm was near Johnson City, Tennessee, along a main route of battle. Consequently, they were victimized by both Union and Confederate troops. The infamous renegades called the Bush- whackers ravished the farm and killed the grandfather during a frightening raid, while his wife and children looked on. The terror was beyond belief; his wife held him as he was dying, but the raiders forced her cruelly away from him, ordering her to the creek to wash the blood from her clothing. When the Union troops invaded the place, they took blankets from the chil- dren's beds. Jim McEwen's maternal grandfather fought for the Union Army as a lieutenant and was killed somewhere in Tennessee. After the war, the family looked for his grave, but couldn't find it.

When Jim was eighteen years old, he received a letter from James Shoun, a relative living at Harney City, Oregon, urging that he come West. He decided the opportunities might be far greater, so headed for Oregon to look around. He survived a head-on colli- sion of the passenger train with a freight near Lexington, Kentucky, and upon reaching Idaho received some good advice on getting ahead that lasted him a lifetime. An old soldier on the train, seeing that he was a greenhorn, took him in charge. When the train made a meal stop, the passengers pushed and shoved into the depot to be well up in the line. Jim held back, but the soldier grabbed him by the arm, hauling him along, urging, "Come on, young fella. You'll never get any place in the back of the line." Jim McEwen declared that he never again stood at the end of a line.

In March 1899 Jim arrived at Ontario and boarded the stage to Harney City. It took nine days to make the trip, Jim walking most of the way. A man named Kellogg operated the stage line. He had no change of horses and the weather was foul. On Bendire Moun- tain the snow was a foot deep and Jim had to walk up the grades, for the horses were tired and old. It was all they could do to pull the empty stage up the grades.

Arriving in Harney City (the former Camp Harney), McEwen was down to his last fifty dollars. Since times were tough, he sent this remaining money back to his sisters. Shoun owned a piece of land in Tennessee, and Jim, deciding to remain in Oregon, made a deal for the property which he sold to his brother. The following winter he worked for Milt Davis, a horse trader who shipped animals east and peddled them to farmers and ranchers for considerable profit. Jim and another young buckeroo fed and rode the horses for Davis.

"We would rope horses and tie them up in the barn, saddle them, and ride out the gate," Jim remembers. "You couldn't steer them and it's a wonder we didn't get killed."

The next spring things began turning more in his direction. Hiring on with August Miller, he began learning about sheep. The next three years were spent herding, and although Miller and his wife were like second parents, he didn't think much of August's operation.

"He was the poorest manager I ever saw," McEwen said. "His herders were losing sheep and not trying to keep them together. I told him if he didn't start giving those men hell for it, he would go broke. You didn't have to put up with what you do today with help."

McEwen suggested that August put three thousand head in a band, get *good men* to watch them, and perhaps the trouble would be eliminated. The sheep were run in the Blue Mountains, but they "didn't dare run them in cattle country because the cowmen would kill the sheep."

Miller sold out in 1903, and McEwen helped to trail a herd of six thousand head, using two herders and two tenders, to Elko, Nevada. Upon his return, he was surprised to learn that he was "experienced." Others now sought him out. A man from New York, named Linnup, offered him a partnership if he would run sheep for him. Linnup said he would buy four thousand sheep at two dollars a head. Jim declined the offer, realizing too late that it was a good proposition, for the wages were thirty dollars a month and the range free. He lacked confidence in himself.

"He put his money up against my judgment, and I could have made it, but was afraid to take such a big step," McEwen said.

Instead, in the fall of 1904 he went to work for Tom Turnbull in Barren Valley. Uncle Tom and Johnny Wood had been settled for some thirty years on the Duck Ponds, about half way between the Crowley Ranch and Riverside, on what is now known as Crowley Road. It became their headquarters, from where they distributed their flocks over the Blue Mountains and the Sheep's Head. From 1880 into the 1890s, Turnbull and Pick Anderson were the two largest taxpayers in Malheur County, Turnbull in sheep and Anderson in sheep and cattle.

Jim's first task working for Turnbull was herding a bunch of sheep to the Ontario railhead. He ran Turnbull's for two years, receiving half interest in the sheep at that time and then going into full partnership with the Scotsman. Jim started at a bad time, during the depression of 1907 when he was unable to draw his money from the bank. Then the bad winter of 1907/08 hit them.

"Winter started on Thanksgiving and I got snowed in on top of the flats above Swamp Creek," McEwen said. "I had to break trail to Barren Valley for the sheep to follow. I could see it was going to be tough, so I went looking for feed."

He stayed overnight at the Jordan Valley Hotel, then went on to Caldwell where he was able to buy corn. The corn was freighted to Duncan's on the

Owyhee, then hauled by four-horse team to the desert where the sheep were located. The Skinners had hay for sale at the Ruby Ranch and many sheepmen headed that direction.

"Before the winter was over," McEwen added, "Skinners were feeding thousands of sheep."

The same year McEwen came into full partnership, he took another giant step, marrying Turnbull's niece, Jemima Scott. Mima had migrated to Canada from Scotland when only eight weeks old. From there, her family moved to Illinois and then to Oregon. After trying a number of Pacific Northwest localities, they were convinced by Turnbull to come to Barren Valley. Scott left the Willamette Valley at McMinnville in 1892 with family and possessions, traveling across the Cascades in a covered wagon by way of Eugene and Prineville. Mima's first memory of their new home was a large bunch of deer gathered on a hill near the two-story frame house.

The father died the first year the Scotts were in Barren Valley, placing additional hardship upon this young family in a strange land. Uncle Tom provided for them. Mima and her two sisters, Margaret and Eleanor, went to private school at Swamp Creek. The sisters were the only pupils. Turnbull hired a male teacher whom Mima didn't like. She would play hooky by hiding in the willows between the house and the school until about ten o'clock. Then growing weary of this tactic, she would return home where her mother would comb her hair and send her back to school. Later, she attended school for five years in Portland, through the ninth grade, riding from Ontario on a train having a wood-burning locomotive with a long-drawn-out whistle which was unforgettable.

Mima returned at seventeen to Barren Valley to stay. She found it now a very busy place, for the desert was populated by many homesteaders and their families. There were streams of travelers, freighters,

cowboys and sheepherders who were always eager
for social gatherings. At the Turnbull place, the three
young Scott girls were a prime attraction with the local
bachelors. There were many dances, drawing people
from a fifty-mile radius.

"When a dance was held," recalled Mima, "a rider
would go up one end of the valley and another the
other way, and they would bring back as many as forty
or fifty people. We used to ride horses from Barren
Valley to the Peterson Ranch to dance. We danced
all night, ate an early breakfast and were home for
dinner. I played the organ for the dances. I like to
dance and ride horses, and liked to walk a lot. People
were more friendly then and enjoyed each other's
company."

Mima married Jim McEwen in 1909 at the Drexel
Hotel in Vale. After a short honeymoon, they returned
to Barren Valley — and the sheep. It was no spur-
of-the-moment affair, for they'd known each other for
years. Their first home was typical of many found on
eastern Oregon homesteads, a simple cabin with a
plank floor and heated by a wood range. Mima said
she spent the rest of her life caring for children and
feeding sheepherders and buckeroos. Anyone who
came along was welcomed for a meal, and there
seemed always to be people passing through the
valley. When the three children were of school age,
Mima moved with them, first to Riverside and then
to Ontario when they began high school. They lived
in town during the school year, returning to the Visher
Ranch summers, which were spent cooking for the
crews. Occasionally the summers were highlighted by
trips to the Blue Mountains where Jim McEwen
grazed his sheep near Calamatie Creek.

The Visher Ranch was Jim's headquarters,
purchased from Peterson. It has remained so to the
present time. McEwen operated as a partner with
Turnbull until 1919 when Uncle Tom became ill and

Jim McEwen with his new bride, Mima, on their wedding day in Vale, Oregon, 1909.

Bill McEwen herding sheep on Steens Mountain, 1910. He has his rifle for protecting his sheep from coyotes and his dog for assistance.

Jim bought all the sheep. He took over management of the entire outfit, running not only Visher but the ranches at Swamp Creek and Barren Valley. He and Mima have lived out their lives in this land where they homesteaded. The year 1969 marked their fiftieth on the Visher Ranch and their sixtieth wedding anniversary, truly pioneers whose memories extend far back into the early days of this part of the West.

Sheepmen had their own practiced methods for handling their flocks. In marketing the herds, they learned through trial and error. Lambs were never sold in the early days, because wool was the principal market. Wethers ran until three or four years old, for the wool, and then were taken to market. During the spring sheep shearing time, large crews would gather at a designated location to fleece the various bands of that area. This was a time of hustle and frivolity, with festival overtones. The shearers were a colorful lot who liked their whisky straight, adding to the revelry along with the nervous bleating and bawling sheep, and raising dust and racket a far distance across the desert.

In 1910 McEwen and Turnbull built a sheep-shearing plant at the Duck Ponds. Thousands of sheep were relieved of their wool there. The huge fleece sacks were hauled by freight strings to the railroad at Riverside, twelve miles away. In earlier times, the sheep were trailed long distances to market. On such treks the bulk of the herd were wethers which could stand the trail's rigors better than the ewes and lambs. The stock had to be driven to Winnemucca, Huntington, or Ontario. When the railroads came closer, through the persistent efforts of men like Bill Hanley, the marketing system changed as it also did with cattle. Now sheep were moved to Riverside, Crane, and Burns.

"We would load up at Riverside and take the sheep east until we found a market where the price was right," explained Jim McEwen. "The first day out from Riverside, the sheep were unloaded and fed at Caldwell or Nampa, the next day at Ogden or Laramie. If we didn't sell them, we went on to Chicago. I always sold at Omaha, if I couldn't sell at any other place because it cost too much to go further. Some took theirs on into Chicago, but I never could see it."

When wool was the mainstay of the sheep business,

Rambouillet sheep were used in the range bands because of their wool producing ability. When mutton became important, Rambouillet ewes were crossed with Black Face (Suffox) rams for mutton and wool. By the end of World War I, wool began to lose importance and lambs were run for mutton. Suffox sheep replaced Rambouillet entirely, until it is now impossible to find a Rambouillet in this country.

For breeding stock, Turnbull and McEwen bought good bucks for their bands. They purchased many Rambouillet bucks from Butterfield in Weiser and others in Salt Lake City. These same sources later supplied them with Suffox bucks.

I have always heard that there was much more money in sheep than in cattle. There must have been, for contrary to popular belief, large cattlemen went occasionally into the sheep business. The Western novelists who romanticized the cattlemen failed to say anything about it. Bill Hanley, for one, made several trips to Canada looking for better quality sheep to run in his bands. Pick Anderson had thousands of cattle from Juniper Mountain to Winnemucca, but he had bands of sheep running on the desert, too.

It's true that cattlemen and sheepmen had their problems; they were two kinds of stock owners. But it wasn't just because the cattlemen hated the sheepmen, as historians and novelists have been saying for years. Nor because cattle and sheep couldn't exist side by side on the same range. There was more to it than that. The old established sheep and cattle operators got along fine, respecting each other's rights on the range. Both had base property for their operations and made a point of maintaining good feelings with their neighbors. It was the tramp cowman and tramp sheepman who caused the friction. They had no base property, so mooched off those who had put together an outfit. Cattlemen and sheepmen alike fought these itinerant individuals, but the historians have lumped the problem under one heading — cattlemen vs. sheepmen. However, the competition for range was critical at times and brought on such incidents as the range wars in central Oregon when many thousands of sheep were slaughtered by masked night riders.

After that time, both cattle and sheep operators tried to limit the use of the range by tramp operators. They went to Congress to plead their case, charging that the range was being destroyed from indiscriminate use by these people. Bill Hanley, who personally knew President Theodore Roosevelt, tried to interest the Rough Rider — himself a Westerner — but nothing was accomplished for another thirty years until the coming of the Taylor Grazing Act of 1934 brought some stabilization to the range lands. Meanwhile, incidents, including killings, brought on animosities that come down to the present.

In the Lakeview area, the many Irish sheepherders had overgrazed the lands to near-ruin and were taking their sheep elsewhere to repeat the damage. One of them moved onto Bill Hanley's range of the Double-O. Uncle Bill was a diplomat and bided his time. He told an inquiring friend that he was in no hurry. The sheep were in poor shape, winter was coming early, and all the while the herder was growing braver, edging closer and closer to the Double-O.

Hanley traveled to Portland, where he ran into a woman who headed the Oregon Humane Society. She was something of a character in her own right who had been in the Klondike gold rush of 1898. When it came to protecting animals, she was tough and aggressive. Once (it was told) she saw a man mistreating a pair of mules. She pulled a .45 Colt revolver from her handbag and shot the animals.

Hanley dropped the comment, "Sure too bad about those poor sheep out by the Double-O."

"What sheep?" the woman snapped. By the time Hanley had the answer out, she was at the starting gate, anxious to hit for eastern Oregon to see for herself. She took one look at the starving sheep and forced the herder into two choices of action: he could either sell the sheep or buy hay from Hanley. The herder bought the hay, but the word spread that the Double-O was inhospitable and a poor place to set up camp. That ended Uncle Bill's troubles with tramp sheep operators.

Jordan Valley was a center for sheepmen and especially the colorful Basques. But there were others too; this is a group of Scot herders who passed through the towns of the Owyhees.

Most of the sheepherders of eastern Oregon and Idaho — throughout the West, for that matter — were Scots, Irish and Basques. The growth of a large Basque colony in the Jordan Valley region presented new and different problems for established ranchers. Young men of all three nationalities were pursuaded to leave their homelands and come to America to take herding jobs. There was a great need for herders who had to be a certain type, liking the lonely life. And in the early years of this century, there were hundreds of thousands of sheep and cattle running on federal lands until over-grazing became a serious problem which would lead to controls.

The forests were under federal control long before the desert range lands. The operators in the Blue Mountains, among them Jim McEwen, were given blueprints showing the areas assigned to their live-stock. The maps were based on earlier surveys; boundaries were designated by section markers burned into trees. By 1907, when the U.S. Forest Service took control, these section marks had been obliterated by growth, so that it was difficult to determine the exact boundaries. That made it a simple matter to fudge onto a neighboring section.

The stockmen resorted to other methods of nudging another flock.

"Roby Potter, a herder for Barnhouse, had trouble with another sheepman over the exact boundary of his range," said Jim McEwen. "Roby had lived in Portland and owned a taxi driver's badge, so he dressed up, pinned on the badge, and visited his neighbor. Told him he was a U.S. marshal and to move on, at the same time shoving the badge out for the man to see. The man moved on, because he couldn't read."

McEwen never had any trouble with cattlemen "because Turnbull came into the country before many of them did." But he knew of many cases where sheep and cattle operators tangled. And a Turnbull herder,

Jimmie Leonard, was shot and killed by another herder named Williams at a camp on Rail Creek below Fish Lake on Steens Mountain, but the quarrel had nothing to do with cattle.

"Roughnecks worked as henchmen for the cattlemen and ran the sheep ranchers around," said McEwen. "They went out of their way to put heat on the Basques. With one Basque outfit, they ran off their pack string. I loaned them horses till they could get theirs back. The cattlemen had run them out to the desert."

Cattlemen shot into Ord's herd in the Blue Mountains, killing sheep in the flock, and herder Harry Kerry declared that "I ran so fast my tracks are there yet." Pat Connelly also had sheep killed by cattlemen. But there was bad blood, too, among the sheepmen over territorial rights and often it involved so-called "foreigners." At Downey Canyon, there was another fight over a campground. Bill Skinner's man was there and a herder for Jhonny Acarregui tried to move in on him. Skinner and his partner, Alex Blanchard, were lambing. The Basque went to town to ask Jhonny what he should do. Jhonny told him to move his sheep away from Skinner's, as he was there first. Instead, the hotheaded herder bought a gun and had Pete Flora show him how to use it. Returning to the camp, he began shooting at Skinner's herder who returned the fire with a shotgun. The Basque was wounded, but not badly. Next day the Basque came back and this time Skinner's herder killed him with a shotgun blast through the chest. It was later learned that the Basque was a dangerous man who wouldn't hesitate to kill. Some folks said he had killed George Nickels in a fight at Trout Creek over scrip land that Nickels claimed. A surveying error put Nickels on the wrong forty acres and the Basque tried to jump it. A fight developed and Nickels turned up dead, but the identity of his killer could never be proved.

Jim McEwen and his sheep once got into a hassle with Ringling Brothers, the great circus outfit. It involved Bill Hanley and resulted in a lawsuit.

"I rented pasture from Bill on the Juntura Ranch," McEwen remembered. "Ringling Brothers wanted my lambs and put seventeen hundred dollars as down payment. They never came to get the sheep and the pasture was about gone, so I called Ringling and they said Bill Hanley had the sheep. I then called Bill and he said, 'I'm dealing with Ringling.' (Hanley evidently felt that, since McEwen already had the down-payment, the sheep were out of his hands.) I loaded the sheep on the train and shipped them to Omaha. Ringling stopped payment on the check and I had to put up a bond to stop them from arresting me. It took three years settling the case in court. I had to pay back the seventeen hundred dollars advance of Ringling's, but I made money on the deal because the price of lambs went up."

In his dealings, McEwen didn't let much get by him, and didn't allow government agents to shove him around.

"In the early thirties — during the Depression — I was broke," he declared. "The government had taken over all the sheepmen in the country. They made budgets and only gave me two hundred fifty dollars a month to run ten thousand head on. I went to Boise to see the bastard in charge. On the way down the canyon I had a car wreck and I wasn't in any mood for playing around.

"When I got to Boise, they kept pushing me around, but finally I found the son-of-a-bitch in charge. He told me he couldn't do any better. So I told him when I walked out that door, he was owner of ten thousand sheep — and they weren't worth a damn thing then. A man across the hall in another office, and who knew me, came running in and said, you had better listen to McEwen; he means what he says. The head bastard

asked me if I could lay over, and I told him if I didn't
get any money, I had just as well not go back at all.
I told him that I came to this country without a damn
thing, but now I had a wife and three kids and would
make it anyway. . . . He called a special meeting that
night and they gave me twenty-five thousand dollars.

"They don't fool me. I've seen it all and know
what it's all about. . . ."

THE COLORFUL BASQUES

NEAR THE CENTER of the town of Jordan Valley, behind the hotel, stands a strange stone structure, which puzzles by-passing motorists. It is a *Pelota Frontone*, built more than half a century ago by the Basque people for the playing of their traditional national sport. Now having fallen into disuse, the structure remains a formidable landmark to a people and a culture which in this century have gained more fame for Jordan Valley than the area's robust Western heritage of mines, cattle, freighting and stagecoaching.

Ambrosio Elorriga began constructing the Pelota court in the spring of 1915, assisted by Basque masons using native stones. The stones were hand-hewn with the imaginative skill of a trade that extends far back into the history of Spain and southwestern Europe. The court was completed in 1917 to become the scene of many exciting contests. Pelota is a form of handball, with two, four or six players throwing the ball against the wall which towers high above their heads. The sphere, about the size of a hard baseball, has a rubber core and is wrapped with string and a stitched leather cover. The ball must hit the wall two and one-half feet above the floor to be legal. The game, with its fast action, typifies a people who brought their culture halfway around the world to the West of Idaho, Nevada, and eastern Oregon, and have strived to preserve it.

There are many versions as to how and when the Basques first began coming to the Owyhee country. One is that in the 1870s a Basque sea captain traveled to Winnemucca on the new transcontinental railroad. Attracted by the rolling land and good grass, he fell back on the traditional occupation of his people — raising sheep — made a fortune, and returned to Spain to spread the word of what a great sheep country existed in the New World. Another version is that young Basques immigrated from the Pyrenees, entering the United States at New York and drifting West until they found a place that was similar to their homeland, where the Basques had lived for centuries in freedom and solitude in the Pyrenees Mountains, behind the Bay of Biscay.

The first Basques into Jordan Valley permanently were José Navarro and Antonio Azcuenaga, who arrived in 1889 on the heels of that terrible winter, and Augustin Azcuenaga, who came the following year. José and Antonio almost didn't make it, learning from the outset what a harsh country it could be. Not far from McDermitt they lost their horses on the desert and were forced to walk. The going was tough in the spring mud and slush. When they reached the Owyhee Crossing, the river was flooding. The ferry raft which took them over the Owyhee nearly swamped. They might well have drowned.

Pedro Arritola, Luis Yturraspe, and Cipriano Anacabe arrived a bit later and soon there was a thriving Basque community. The pattern was for the men to come first to get established; then the women followed with the children. It was a stark, if not frightening change from the Pyrenees with its small plots and many limitations. The land here seemingly spread forever and there appeared to be plenty for all. As one Basque put it:

"I don't know where they could have gone in the world where there was such an extreme change."

The land held its dangers and its surprises, for it was a different world and demanded a different pattern of life. Upon arriving, the men spent a few days in town, getting their bearings and talking with other Basques. Then they took mortgage on a band of sheep to look after. It was rough out on that lonely desert, but amazingly, none of them died from exposure. Native instinct, fortitude, frugality, and determination, which had spelled survival for these people for countless generations, again kept them alive where lesser men might have succumbed or given up. Some of them stayed for years on the lone prairie until substantial wages were accumulated to purchase their own sheep bands and ranges and send for relatives and friends. Usually a brother or cousin came first.

The Basques were treated roughly in the beginning by the other ranchers, primarily because they were sheepmen adding pressure to the range. It was an attitude many of them found difficult to comprehend in this land of freedom. But when the Basques began owning cattle, they didn't get along with sheepmen either, even their own kind. Later, many American ranchers sold out to the Basques, because of an economic depression or because their fortunes were made.

The colony continued growing. Not all Basques became sheepmen; they turned to trades, skills, and business enterprises as stone masons, miners, hotel keepers, and merchants. There were several Basque hotels in Jordan Valley. The biggest influx came at the time of World War I as the Basque people in Europe continued staunchly resisting attempts to infringe upon their independence and control by outside forces.

Like the Gypsies, the origin of the Basques or *Euskaldanak*, as they called themselves, remains in doubt. They are descendants of a people who inhabited Spain before the Celts and claim to be "the oldest unmixed race in Europe." But unlike the wandering Gypsies, the Basques stayed primarily in the Pyrenees until they discovered the remote portion of the West in Nevada, Idaho, and Oregon. They settled not only at Jordan Valley, but at McDermitt, Fields, Andrews, and Ontario. There were early Basque settlers near the Steens Mountain. Idaho has a large Basque population, and there is also a major colony today in California.

Infringement on their rights and the need for self-determination weren't the only reasons why the Basques left the Pyrenees. There was internal friction, too, from overcrowding and a lack of opportunities for young people. There were pressures from the officials of the Catholic Church. An elderly Basque immigrant, who came to Jordan Valley as a young man, explained it thusly:

"If you had two, a chicken, one fat, one skinny, the Priest he would take the fat chicken. If the fat chicken die, he take the skinny chicken. Let the people starve. Poofa! No good."

The sheep herds grew larger, healthier, and more numerous, as did the settlement. At the peak of this era, there were some two hundred thousand sheep ringing Jordan Valley. During the 1920s and 1930s, Jordan Valley was one of the foremost Basque communities in the United States. There were approximately two hundred fifty to three hundred Basques living in the area, and at times their language seemed to be the town's predominant tongue. Children began school without knowing any, or very little, English, posing a critical problem for the teachers. Later, the young ones learned English from their older brothers and sisters who had been taught in school. While the instructor may have had a struggle teaching the language, discipline was no problem whatsoever. That was well-learned at home. But one small Basque boy who didn't begin school until he was eight got off to a shaky start. His parents had given him some money to fill his school needs, but he thought the coins were buttons and the other boys tricked him out of them.

The years of the Great Depression were hard on the colony, which had become used to the booming times as "normal." From thirty to thirty-five sheepmen went out of business. In 1934 lambs brought only five and a half cents a pound, and steers around two and a half cents.

"Everyone almost broke," remembers Aurora Madraiaga, an elderly Basque woman who came from the Old Country at age sixteen. "People with money lose money when the Jordan Valley Bank closed. All Fernando and I have was five dollars and thirty-five cents. Tim Lequerica (one of the owners of the Azcuenaga Ranch) bring us a quarter of beef. Next money we had we put in Boise Bank and it closed. We didn't have much, but we lost it."

During the twenties, some of the colony had participated in Jordan Valley's moonshining activities, but the end of Prohibition closed out this source of revenue, too. Yet the Basques didn't normally defy the laws of their adopted homeland. They were found to be a thrifty, energetic, peaceable people. Few of the early arrivals became naturalized citizens; many of them intended to go back to Spain. Later generations became a permanent part of the American scene, turned to other occupations far removed from sheepherding, and were gradually assimilated into American cultural ways. Yet the thing that struck me in talking with the Basque people is their intense loyalty and sincere love of this country. The older ones remember the hard times in Spain and look upon this as truly the Promised Land.

For many decades the Basques, or Bascos as they are often called, provided a colorful and fascinating interlude to Jordan Valley life which attracted newspaper and magazine feature writers and photographers from near and far, so that Jordan Valley became nationally known as the home of the colorful Basques. But this is no longer true, for so far as Jordan Valley is concerned, one must look hard to distinguish a Basque from anyone else in this area. Their life-style has greatly changed and they have become completely "Americanized." There are no festivals or local color, through costumes and customs, now to be found in Jordan Valley. And while it appears that the Basque people regret seeing their customs lost, it has become increasingly difficult to preserve them for succeeding generations, since there has been much intermarriage. Actually, the Basque population of this region now centers in Idaho which has from eight thousand to twelve thousand Basques, large numbers of them located in the Snake River Valley. There are also sizable colonies in Nevada and northern California. In Idaho, efforts are made to preserve the old customs, cultural ways and music, dance, and art forms through such groups as the Euzkald Society which holds an annual ball at Boise.

Idaho is now known for its Basque colony, as was once Jordan Valley. It was a combination of the Idaho hills and the Basques which reminded Ernest Hemingway so much of his beloved Spain that he established his last permanent home there. But thirty years ago, Jordan Valley was a place of Old World charm and color, and it is best that we view the era of the Basques as things were at that time.

The original Basque homes were built of native

Tim Lequerica and his sons were the last of
the Basque sheepmen located in Jordan
Valley, holding to a proud tradition. He came
to the Owyhees in 1903 to work for his father,
who pioneered the famed Basque settlement
in Malheur County.

stone, Pyrenees-style. The house was low and divided
into small rooms to insure warmth in winter and cool-
ness in summer. The rooms were furnished in colorful
shades and often filled with beautiful handiwork,
which is almost a lost art to many Americans. The
work was displayed at that time in fairs and festivals.
As with other ethnic groups, the conservative Basques
feared that their centuries-old customs might be swal-

lowed up by the overwhelming American life-style — as indeed many of them have been. They were, therefore, striving hard to preserve them.

Native costumes were worn for special affairs and festivals, providing flashes of gay color and fashions reaching back countless generations in Europe. Away from their work, the Basques were a happy, light-hearted people with a great love for feasting, music and dancing, games and contests. The Basques are known for their clear olive skin, sparkling dark or blue eyes, good teeth, very red lips, and warm smile; and the women especially for their dark beauty. There were touches of old Spain in their dress, with graceful lace mantillas draped Spanish-style over high combs. Wherever two or more men gathered, there were contests of endurance — throwing rocks, weights, even crowbars. Athletic prowess was important to them. Every Memorial Day there was a festival at DeLamar, which included street racing, contests and dancing.

There were three Basque hotels in Jordan Valley — the Madariaga, Elorriaga, and Marquina. The buildings shook each night with the lively dancing to happy rhythms of accordion, guitar and harp, and the clapping hands and stomping of feet. The Basques sang and danced as they had done in the Pyrenees. Occasionally during the twenties, there were interruptions. Once federal men raided all three hotels simultaneously, looking for "moonshine." It didn't much ruffle the Basques. When they hit the first place, the others were quickly tipped off and the illegal booze safely hidden. Thereafter, like the people in the novel about Santa Vittoria, whenever government men left the Snake Valley headed for the Jordan, word traveled ahead of them.

The romance of old Spain is brought to life in the Basque folk dances — the fandango, farandole, and arreska. Some of the lively routines seemingly have their origins in ancient Egypt and then were passed on to the Romans. There are the vintage dance, the weaving dance, and *Txankareku*, a sword dance. The weaving dance inspired the familiar Maypole known throughout this country. Then there is La Jota, the national folk dance. La Jota strongly resembles the Irish jig and the Scottish Highland fling, and perhaps all three have the same origin. The Basques of this region have an organization which has as its aim the preservation of the old music and dances as performed by the Oinkari Dancers, who are widely known — they have performed at two World's Fairs and the National Folk Dance Festival — and very popular for their lively, colorful appearances at fairs, festivals, and annual Basque events. An annual picnic and festival is staged each August at Mountain Home, Idaho. There are also festivities about the same time at Boise and Winnemucca, and a Sheepherders' Ball each January. Colorful peasant costumes are worn by the Oinkari Dancers (*oin* comes from the foot, *kari* means fast) — the girls in full red skirts, with black bodices over white blouses, and the men in white with red sashes and black berets. The costumes carry out the colors of the Basque flag. Fifty dancers comprise the troupe. Music is provided by accordion, tambourine and a flute called a *twistu*. There is much snapping of fingers, singing, and genuine laughter in performing such routines as the Arco, a hoop dance, and the *Esku Dantza*, which tells a story with gestures.

In decades now long past, Jordan Valley was the setting for many a Basque celebration. The year's end holidays had special meaning. In many localities, the Basques had their own churches, their faith being Catholic, but the priests conducted the services in their own tongue. This wasn't true in Jordan Valley. Before the Catholic Church was built, services were held in various Basque homes, but not since; and the services in the church were regular ones, for Basques and all alike. The first Basque marriage ceremony in

Oregon, it is said, could not be held until the correct ritual could be brought from Salt Lake City, as the traditional service was the only one recognized at the time to bring about the marriage. The men were allowed to marry outside the colony, but never the girls. In later years, there has been much intermarriage among the Americanized younger generation which helped to bring about the breakdown of the old traditions.

Christmas, New Year's, and Three Kings Day on January 6 were, and are, the three most important days in the Basque year. The latter honored the Wise Men who visited the Christ Child from the Far East. As with all their social events, the holidays were observed with much frivolity and music, and everyone was in a gay mood. The musicians played their native instruments and the celebrants stood in a circle, hands on shoulders and singing the melodious Basque airs, plaintive songs of old Spain, and French folk tunes. The Basques were lovers of good food, too, and today, Basque restaurants are to be found where there are substantial Basque populations, or in tourist centers like San Francisco. The operation of restaurants became another Basque means of livelihood, and Basque cookery a specialty. In recent years a Basque cookbook has been published in Idaho; and among the most noteworthy cooks for special Basque dishes was Gloria Batis, who cooked at Ketchum's Rio Club and from 1950 to 1967 at Sun Valley's Trail Creek Cabin, which Ernest Hemingway often frequented for his private social affairs.

The Basque language, called *Eskuara*, or the colloquial name "Basco," is a tongue-twister to most people, with a certain mystery about its origin. Philologists believe it is similar to Egyptian. The characters are Roman. It is smooth-flowing, with many vowels, but the verbs contain allied parts of speech and as many as fifty forms for one person. Proper names have spellings and pronunciations that confound the average American, including people with much education. One of them was Dr. Jones of Jordan Valley who had quite a time with the spelling of Basque names in his record book. Among the tongue-twisters, which have a musical sound when pronounced, are Pascal Arritola, Floyd Acarregui, Tony Yturri, Alfonso Acordagoitia, Emilia Chertudi, Carmen Guerricagoitia, Pilar Eisaguirre, Jesus Arristola, and Damaso Cortabitarte. The names and language have a musical ring to them, but it is no wonder that French peasants declared that the devil himself failed to impregnate the Basque religious faith. He studied the language for seven years and mastered only two words.

But to most people, the Basque conjures up an immediate picture of the sheepherders keeping their lonely vigils on plains, desert, and in the high mountains of the Western states. In summers, their flocks and covered wagons on rubber tires, with twisted smokestacks, dot the landscape of Oregon, Idaho, and Nevada. These are men of a particular breed and their work a way of life that hasn't changed much over the centuries. They may go for weeks without seeing another soul, only their dogs and the sheep, although life need not be as lonely as it was, what with portable radios and even television sets. The sheep dogs are as important and necessary to the Basques as their families, for the herders could hardly handle the flocks without them. And the herders cling proudly to the ancestral occupation of generations, as reflected in one of their songs:

"Far nobler in the mountains is he that yokes the ox, and equal to the monarch, the shepherd of the flocks."

Tim Lequerica and his sons, John and Rufus, were

John Lequerica is heir to a proud tradition
as member of the last family of sheepmen in
Jordan Valley. The family operated the
Azcuenaga ranch.

the last sheepmen in Jordan Valley. They held to this
proud tradition. There are other Basque sheepmen
running in these mountains, but they are based in
the Snake River Valley. Tim Lequerica came to the
United States in 1903 to work for his father, who lived
at the Owyhee Crossing on the Birch Creek Ranch,
better known as the Hole in the Ground. His father,
Domingo Lequerica, and Martin Achavia were the first
Basques to come to the McDermitt area in the late
1880s. McDermitt became almost wholly a Basque

settlement. Lequerica and Achavia worked at first for Pick Anderson, then Bob Wilkenson, who had them take a band of sheep to South Mountain from McDermitt.

Tim expected to work at Birch Creek where his father had settled. But tragedy struck just prior to his arrival. His father was driving a freight wagon down the steep Birch Creek grade when the wagon's brake beam broke. The frightened team ran away and Domingo was thrown out, the wagon running over him. His legs were broken and he was near to death. He tried crawling down the grade to the river for water, having presence of mind to leave an article of clothing and his knife along the way so that he could be found. Domingo died before reaching the river and was first buried there, although later the body was removed to Jordan Valley.

In the old days, Lequerica remembers, they herded the sheep wherever there was grass and water. They would move to the valleys in the winters, then follow the grass upward with the spring. The coming of the Bureau of Land Management and the Taylor Grazing Act changed the system.

When it was time to sell the lambs, the sheepmen took them to the railroad at Murphy, Idaho. To the sheepmen, Murphy was what Wichita, Dodge City, or Winnemucca was to the cattleman. Sheep from all parts of the Idaho-Oregon country were shipped from Murphy. Sometimes they parted the lambs from the ewes and took in the lambs alone; other times they took both ewes and lambs, and parted the lambs there.

"This was risky," said Lequerica, "because sometimes the ewes would get too hungry when they hit the Murphy Flat and would eat the greasewood which would poison them."

The Lequericas lambed at Mud Lake or near the crater, and kept moving while lambing. This was called the "drop band" because each time a ewe had a lamb, she was "dropped" to be picked up later with her offspring. The sheepmen would leave them on water, then a crew of three or four men came along to tend to the ewes and lambs. Two men could handle the drop band.

Shearing plants were built at various locations — Baxter Creek, Trout Creek, the Corta Place, Antelope, Sucker Creek, and the Duck Ponds. The "plants" were comprised of huge sheds with stalls for removing the wool and large corrals for handling the great numbers of sheep gathered there at shearing time. A shearing crew of twenty-four men was mostly Mexican. When the fleece was shorn, it was thrown onto a platform where a man shoved it through a wooden rim which had a wool sack attached. He would tromp the wool into the sack, a task requiring much skill and know-how to pack it just right.

When Tim Lequerica was in partnership with Azcuenaga they ran twelve thousand head of sheep in six bands. They had many horses and pack mules in their camps. In those days they didn't use wagons.

Modern sheep handling and "shed lambing" is far different from that earlier time on the open range. The drop bunch is the "big bunch" or herd. Ewes with lambs are removed from the drop bunch. The singles — ewes with only one lamb — are placed in pens of twenty-five to thirty. They are left for four or five days, then put in a bigger bunch.

Twin lambs pose a different problem. They are more difficult to care for and more time is required, since it takes a while for the ewes to get used to the double offspring. Ewes identify their lambs by both sound and smell, but can be rather stupid in keeping track of them. If too many are put together, too soon, the ewes likely lose their lambs. The system used by the Lequericas was to place the twins in pens of five ewes, keeping them there for about four days. Then mothers and youngins were moved to pens of ten ewes for another four or five days, then shifted to pens of twenty. After a week, they went into pens of sixty and then into pens of one hundred. The sheep were taken to range in bands of three hundred ewes with their twin lambs. The singles were moved to the range in bands of four hundred, with their mothers. The sheep ran in these separate bands until May 1; when they were bunched together and moved to the mountains. In early August, the lambs were shipped.

But today, says Lequerica, the sheep business is like cattle ranching. The price is too low. They are getting thirty-five cents a pound for wool "and we got that during the Depression."

"A fleece averages three dollars apiece, but if you go to buy a wool suit, it will cost you at least one hundred dollars," says John Lequerica. "It would look like things would be better, since there aren't as many sheep as there used to be. Supply and demand don't have anything to do with it." The Lequericas sold their sheep in the late spring of 1972.

All in all, the sheep business was never romanticized in the saga of the Old West, as was the cattle operation. Tim Lequerica has his own explanation:

"The cowboy wrote a lot of songs telling about his occupation. He had the time. The sheepman didn't. . . ."

John Lequerica working with sheep in the pens, making ready for shipment.

FRISKY TIMES IN SILVER CITY

IT APPEARED AT FIRST that the boundary dispute between the Ida Elmore mine and the Golden Chariot would be settled among gentlemen, through negotiations and compromise. But one was trying to jump the other's claim. Violence and death replaced reason, for the impatient proprietors and miners couldn't wait for legal proceedings. Soon it approached full-scale warfare, and the streets of Silver City were wrought with danger.

Both sides hired notorious gunfighters, and all were heavily armed. The Golden Chariot secured a cannon as its forces settled down to besiege the Ida Elmore. On the morning of March 25, 1868, they stormed the Elmore fortifications in a running, shouting, and shooting battle that matched any other mining dispute in the West. In the desperate fighting that ensued, John C. Holgate, owner of the Golden Chariot, was shot in the head and died instantly. The fighting continued throughout the day and into the night. Then early the next morning, Meyer Frank of the Ida Elmore was fatally wounded, dying in a few hours. Several men were wounded seriously, among them James Howard of the Ida Elmore. Others received superficial wounds.

Governor David M. Ballard of Idaho acted swiftly, issuing a proclamation ordering both sides to cease hostilities. He dispatched a squad of U.S. Cavalry from Fort Boise to the scene, but before they arrived with the governor's order, the fighting was halted and representatives of both sides met to effect a compromise. The gunfighters were withdrawn; things began to simmer down. But bad blood remained between the opposing sides. On April 1, Sam Lockhart of the Ida Elmore was seated before the stage office at the Idaho Hotel, taking in the scenery. Marion More, Jack Fisher and two or three others came up. Hot words were exchanged. Lockhart who was outnumbered began shooting. Fisher was hit in the thigh and More in the left breast. More ran about fifty yards to escape the gunfire, then fell before the Oriental restaurant. He was taken inside, but nothing could be done for him. He died the following afternoon. Lockhart had taken a shot in the left arm, which had to be amputated. Blood poisoning set in; he died in July. Marion More was well-liked in Idaho. The Masonic Lodge of which he was a member took the body to Idaho City for burial. Several arrests were made, but proceedings were dropped as peace and reasonable quiet prevailed again in Silver City.

But public reaction to this little war was strongly against all the gunplay. An item headlined *The Biggest Yet* in *The Idaho Statesman* declared:

"A monster gun has recently been patented in England. It is of 32-inch bore and will throw a 6,000 pound shot. The length of the bore is 32 feet. This huge cannon is constructed on the air gun principle, the air being condensed to a pressure of 10,000 pounds to the square inch, which will drive the ball at the rate

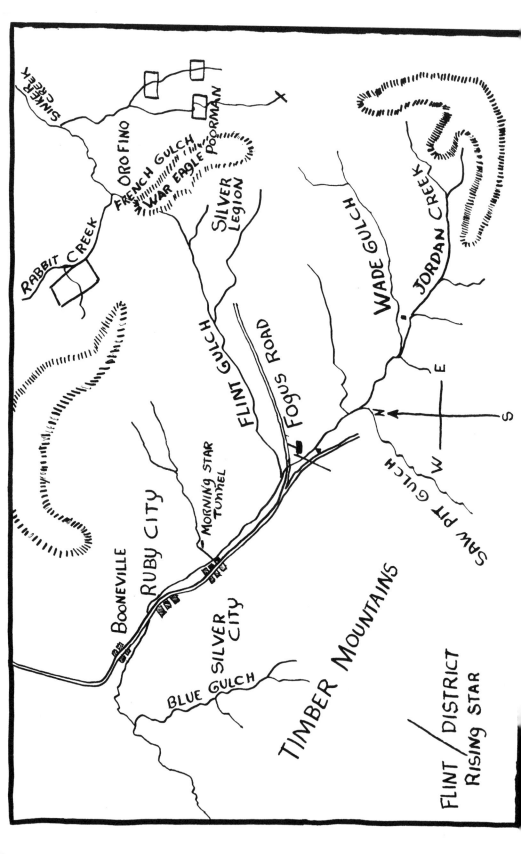

of about 13,000 feet per second. When the next war is inaugurated on the mountain, we will send a couple of these guns and knock War Eagle into a cocked hat."

Mining activity in the Owyhees was both placer and hard rock. Miners worked the surface with shovels, picks, pans, and sluice boxes. Hard rock was done mostly in shafts and tunnels, forming a vast network of mining claims, with two hundred fifty mines recorded from 1863 to 1865. The miners were a rugged lot. Just about every nationality and way of life were represented. Besides the average Americans, there were English gentry, Irish, Australian, Chinese, murderers, thieves, ruffians, to mention a few. An Irish ballad sums up the reason why miners left their home comforts:

> Why do the Irish leave the country?
> Why do the Irish emigrate?
> They're all following the whisky that's exported, crate by crate.
> They also give up digging spuds in Ireland to dig for lumps of gold in Californi---

And it was hard work, often discouraging. It didn't take long for some of the dreamers of easy wealth to give up ideas of the pot of gold at the rainbow's end as a bad go. Corporal William Hillery noted in his diary for May 11, 1866, at Fort Boise:

"A regular who deserted from the guard house some six weeks ago returned last night to his old haunts, preferring a soldier's life to the hard knocks of a miner's occupation. Hard work turned his stomach."

The miners tried to make light of the gruelling work. Wrote one:

> My sweetheart's a mule in the mine.
> I drive her with only one line.

Roaring Silver City, Idaho, was the Queen City of the Owyhee mining camps. This view was taken just after the turn of the century when Silver City experienced a second boom.

> On the dashboard I sit,
> And tobacco I spit
> All over my sweetheart's behind.

Another found humor in the bad booze he was accustomed to drinking in the saloons, gambling halls and brothels of the Owyhee camps:

> When I am dead and in my grave
> No more whisky will I crave,
> But on my tombstone shall be wrote
> There's many a jolt went down this throat.

Law and order were the impossible dream. As one old-timer put it: "If a man was caught doing anything wrong, we just killed him, that's all."

When Lyman Stanford was elected Owyhee County sheriff in 1865, the usual means of establishing law and order was to run the troublemakers out of camp. If a fellow was arrested or if an argument was to be settled, the disposition of justice favored the one with the most friends who had command of the situation. Noted *The Idaho Statesman*:

"On Tuesday last, one Morgan had his pocketbook stolen with a considerable amount of greenbacks in it. He claims that a man by the name of Coleman took it. Our town is infested with quite a number of light-fingered gents who ought to be presented with a ticket to leave or a pick and shovel and started for the mines."

And Corporal Hillery of the First Oregon Infantry also recorded the situation in reporting an 1866 visit of Sheriff Stanford to Camp Lyon:

"The sheriff from Ruby came over to get some of the men who 'went through' the 'whisky mill' up the creek sometime ago, but he did not find anyone he could get hold of."

Thievery, brutal beatings, murder, and other crimes of violence ran rampant throughout the region. The miners feared mostly the notorious Nevada Gang which preyed on all the others and operated similar to the famed Plummer Gang up in Alder Gulch, Montana. The story was of parallel pattern from camp to camp. Miners trying to leave with their pokes were killed and robbed by the road agents, whom they feared more than the Indians. It took a particularly brutal slaying of a well-liked man to arouse the ire of the miners sufficiently to do something about it. That occurred when Lloyd Magruder, a widely known freighter, was transporting supplies from Lewiston, Idaho, to Virginia City, Montana. Magruder was returning from Alder Gulch with thirty thousand dollars in gold dust when he and his traveling companions were killed, along with their pack train of some forty fine animals. The goods were plundered, and everything dumped into a ravine.

Hill Beachy, who would establish a major

stagecoach line in the Boise Basin and through Silver City and Jordan Valley, was operating a stable at Lewiston, from which Magruder checked out his pack animals. Beachy performed a magnificent feat of detection when his suspicions were aroused that Magruder might have met with foul play. Beachy tracked the killers to San Francisco and brought them to justice. He also brought back a plan for ridding the Pacific Northwest of its toughs, based on the San Francisco vigilante movement. Others were thinking along the same lines, including William J. McConnell of the Boise Basin. The result was a regional movement in 1866 of a secret society called the Northwest Vigilantes which cleaned up the country from Jacksonville, Oregon, to Alder Gulch by running out the toughs and decorating the trees, rafters, and bridges with cutthroats and killers.

Idaho Historical Society

Freight wagons rumbled daily through the streets of Silver City during its heighday. The town was a busy one, with a population of ten thousand, and at times, traffic problems that frustrated its occupants as intensely as in modern cities.

Just what the population of the Owyhees was during those rough and tumble years has never been completely determined, but the "Queen City" alone reached around ten thousand. And there were many smaller camps scattered across the mountains and down the gulch toward Jordan Valley. When the miners emerged from their holes and headed for town, they were like the loggers of the timber camps, eager to let off steam. Silver City had innumerable saloons and deadfalls, gambling joints and traps, geared to separate the miner from his treasure. There were said to be eighteen houses of prostitution operating at one time in Silver City. The red light district stretched along Jordan Street in the vicinity of Long Gulch Creek. Among them were Stella's, Mother Nack's, Maude, and Georgie's. After loading up on rotgut whisky and having a few dances at the hurdy gurdies, the celebrating miners headed for Jordan Street. But love wasn't all they found there; shootings and death often occurred. Noted the *Nugget*:

"On Tuesday evening in a house of ill fame at Silver City, an unpleasantness occurred during which a shoulder stricker for the shop, a Finlander named Peterson, shot Herb Davis through the arm. An examination resulted in the exoneration of the shooter."

The saloon proprietors, aware of the keen competition from other deadfalls, bent every effort to keep their customers pleased and interested. Dance hall girls were organized into traveling troupes which when from one mining camp to another in the West, luring great crowds of lonely men who craved the company of a woman. Many of these strumpets were hardy Germans, called "Hurdy Gurdy Girls." The price was fifty cents a dance and fifty cents for the lady's drink, which was the color of whisky but in reality merely tea.

Despite the price — plenty high for the time — and the risk the miners ran of having their pokes lifted,

Idaho Historical Society
Silver City in winter when the snow piled up and temperatures dropped to well below zero. During the long winters, the many saloons and gambling joints were havens from boredom, as they were in the Klondike and other mountain mining camps of the West.

the men loved the diversion which became a part of mining camp life from Central City and Tombstone to the Klondike. One miner expressed his good feelings in song:

> Bonnie are the hurdies!
> The German hurdy-gurdies!
> The daftest hour that e'er I spent
> Was dancing with the hurdies O!

True romance developed sometimes, and the girl would marry her suitor when her dance hall contract expired. Her "take" from the hall was never very large, except what she could make or steal on the side, but the establishments made it big. The *Avalanche* noted:

"We have it on good authority that one hurdy shebang shipped $8,000 as net proceeds of its July business. As the bar gets one-half, it makes in all over $16,000 in one month. Thus it will be seen that these leeches corral more cash than most quartz mills."

Occasionally traveling troupes of show people arrived in Silver City, giving the camp the treat of more refined entertainment. One of these was John Kelly, a famous violinist of his time who had as an assistant a small Paiute boy, the lone survivor of a battle along the Malheur River. In 1865 they performed at Ruby City and it was said of Kelly that "as an artist with a bow, he had no equal." Word was passed from camp to camp,, and the night Kelly played at the Magnolia Saloon, the place was jammed with lonely men. His selections reminded them of far-off firesides and of their childhoods, and brought tears to their eyes. When Kelly was finished, the men cheered long and loud, and drank a toast to him. But then atmosphere quickly changed as they returned to the gambling tables and the fair but frail.

There were other diversions, some of them refined and uplifting. The Masonic and Odd Fellows lodges had their meetings and social activities. The first Knights of Pythias lodge in Idaho was organized in the Owyhees. And the "Owyhee Boys" were challenging anyone in the territory to a "snow shoe" or ski race for a purse of between one thousand and two thousand dollars.

"We understand that parties have made it from the top of Florida Mountain to Ruby in twenty-eight seconds," commented the *Avalanche*.

Certainly the Owyhees were a place that "needed

saving," attracting many circuit riders and Catholic missionary priests. The *Avalanche* took note, in good humor, of the "ungodliness" of Silver City, and that the spiritual and moral condition of the wild camps was something of an institution in itself. Reported the newspaper:

"Last Sunday was an unusually lively day for Silver — boss packers, bullwhackers, etc., acted as if they hadn't had anything to drink but Snake River for two months."

The first church constructed in Silver City was St. Andrews in 1869, built near the Morning Star Mine. It was later torn down as being too far removed from the residential part of town. In 1882 the Graham Building was purchased from Regan Brothers and converted into the Church of Our Lady of Tears. Father Nattini was instrumental in installing a bell in the steeple. When the editor of the *Avalanche* heard about it, he was inspired to write:

"We'uns of Silver City feel quite civilized when we hear the church bell which, thanks to the energy of Father Nattini, now peals forth in clear, ringing tones, calling people to worship. Just wait now till the new fire engine arrives, and we guess Boise City won't put on so many frills, and call us 'that little one-horse mining camp over in the snowdrifts' ain't it?"

When the Right Reverend Daniel S. Tuttle was appointed missionary bishop of the Idaho Territory, he set about immediately establishing Episcopal churches in Boise, Idaho City, and Silver City. The Catholic Church has, in recent years, purchased the Episcopal Church property in Silver City and once or twice each summer, mass is said there. The Catholics appeared to have been more aggressive than their Protestant counterparts in Idaho, for there were only three Protestant churches in the territory prior to 1871. Had the Reverend Tuttle not been appointed missionary bishop of the Idaho Territory, the count might have been zero.

Schools for educating the children of the mining camps weren't forgotten either, despite the central interest being the treasure in the ground. But it was often makeshift. School was held in any vacant building or a private home. The need was obvious. In 1865 the Owyhees had ninety-three pupils enrolled in three schools.

The Fourth of July celebration was the wildest whingding of the year. The good citizens of the camps outdid themselves beyond any Saturday night. Build-

Idaho Historical Society

The Fourth of July was always a rousing time in Silver City and other mining camps of the Owyhees. Celebrants gathered along the main streets to watch special events. This happens to be a drilling contest, familiar in all mining camps, during the Independence Day observance in 1898.

Labor Day was also observed with a big parade and special events. In the parade of 1898, an observer reported that "we counted one hundred seventy miners in the line," the first of the marchers seen just behind the band that is rounding a corner. Silver City was the scene of much labor strife.

ings and vehicles were draped in bunting for the street parade. The lodges marched in full regalia, to the spirited playing of the bands. The excitement, noise, and fireworks made the horses rear and plunge; and every so often, some buckeroo from the lower country would try his skill with a bronco in the street, attracting an immediate crowd to this spontaneous show.

The streets were cleared for foot racing, tug-of-war, horse racing and other games and stunts. The stakes ran high. For years old-timers reminisced about the "Fight of '66" when James Dwyer and Patsey Foy fought eighty-four rounds in two hours and five minutes for a five hundred dollar purse. Hand drilling was another exciting sport, the winner being the one who drilled the deepest hole in stone during a certain set time. Drill holes from these contests can still be found in the rubble around Silver City. When DeLamar was a going camp, the town had a band rated the best in southwestern Idaho and often adding a touch of refinement to the Fourth of July celebrations. There was a certain rivalry between the camps, and when Idaho gained statehood in 1890, the DeLamar boys took great satisfaction in observing the occasion by whipping the Silver City baseball team on the banks of Jordan Creek.

The Oriental population, which was of substantial size, had its own noisy celebration in early February — the Chinese New Year. Silver City had a "Chinatown" at the upper end of Jordan Creek. There were business houses, stores, two Chinese Joss Houses, and a Masonic Temple to accomodate the hundreds of Chinese scattered throughout the region. The Chinese New Year celebration was a colorful affair, the Oriental community parading their huge dragon through the streets and showering candies and nuts, direct from China, on their white neighbors as symbols of good will. To them, this was a time to forget differences and to begin the New Year right by renewing friendships not only with fellow Chinese but Caucasian miners.

The Idaho Statesman in February 1869 gave some indication of the size of the Oriental population by reporting that "at least 3,000 Chinamen are expected to arrive in the basin between this and the first of May." By the early 1870s, there were approximately seven hundred Chinese scattered throughout the Owyhees, with the largest group centered at Silver City. There was a ban on them at first, placed by the Idaho Territorial Legislature to keep alien Chinese from mining in the territory. But it wasn't long before the white miners felt the need for cheap labor, for the work was tough digging on the claims. The miners encouraged the Chinese to come to Idaho; and then the legislature, letting down the barriers, passed a tax assessment of six dollars per head for alien miners. The tax revenue was divided between the territory and the county where the aliens worked. The placer mine owners got around the tax by subletting the claims to the Chinese.

Unscrupulous promoters and merchants took advantage of the Orientals in urging them to go to the mines. One promoter outfitted several large groups of Chinese with wooden rifles to "scare away the Indians." It didn't work; the Indians killed ninety-four Chinese armed with wooden guns on their way to Idaho City in 1866. The warriors surrounded the terrified Orientals and the women killed them. And Chief Egan and his Paiutes attacked that group of fifty Chinese as they neared the Owyhee Crossing, at the place where the present-day ranch of Bob Dowell is located. Only one escaped death when he hid under some driftwood along the river bank. I-John, who lived for many years in Silver City, said while he was hiding under the wood and brush an Indian woman sat atop the pile nursing her baby, while the warriors killed his comrades.

The Chinese were first brought to the West Coast during the California gold rush, when mine owners learned that whites wouldn't labor for low wages and under poor working conditions. They imported coolie labor from China. Thousands were brought in, too, to build the transcontinental railroad across the Sierras, and into the Pacific Northwest by Ben Holladay to construct the Oregon-California railroad. Coolie needs were simple; they were willing to work for far less then their white brothers, but while the whites refused to do the same jobs, the Chinese provoked ridicule, bullying, racial prejudice, and violence. But the Orientals proved industrious additions

Silver City had a huge Chinese population working in the mines and the tailings, and providing other services through small businesses. They grew and peddled vegetables to the camps. Chinese New Year's always touched off a noisy celebration which could be heard throughout the town.

to the West. They labored not only in mines and on the railroads, but ran restaurants, laundries, and grew vegetable gardens, selling the produce for a good profit. The whites were jealous of the industry shown by the Chinese. They chased them through the streets "for fun," threatening to "cut off the Chink's pigtail," so the Chinese kept to themselves as much as possible in the camps, bowing humbly and silently enduring before the miners who called them "dirty Chinks" and "heathen Chinee" because of the Joss Houses in which they worshipped their own gods. Worshipping and gambling were two special Oriental activities. It mattered little that many miners had never seen the inside of any church. The fact that the Orientals had developed a civilization long before the western world left the cave didn't matter. They were different, and that was sufficient.

The Orientals, like the Indians, loved to gamble and had their own special games. Sometimes the noise was terrific. A newspaper editor took note:

"Greenbacks, opium and Joss-gods were the stakes. . . . We don't know and don't care how many years they claim to have been infesting the earth, and only wish they would go to bed like decent people and stop playing their infernal button game of 'Foo-ti-hoo-ti,' so a fellow could get a nap."

But not all the strife could be blamed on the whites. The Chinese carried on their own tong wars where there were injuries and killings in an effort to "save face" and settle a feud.

The Orientals followed the gold strikes from camp to camp, because this was where the action was for them. They could always find work. That fact drew them to the Owyhees. Their work ranged from digging miles of ditches for the mining companies to cleaning up the town. Although held down to a very low level of the social scale, the Chinese were never slaves to the white man in the strictest sense. In addition to their own business enterprises, they often "worked the tailings" of abandoned mining claims, patiently grubbing out the ore in amounts too small for the whites to deem worth the trouble.

When a Chinese died, burial was considered "only temporary," for the remains were shipped later back to China. It was the ambition of most Orientals to go back to China, dead or alive, and many of them saved frugally to return home alive and well to live out their lives and marry the girl they left behind them. A Chinese funeral was nevertheless a lavish affair, as described in one account:

"A Chinese funeral was carried on with all the pomp and ceremony, and much feasting. In due time the deceased would be carried up Slaughter House Gulch to the cemetery, accompanied by a long line of marchers. The shrill rhythm of the Chinese band blared along the way. According to ancient tradition, thousands of little red papers were strewn along the route of the funeral procession. The 'devil' would have to pick up all these bits of paper before he could overtake and possess the deceased."

To appease the evil spirits even further, large quantities of food were placed on the grave. There's a story about a white man asking his Oriental friend if he really believed the deceased would arise from the grave to eat the food. Replied the Chinese wisely:

"Just as white man will come up to sniff the flowers."

On one particular occasion in Silver City, the Chinese couldn't get together an Oriental band for the funeral procession. So they hired an Irish band. After taking on much food and drink at the funeral feast, the fun-loving Irishmen got into the true spirit of the wake. Starting up the gulch, the boys struck up "There'll Be a Hot Time in the Old Town Tonight." As the deceased was being lowered into the grave, they played "Down Went McGinty." No other Oriental in history was ushered into the World Beyond with such flourish, and the Chinese were very pleased with the send-off provided by their friends of old Eire.

The mining boom or bust roared ahead and the Owyhee camps flourished until the Bank of California failed in 1875. That brought a money crisis; promoters were now unwilling to invest capital in the mines. The results were disastrous. Operations ground to a halt. Mines that had produced thirty million dollars filled with water and the properties shut down, tied up in litigation. The people who had survived the hard winters and the rampaging Indians to work in the Owyhees were forced to leave or to face destitution and starvation. The crisis came to a head in June 1876.

Following the panic, the Golden Chariot came under the management of M. A. Baldwin. The mine was able to meet its responsibilities for a time, but then lapsed two months without paying wages. The men went along with it, because Baldwin spoke in glowing terms and the Golden Chariot appeared to be an economic miracle in the face of disaster all around. Baldwin continued making promises, but nothing materialized. When the company began moving out valuable equipment, the miners, who were facing starvation, grew suspicious that the Golden Chariot had thrown more than just a wheel, and that the mine was about to close. It was therefore time to act.

About midnight on the last day of June, some one hundred men who were Golden Chariot employees, and miners from other diggings, marched on the company office. They kidnapped Baldwin, taking him to a house in Fairview and placing him under guard. He was being held for ransome — their wages. Word was telegraphed to San Francisco. When company officials assured the miners that they would shortly receive their pay, the trusting band allowed Baldwin to leave for the Bay Area. But woe be unto him if he didn't return with their money. A month later he was back and the men were paid off, but that was the end of the Golden Chariot. It never opened again.

Idaho Historical Society
Occupants held special celebrations at the drop of a hat, all through the canyon leading to Silver City. What this occasion was isn't recorded, but it was important enough to include a brass band. It may have been the Fourth of July or a welcoming committee for a visiting dignitary.

When the big mines closed down, the small independent outfits kept the camp alive, although things were in a decline which lasted some fifteen years. There was a revival of the mining boom in Silver City in the 1890s, but it was on wobbly footing, since it came largely from the ambitious efforts of Colonel Dewey. For a time it was hoped the new boom might equal or surpass the original bonanza years, but then the steam went out of the promotional flourish. A factor was labor, for the plight of the miner in this new era was a sad one. The national wage scale between 1876 and 1906 rose some thirty per cent, but there were few rewards for the miner. They worked brutal eight, ten, and twelve hour days, the length of the shift vary-

Colonel Dewey, whose enterprise and vigor made him wealthy. He established businesses in the Owyhee mining area, including an ornate hotel in the town bearing his name.

ing from camp to camp. Even new methods didn't help. The work with dynamite was dangerous, and the new drilling machines so heavy and unwieldy that they were known as "widowmakers." The steam hoisting machinery was equally cumbersome. The task of surfacing the ore remained one primarily of sheer muscle and brute strength. The mines were dangerous from poor ventilation and drainage systems. There was the ever-present danger of cave-ins and fire far underground, in tunnels shored up by millions of board feet of timber.

Idaho Historical Society

DeLamar was another Owyhee mining town, part of which is shown here. Note the loaded wagon and stagecoach. DeLamar was founded by a former sea captain who named it for himself. Part of the place was called "Tough Town" for its many saloons, gambling dens, and bawdy houses.

Colonel William Dewey walked into the Owyhees in 1863 without a penny and during the South Mountain activity of 1871-75, Dewey owned about half the camp. He had interests in many other properties which he actively promoted for profit. Among them was the Black Jack group which he sold in 1889 and the Trade Dollar, sold in 1892; and in 1896 he organized a company of the Booneville mine group on Florida Mountain. That same year, Dewey incorporated the Boise, Nampa & Owyhee Railroad for linking the Owyhees with the outside world. The line never arrived, however, stopping short at Murphy.

Dewey the promoter and visionary had dreams of creating a boom that would overshadow the first one. He bought the site of old Booneville, modestly renaming it Dewey. Nothing ever much stopped the Colonel in what he wanted to do. Considered an authority on liquor (Dewey could reportedly tell the age of whisky by running it over the back of his hand) he was once lured into a cellar on the pretense of sampling some booze by a saloon keeper who wanted to kill him. The man got off the first shot, but unfortunately for him, missed the Colonel who gunned him down in a fast draw. Dewey was tried but acquitted.

The Colonel set about busily building his new town and preparing for the arrival of the railroad. He erected business houses, livery stables, office buildings, miners' quarters, and a fine home for the mining superintendent. All this provided a setting for the town's most formidable structure, the ornate and elaborately furnished three-story Dewey Hotel. The sprawling building was Southern style with a double portico, large cupola, and magnificent internal furnishings. Steam heat and electric lights were provided from the Florida Mill. On the third floor was a hall for theatricals and dancing. The hotel had no equal anywhere in the Owyhees.

The town of Dewey, much to its benefactor's pride,

also boasted an elaborate water and sewerage system. There were twelve fireplugs strategically located throughout the central core area. But even this modernization didn't prevent disaster. Fire raged through the hotel after the turn of the century, burning it to the ground.

The new boom wasn't confined to Dewey, despite the promotional enthusiasm of its benefactor. Another promoter who contributed much to the revival of the mines was a former sea captain, Joseph L. DeLamar. Several mineral claims were purchased in 1888, the first by J. W. Stoddard and another by John A. Wilson. Captain DeLamar began developing his properties and a town which was naturally called DeLamar. The camp included mill buildings, mercantile houses, offices, shops, hotel, and bank buildings. In the lower end was what was known as "Tough Town," which according to the Idaho Blue Book of 1898, printed in Silver City, ". . . in mercantile activity fully equals that of the town proper." Continued the Blue Book:

"From there the road to Oregon is skirted by residences of ranchers, teamsters, dealers and woodsmen, with here and there an occasional evidence of mining industry such as the Henrietta Mill, Jones Mill, and John Scales Mill at Wagontown. A flourishing miners' union, a lodge of Odd Fellows, with Rebekah Lodge, comprise the secret organizations, and the welfare of the town is generally looked after by the *DeLamar Nugget*, a spicey and entertaining newspaper started in May 1891 by Lamb and York, and which is still ably edited by Judge Lamb."

Not mentioned in the promotional style of the Blue Book's editors was the more realistic character of DeLamar's Tough Town. Nearly every building in this section was a saloon or gambling den. Those that weren't were bawdy houses, each with about five members of the fair but frail and overseen by madams with such names as Old Lady Bradbury, Daisy and

Idaho Historical Society
Roads to and from the mines were narrow and very crowded. Here at lower
  DeLamar, one freighter tries to pass another along the narrow dirt road.

Old Lady Yell who was a strapping six-footer and had
the voice to match. Tough Town was the favorite hang-
out of the sporting crowd from all the surrounding
country. Jennie Mitchell and her girls moved over from
Hailey to set up one of the largest and most thriving
enterprises in DeLamar, the list of strumpets headed
by a lady known as Long Toed Liz.

Frank Swisher who delivered milk from the family
dairy to DeLamar when a boy in the 1890s was impressed with the fancy team driven by the town's
Negro barber, Lewis Walker. Tough Town also had

many dogs which took after Frank whenever he made his rounds. Frank cut down the dog population by boiling sponges in bacon grease. As the sponges absorbed the grease, they were reduced in size. When Swisher made his next delivery, he took along a pocketful of these "dog buttons," tossing one to each mutt that made a pass at him. The dog would swallow the tasty sponge which would return to its full size when the grease left it. It meant death for the dog, but a boy delivering milk in Tough Town had to take care of himself.

Silver City was flourishing again in the nineties with six general merchandise stores, two hardware stores, a tin shop, two meat markets, two hotels, four restaurants, eight saloons, an undetermined number of houses of ill fame, a bakery, shoe shop, photograph gallery, brewery, soda bottling works, two livery stables, feed store, three drug stores, jewelry store, three blacksmith shops, furniture store, two lumber yards, tailor shop, three barbershops, a newspaper, four attorneys, two doctors, and a fine courthouse containing the county seat. It was a bustling place and wholly dependent on the mining industry. The mill whistles, the muffled roar from giant powder blasts which shook the earth, and the noise from four stamp mills with an aggregate of fifty stamps and two arastras — all were a symphonic orchestration to the ears of the business men. Silver City had a new social outlook, too, as described by the Blue Book:

"The social life of Silver City is free from the petty jealousies and heart burnings that are so common in small places, the 'upper ten' and the 'cod fish aristocracy' swell over their inferiors. Here there is a pleasant, natural commingling between all classes, and a cordial hospitality rules society. Church services are conducted at odd intervals, there being no resident ministers. The Masonic order has two lodges in Silver City — Chapter and Blue Lodge — and the Odd Fellows

Silver City life had an air of refinement above the average mining camp, as indicated in this fine home, the Jack (or J. W.) Stoddard house with its ornate gingerbread trim.

three — Encampment, Subordinate and Rebekah. The Knights of Pythias are also represented with a strong lodge."

Yet with all this bustling activity, the plight of the miners remained unimproved. The hard rock miner saw unionism as his only chance for escape from a hopeless situation. The Western Federation of Miners, begun long ago in 1869, now was growing in strength, and it had found a leader in Big Bill Haywood who had risen from the ranks of the federation local right in Silver City.

Repeal of the Silver Purchase Act in October 1893 touched off a panic and worsened already deplorable conditions. The act had guaranteed government purchase of 4.5 million ounces of silver each month, almost the country's entire output. Sixteen thousand

Idaho Historical Society

Silver City occupants, in their Sunday best, posed for this group portrait which proved a thigh-slapper when developed. Man in center is whispering to girl in leg o' mutton sleeve blouse, and she smiles coyly. The girl in center is bending an ear, trying to catch the words. Meanwhile, boy in window tries to get into the act, which he obviously did.

businesses, five hundred eighty banks and mines, mills, and smelters failed throughout the West. However, the Owyhee country was unique in that it was more stable, without all its eggs in one basket. The Owyhees weren't dependent on silver alone; there were also gold, copper, lead, zinc, antimony, diatomaceous earth, opals, manganese, and nitrates. The district managed to weather the storm. Cripple Creek, Colorado, was the richest silver producing area and seizing upon opportunity, Bill Haywood quit his job with the DeLamar Mine to go to Colorado.

Haywood was elected secretary-treasurer of the Western Federation of Miners and became a powerful influence within the organization. He was a militant with strong socialistic leanings. He advocated violence and was a dynamic speaker. Conditions grew increasingly worse in the years surrounding the turn of the century. Thousands of miners were out of work, idled by strikes, strikebreakers and a shortage of jobs. The wealthy mine owners were growing richer, the miners poorer, and the mining federation flourished. There was violence and killing on both sides as tempers wore thin. Public sympathy was with the mine owners and the Western Federation was charged with being "openly socialistic."

Thirteen were killed and twenty-four injured in dynamiting of the railroad depot at Independence, in the Cripple Creek mining district. The public demanded that the Western Federation be crushed because of its violent tactics which achieved nothing for the average miner. Among the most vocal against the federation was former Governor Frank Steunenberg of Idaho, who had embittered Bill Haywood for his actions against the 1899 strike in Idaho. While working in Silver City, Haywood wrote out a resolution against Steunenberg symbolically on the side of an empty powderbox. Then he introduced the resolution, which was adopted at the next meeting

The rough and tumble crew of the Trade Dollar mine paused long enough to be photographed. Big Bill Haywood, who became one of the leaders of the Western Federation of Miners, got his start in the Owyhees. He is shown fourth from right in front row, looking off toward the left.

of union local No. 66 and published in the *Miner's Magazine*.

Someone set a dynamite boobytrap on the gate at Steunenberg's home in Caldwell. When he opened the gate, the bomb exploded, killing him. The public was shocked. Haywood and Charles H. Moyer, president of the federation, were arrested and charged with the murder. The prosecution's only witness was Albert E. Horsley, the infamous Harry Orchard. He confessed cheerfully to a string of twenty-six killings including Frank Steunenberg and the mass murder at Cripple Creek. All were instigated, he said, under the orders of William D. Haywood and the Western Federation of Miners. But the confession wasn't sufficient to convict Haywood and the other federation leaders. A year later Orchard was convicted and the death sentence commuted to life in prison. He spent the rest of his days in the Idaho Penitentiary at Boise, dying there in 1954.

Haywood was ousted from the federation the year of Orchard's conviction. He continued his radical ways with the Industrial Workers of the World — the Wobblies — and was arrested, drawing a sentence at Leavenworth prison. Out on thirty thousand dollars bail, Haywood fled to Russia where he was at first treated as a hero escaping from the dungeons of capitalism. Haywood hoped for an important position in the Soviet councils. However, he was forced into a position of obscurity and died of diabetes in 1928 in Moscow, where he is buried. Twelve years before, the Western Federation was granted permission to join the respectable American Federation of Labor. It tried further to disassociate itself from a lurid past by changing the name to the International Union of Mine, Mill and Smelter Workers.

Activity in the Owyhee mines continued until the crash of the stock market on Black Friday, October 29, 1929, despite the fact that much of the hustle and bustle had been on paper rather than actual worked ore. More activity was created during the thirties when people were out of jobs and the old mine dumps were being worked over, much as the Chinese had done earlier. A fifty-ton ball mill was installed at the Dewey Mine, a one hundred-ton mill was opened above DeLamar, and some development was done on the Rich Gulch property between the Trade Dollar and DeLamar mines. But the steam went out of these new projects, and in 1934 Silver City lost the county seat to Murphy. Since then Silver and her sister camps have been primarily ghost towns, sometimes haunted by buffs of Western history and a few wandering hippie-types. In recent years the Queen City of the Owyhees has had some revival summers as a tourist attraction, a few summertime residents live there, and there have been proposals to establish the camp as a state or national historic site.

A few old-timers remained after the mines closed down for the last time, partly from loyalty to the past and partly because there seemed no other place to go. It was cheap if not progressive living in this back-wash of the West, but at least things weren't crowded, and there wasn't any traffic or smog problem. Last of these old-time permanent residents was Willie

Ellis Lucia Photo

Many rustic old buildings still stand in Silver City, over-shadowed by Florida Peak. Thousands visit the old camp during the summertime, but it is generally left to its ghosts in the long winters.

Hawes who died in 1967. Hawes was for years the self-appointed guardian of Silver City, adding to the color of the proud old camp with lively tales of its boom town days.

Colonel Dewey retired to the Dewey Palace Hotel he'd built in Nampa when he was promoting the Owyhees and his railroad. The hotel was long a landmark of southern Idaho, but after Dewey's death in May 1903, the old hostelry fell into disuse and was eventually torn down.

Below DeLamar, down Jordan Creek toward Jordan Valley was another village called Wagontown, for the numerous wagons parked there in the days before the road was finished up to Silver City. Wagontown was also a stage station for the Ruby City-Chico stage and later the Silver City-Winnemucca line. In the 1890s the Henrietta, Jones, and John Scales mills were located there. In 1891 Scales conceived the idea of building a dam across Jordan Creek to catch the tailings of the big mill at DeLamar and netted a fortune. When worked a second time, the tailings yielded three ounces of silver and five dollars fifty cents in gold to the ton.

But Wagontown had other attributes. One was the large level area along the upper creek, ideal for racing and celebrations, attracting riders and citizens from a far distance. Once *The Idaho Statesman* announced:

"Pony Young and Eph. Ball leave today for Wagontown, Owyhee County, to attend the races to be held in that place. There are two $300 purses to be run for, and Pony we believe will take one of the purses with the 'Early Filly' and 'Crooked-backed Bill,' providing he has the fastest horse. We hope he will make a good showing and bring some of the Owyhee men and horses to participate in our races next week."

Sometimes a dark horse topped all the others, to the surprise of the spectators, especially if it was ridden by an Indian.

"The aboriginal Americans," declared the *Nugget*, "got away with prizes at the Fourth of July races. White men were not in it. The Indians have a poker stake now."

During the short-lived revival of the camps in the thirties, Wagontown's race track was dredged up with most all the upper valley. Only huge gravel piles now mark its location. It was the grand finale for the mining district, although a few determined prospectors each year join the souvenir hunters poking around the old towns and creekbeds, trying their hands at panning gold, and finding occasional nuggets. And every so often, too, a mining company will send in a crew to work their properties. Could be that the day will yet come when the Owyhees are again a bustling mining district.

DOG TOWN GROWS UP

THE PANIC THAT FOLLOWED failure by the Bank of California paved the way for old Baxterville, alias Dog Town, to come into its own under a new name — Jordan Valley. Residents of the mining camps drifted out of the mountains and down to the lower levels, suddenly developing an interest in ranching and farming. Defeat of the Indians, too, had something to do with it, since it was now reasonably safe to settle away from the protection of the mining camps.

The first permanent settlers in the vicinity of the present town of Jordan Valley were John Baxter, Alex Canter, Jared Lockwood, and Frank Cable, who all came in the summer of 1864. Silas Skinner hadn't built his toll road through the valley yet, so it was a pretty isolated place. Canter later said that when he first came to Jordan Valley, he found two Indian camps — one on the site of the present Cowgill Ranch, where Lockwood and Cable settled, and the second where the town of Jordan Valley stands.

Silas Skinner, who built one of the major toll roads in the Owyhees,
with his wife, Annie.

Baxter had a horse mowing machine, the first in the area, and started cutting native hay. Indians ran off his horses and with the help of a group of miners, Baxter went after them. While he was gone, he loaned the mower to Canter whose horses the Indians missed. When Canter finished cutting his hay, he didn't have a pitch fork so stacked it with one he made out of willows. Hay was worth up to three hundred dollars a ton delivered at Ruby City. He delivered several tons by pack mule, then sold the remaining four tons at his new homestead for one hundred dollars a ton and considered it a bargain.

Lockwood and Cable put up enough hay to feed travelers' horses. They also served meals, starting the first settlement in the valley, but they charged exorbitant prices and were offensive to their customers. Within a year, they lost their business to John Baxter six miles up Jordan Creek.

As early as 1865, James Gusman was farming on his ranch in Pleasant Valley, using ox teams to raise crops of grain and hay. In 1871 he ordered Jordan Valley's first threshing machine, all the way from Buffalo, New York. The machine was shipped by the transcontinental railroad to Winnemucca and the excited Gusman met the train with his freight team and trailed the equipment across the desert to its new home.

Others made a profitable business hauling hay to the camps over Silas Skinner's toll road. Abandoned Bullion City on South Mountain furnished construction material for the new ranches by moving and tearing down the buildings. The sawmill on South Mountain spewed out more lumber, this time for ranches rather than for mines and mining towns. On our ranch in Jordan Valley, all the buildings are of lumber from Bullion City. The weathered old boards contain broken square nails from the original buildings, plus "newer" square nails used in constructing the ranch buildings. A quick way to tell whether a building is

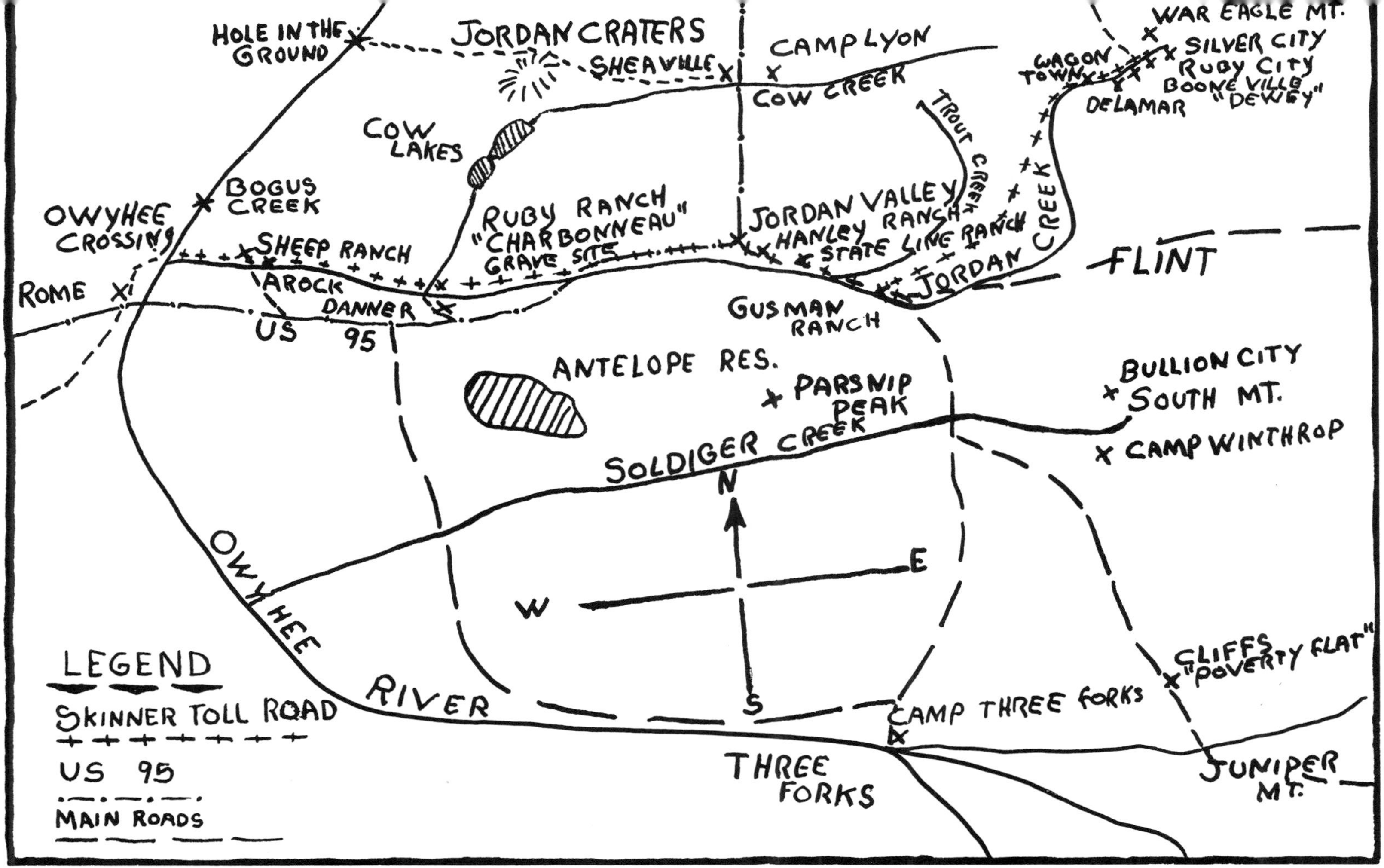

HOLE IN THE GROUND
JORDAN CRATERS
SHEAVILLE
CAMP LYON
COW CREEK
WAGON TOWN
WAR EAGLE MT.
SILVER CITY
RUBY CITY
BOONEVILLE
"DEWEY"
DELAMAR
TROUT CREEK
COW LAKES
BOGUS CREEK
OWYHEE CROSSING
SHEEP RANCH
RUBY RANCH
"CHARBONNEAU"
GRAVE SITE
JORDAN VALLEY
HANLEY RANCH
STATE LINE RANCH
JORDAN CREEK
FLINT
ROME
AROCK
DANNER
US 95
GUSMAN RANCH
ANTELOPE RES.
PARSNIP PEAK
BULLION CITY
SOUTH MT.
CAMP WINTHROP
SOLDIGER CREEK
N
E
W
S
OWYHEE RIVER
CLIFFS
"POVERTY FLAT"
CAMP THREE FORKS
THREE FORKS
JUNIPER MT.
LEGEND
SKINNER TOLL ROAD
US 95
MAIN ROADS

The historical little town of Jordan Valley, near the Oregon-Idaho border, still contains much of the flavor of its roaring past. Many of its original buildings still stand and are in use.

truly "old" is to look for the square nails. In our barn is a thirty-foot timber hewed with a broad axe and held in place by wooden pegs. These old buildings go back a hundred years and have seen a lot of Western history. . . .

There were many small landholders at first in the Jordan Valley region, but gradually they were bought out and the holdings consolidated into the ranches of today. Our ranch, for example, is comprised of five homesteads. The sites of each may still be located by the old foundations which form permanent markers of the old homes and out-buildings.

Old Dog Town or Baxterville became the hub of activity for the area called Jordan Valley. Finally the town adopted the name as more dignified than Dog

Town. The place has seen a lot of action of many kinds, since it was long a stopping place for a steady stream of traffic to and from the mines. John Baxter, for whom the place was originally named, saw its potential, so erected a large hotel there in the 1880s, moving into it from the little stone house where he'd survived for about two decades.

"He was serving meals, selling goods and keeping travelers all under the same roof," remembered one early visitor who happened to be there when Jones & Adams from Wagontown were fitting the window sills on the hotel. The new hostelry was built to accommodate a growing flow of travelers. When ranchers came to town, they needed a place to stay overnight.

Main Street, Jordan Valley, in the early 1900s, before the town saw much of either autos or paved streets.

The old Jordan Valley Hotel, built originally by John Baxter who had founded old "Dog Town" on the main route to the Owyhee mines. It was later expanded and had the community's first ballroom on the upper floor. Baxter built the first part of the building in the 1880s.

Jordan Valley also had its own racetrack on the edge of town and during the racing season, the place was swarming with fans. John Baxter was right; the hotel became a profitable enterprise. Then in 1909 Mr. and Mrs. J. A. Schas took over the management and Harry Bassett was chief clerk. But three years later the historic hotel burned, to be replaced by a more substantial stone structure which stands to this day at the main intersection in Jordan Valley.

"I ate my first meal in Jordan Valley on the Goodrich Ranch," recalled old-timer William F. Schnabel in the *Jordan Valley Express*. "The first meal was cooked by a woman, Mrs. William Beers. The first thing I ever bought in Jordan Valley was two bottles of sarsaparilla from J. R. Baxter in the little stone house. We had no liquor then in Jordan Valley, no hotels, no saloons, no restaurants. . . ."

Next time Schnabel came through, he noted changes were taking place. There was a small shack with a sign, "Dew Drop Inn," the first saloon in Baxterville.

Many Jordan Valley homes contain antiques and trappings from the pioneer and gaslight eras, when life was at an easier pace. Shown is one such collection. Mrs. Tom Skinner, left and Mrs. William Dentel.

"I rode up and took my first dose of tarantula juice in Baker County," Schnabel confessed.

John Baxter put up a store next to his hotel "and things began to hum." A Mrs. Adams built a restaurant and lodging house, and on the second floor was the first ballroom in Jordan Valley. Billy Williams and Nick Maher opened a "first class" saloon, while Johnny Brown gave them competition a short distance away. Jim McMahon opened a blacksmith's shop, Prince, Atherton and Russell a store opposite Williams' watering hole, and Ben Boyer began a carpentry business. In a short time Boyer built a two-story house, using the lower floor for a post office, store, stage stop and carpenter's shop, and the upper floor for another ballroom. Later, Baxter sold his hotel to Billy Williams who expanded the hostelry and attached to the saloon a barbershop, billiard room, large dining room, and a fine ballroom.

"Now old Jordan Valley began to roll," said Schnabel. "Things became interesting. People came from all parts of the West, some good, some bad. Strings of cow horses were hitched all day to the racks and cattlemen were moving at all times. The yell of the cowboy and the crack of the six-shooter were familiar sounds. Then a race course was built and Jordan Valley became the drawing card for hundreds of miles around. There was gambling, racing, fighting and dancing galore. A man could get any kind of a game he called for. Then Jordan Valley wanted the county divided and a county seat. They got the county divided and it was called Malheur, but they did not get the county seat. From that day on, Baxterville disappeared and Jordan Valley was called to life, and it is Jordan Valley today."

Loss of the county seat by twelve votes to Vale in 1888 was a low blow to the ambitious promoters of the town who hoped of a grand future. Had Jordan Valley won, the continuing squabble over the southern party of the county being slighted by the northern half might have been reversed. I doubt that it would make much difference, however, for Jordan Valley is certain that Vale and Ontario are neglecting the rest of the county; and then there is McDermitt, on the Nevada border, whose citizens are dead sure the rest of the county hardly knows of their existence. Especially they claim this is true of Jordan Valley, contending that whatever money gets away from the Malheur Valley doesn't go beyond Jordan Valley. The distances are long, even with today's high speeds, and the county seat and courts seem very far away. So sometimes we settle our differences locally without taking the time and trouble of going clear to Vale.

But Jordan Valley has a great tradition of being a fun-loving place, and at times it was rather wild. An itinerant evangelist told the *Silver City Nugget* that Jordan Valley was "the most wicked settlement he had ever seen." But the *Nugget* quickly added: "The admiration seems to be mutual as the Jordanites didn't seem to cotton to the reverend gentleman, if all reports are true."

After losing the county seat, the proud citizens decided to show the rest of the world by having a whing-ding Fourth of July celebration. A big picnic was held in Parks' Grove, plus a parade, horse racing, gambling and generally whooping it up. Floats were built for the parade, but the sponsors learned to their horror that there was no band. Jim McMahon saved the day by making a snare drum from an old tin pot at his blacksmith's shop and stretching beef bladders for the drumheads. Bill Schnabel was the only drummer in the area, so he did the honors at the head of the parade "and beat the hell out of that drum." A four-horse coach, driven by an old stage jehu named Libby was kept busy hauling folks from the hotel to the playgrounds and back, at twenty-five cents a ride. The dance lasted all night, beginning at 6:00 p.m., at five dollars per ticket per man, and ending — for a brief time — with breakfast the following morning. Then the dancing began again, lasting until noon.

More substantial businesses built up around Baxter's hotel in due course and by 1907, there was quite a thriving community. Among the leading enterprises were: the Bank of Jordan Valley, the J. R. Blackaby Mercantile Company, Jordan Valley Mercantile Company, Grand Central Hotel, newspaper, drug store, hardware store, blacksmith shop, men's store, the Monopole Hotel, livery stable, soda works, slaughter house and miscellaneous endeavors. The first city council was organized on March 27, 1911, with Henry Scott as mayor; F. R. Miller, treasurer; Richard Malloy, city recorder; and John W. Wroten, town marshal. Sitting on that first council were Fred J. Palmer, Jasper B. Duncan, Clyde Foster, Clyde Roberson, James McCain, and George Parks.

The Blackaby general store was among the early businesses that sprung up near Baxter's hotel. The proprietors, Mr. and Mrs. J. R. Blackaby, are shown with the bicycles at left and center of photo, taken in the 1890s.

Jordan Valley got religion, too. Until 1912 the Methodist Church held its services in the schoolhouse and the Catholics in private homes. The Methodist Church then built its own edifice, financed by donations. There were no resident Catholic priests in Jordan Valley until 1914 when the Diocese of Baker sent Bishop Charles O'Reilly to the town. He remained for some little time and administered the sacraments to twenty-two persons. Much impressed by his visit, Bishop O'Reilly wrote in his diary: "Great country! Church to be built there as soon as possible."

On July 15, 1915, Bishop O'Reilly appointed Father Hugh J. Marshall the first resident pastor of Jordan Valley. Encouraged by the Bishop and the enthusiasm of the local people, Father Marshall began plans immediately to build a church. He was well liked by both Catholics and Protestants, and when quarrying of the stone began in Willow Creek draw, four miles east of Jordan Valley, they all turned out to help him. The church was built under Father Marshall's supervision. He also did much of the work fitting together the stone and carving the crosses on the church, which has been described today as "a striking example of desert architecture." Father Marshall poured all his energies into the project, impairing his health. About 1916/17 he was transferred to Klamath Falls, but a few years later, in 1923, returned to Jordan Valley. He then was moved again to Hood River. But his health deteriorated rapidly and he died in 1929.

When Father Donald D. Sullivan was appointed pastor in Jordan Valley in 1958, he took up where Father Marshall left off. He promoted construction of a new church at Arock, a few miles to the west, plus a parish house and parish hall in Jordan Valley, the latter being named in honor of Father Marshall. Both these priests did much for the community, illustrated by the fact that in 1968 when Father Sullivan was transferred, a large farewell party was given in his honor. About half of his many friends who attended were of the Protestant faith.

The new city council had its problems in shaping the destinies of the growing community in the shadow of Pharmacy Butte. There was much more to deal with than the horde of stray dogs of Baxterville, and the cursing freighters and rampaging Indians. Among the actions of its first months in office, the astute body granted permission to Harry Bassett to sell liquor during the fall races, approved plans for a new city jail, took up the matter of widening the main street, instigated a citywide cleanup, directed Marshal Wroten to engage Charles Hicks "or another party" to clean out Baxter Creek and the Parks irrigation ditch, and acted on the acquisition and supervision of lands for a cemetery.

There was certainly a new civic pride reflected

in the actions of the council. But Jordan Valley had problems unique to its setting and isolation, and its heritage of the surrounding wild region. The weight of decision fell directly on the city fathers rather than relying on some higher-up governing body. Three near-epidemics provided periods of crisis when the council had to take whatever steps it deemed necessary to deal with the situation. In 1912 there was a brief scare of a smallpox epidemic with the outbreak of a number of cases. The council voted emergency funds to establish a "pest house" for isolation of smallpox cases; and through the local newspaper, the council urged all citizens to get vaccinations and to avoid all contact with persons suffering from the disease.

Then in 1915 the valley had a critical problem with rabies, spread by diseased coyotes. It threw a scare into everybody, for the coyotes were prevalent on the nearby range lands and were infecting cattle, sheep and dogs. The council took prompt steps:

". . . Inasmuch as an emergency seems to exist that to save the peace and health of our citizens, the

Typical early family (the Cowgills) of Jordan Valley pose before their home.

police are empowered and are hereby instructed to destroy all dogs found on the streets and alleys of Jordan Valley, unless securely muzzled; and in view of the apparent emergency, this resolution shall be in full force and effect immediately."

And during the 1918 nationwide influenza epidemic which caused many thousands of deaths, the town council closed Jordan Valley to all public gatherings, ordered parents to keep their children at home, and posted quarantine notices on homes where there were cases of the disease. The quarantine lasted until the following February.

One of the most frustrating problems was building and maintaining adequate roads throughout the area. The responsibility, now that this was a separate county, was passed to the road department, in the control of the Malheur County Court. The *Jordan Valley Express* suggested, pleaded and prayed for road improvements, pointing out in strong language that "a deplorable state of affairs exists in the condition of roads and bridges leading to and from Jordan Valley, and only in justice to the people of this section, the County Court should take immediate action in the matter of bridge repairs and road improvements."

Heavy rains weakened bridges and spread water at a depth of four feet over a quarter mile area on each side of the bridges. Surveys had been made during the summer for repairs and improvements, but there had been no concrete action. The *Express* editor again went to bat for its citizens:

"We are not censuring the County Court individually or as a group. We have the profoundest regard and esteem for the court, but we are trying to make it plain to these men, as officials of Malheur County, that the people of Jordan Valley have county rights which should be respected and receive some attention and consideration though we do live in the very extreme southeastern part of the county, and almost a hundred miles from the county seat. . . . I don't want to absolve the County Court of all the blame, for I'm sure that there were times when things went astray, but for the most part we'll have to admit that they did a good job considering the needling we have given them through the years."

Jordan Creek was always capable of flooding the valley, and it still is today. The flood of 1909 inspired one citizen, C. W. Faris, to write:

> Take me out and let me stay,
> From the land of Jordan's flood;
> For I am sick, so very sick
> Of the water and the mud.
>
> I was told this land was dry,
> And the story I repeat;
> For I never in all my life
> Saw so much water on a street.
>
> Good impressions are all gone
> Back to native land I go;
> All because the people there
> Didn't make a better show.

The folks of Jordan Valley still complain about the County Court, for the roads continue to give us much trouble, even though they are greatly improved from the old days. On the other hand, the loads carried by the big semi-trucks and trailers are far heavier than those of the early freight wagons. Both caused the roads of their era to break up. The traffic now is heavier too, what with the steady stream of tourists, fishermen, rock hounds, and hunters in the summertime and autumn. Often they leave a mud mess for the local people to travel over in the winters. It is one more reason why we look upon this as the Forgotten Corner.

Today's residents of Jordan Valley and surrounding area are very aware of their colorful past and their heritage. Many families have lived there for several generations and on special occasions bring out costumes and rolling stock from yesteryear. Left to right: Mrs. Dale Sinclair, Julene Zimmerman, Suzanne Hanley, and Sharon Bennett.

Water and its proper use has always been of great concern to Jordan Valley, as it is with much of the West. The Jordan Valley Irrigation Project was created to water the lands adjacent to Jordan Creek. Frank Reas built a reservoir in the early 1900s at the site of the present Antelope Reservoir, but it was washed away in a flash flood. Then in 1909 the Azcuenaga Ranch rebuilt the dam on the guarantee to give Reas water for use of the site. The Azcuenaga Ranch, which was a Basque livestock company, wished to irrigate its lands below the dam. Again the dam washed out, and then the now-famous construction company of Morrison-Knudson rebuilt it for Azcuenagas as one of their first projects.

During that same year, Morrison-Knudson completed a diversion canal near the town of Jordan Valley, emptying into the newly-built reservoir. But the backer of that particular canal and irrigation project died suddenly, and everything came to a halt. Twelve years went by before the project was reactivated. Meanwhile, settlers held onto their lands, waiting for water. Finally in September 1921, they took matters into their own hands.

The Jordan Valley Water Users Association, working with little capital but much determination, began the Arock Project, so-called for the community which acquired its name from a huge rock containing picture writing of Indian origin. The name was suggested by T. Townley Garlic.

Water stored in the Antelope Reservoir was to be released gradually, according to the plan, and picked up in a diversion dam near Arock, from which it would be carried in various laterals to the water users. Contractors Maney and Wells began work on the diversion dam, but went broke when just six feet short of completing the project. Basque stone masons were being employed to do the work. John Yturriondobeitia, a land owner, took over the rock work. His crew finished the dam. The ranchers wanted this project, so it became a single effort by everyone. While Little John's crew labored on the dam, his neighbors scraped together what funds they had to proceed with work on the laterals. Using picks, shovels, dynamite, horse power, and sheer human muscle and will, they got the job completed and began irrigating in 1924.

In 1959 the Antelope Reservoir was raised to the level where it is today, now capable of handling fifty-six thousand acre-feet of water. Land served by the two projects totals eight thousand acres, with six thousand under Arock and two thousand under Danner, the town named for one of its early pioneers, J. N. Danner. However, the projects are entirely dependent on the Antelope Reservoir which has had a frustrating problem since the beginning. The floor of the reservoir is broken lava and the runaway seepage is substantial. In 1969 approximately sixty per cent of the total water flowing into the reservoir escaped through the lava. At the time this book is being written, there is a proposal to raise the dam to accommodate seventy thousand acre-feet. However, the increased acre-feet may mean additional pressure, forcing even more water through the broken floor. Somehow, the cracks must be patched up, and under the project, ranchers can only remain optimistic that the problem will be solved with the same kind of determination that created the water users' project in the first place.

WHEN THE PONIES RAN

HORSE RACING WAS LONG a diversion in the Owyhees, with both Indians and the whites, and since Jordan Valley developed a reputation for the breeding of fine horses, it wasn't surprising that a racetrack should be built there. In fact, together with the track at Wagon-town, the Owyhees boasted quite a racing community, with many familiar faces, coming from hundreds of miles away, attending both events.

The Jordan Valley racetrack was laid out in the late 1870s and the early 1880s on swamp land east of the town, at a time when it was still known as Baxter-ville. It proved to be an ideal location; it was not only handy to what the town had to offer, but it proved to be a "live track." There was enough sod over the swamp to keep the horses from breaking through, resulting in a spring-like effect which gave it a reputa-tion of being the best horse track in the Pacific Northwest.

The racing season was dependent largely upon the

weather, but spring and fall were the popular times. There were usually ten days of racing. Horses, riders and their owners came great distances, the purses and side betting were substantial, and there was always a good time, for Jordan Valley took on a festive air. Miners and citizens poured out of the Owyhees, and business men closed their shops in the camps to take part in the celebrating, join in the excitement, and place a bet or two. Local school teachers found it impossible to conduct classes, and when there was a particularly crucial race, pupils were dismissed so that they might watch the running. Indians from Duck Valley and McDermitt were on hand, too, for the natives had a passion for racing. They set up camp near the track where they could watch and participate in the competition. Folks learned that the Indians and their horses shouldn't be sold short as "also-rans;" often a scrubby-looking Indian pony jockeyed by a plucky young member of the tribe outran the best that the track offered.

Seizing an opportunity, proprietors of the red light district up in Silver City and DeLamar moved down to Jordan Valley to get a piece of the action. They rented houses outside the town or set up business in tents. Long Toed Liz was there regularly, as were Georgie and Lola, and business was most always brisk from the freewheeling crowd of celebrants. The city fathers wouldn't allow any soliciting in town or at the track, but the girls found that Marshal Johnny Wroten couldn't be every place at once, he was likely to overlook some things, and he had his hands full trying to keep the laws enforced during racing season. Once he ran Lola out of the grandstand for "advertising," while the crowd booed the lawman and cheered Lola in her retreat. But Lola and her friends found a way around the narrow-minded city fathers by renting a small house just over the fence from the track, in Swishers' field. It was an ideal location. The law couldn't touch them there, and they could watch the races and advertise their wares, since the track and grandstand were within full view of their back door.

Among the memorable horses that ran in Jordan Valley were Modesk, Red Blood, Quick Silver, Bunch Grass, Pin Ears, Shrimp, Dona Lotia, Beautiful Doll, Mike Cherry, Papoose, Liberty and Bally Beers. Joe Newell and a man named Hailey owned Bunch Grass. In August 1909 they challenged Frank Swisher to a race and Frank bet them one hundred dollars that his horse, Liberty, could beat Bunch Grass. Arrangements made, the race got underway. Frank's jockey had a reputation for fixing races; he had once been shot for it, but recovered and still hadn't learned his lesson. He pulled up the Swisher horse, losing the event to Bunch Grass. But Swisher didn't protest. That night Frank found Newell and Hailey drinking and loudly bragging about their victory in a local saloon. Swisher challenged them to a re-run, for a five hundred dollar stake, and the confident pair accepted. As sure as he stood there, Frank knew that Liberty could beat Bunch Grass. This time, Swisher was more careful in selecting a rider. He chose his good and trusted friend Ed Beers and Liberty beat Bunch Grass by several lengths.

"It paid me to keep my mouth shut," laughed Swisher. "I made a profit of four hundred dollars."

Probably the most celebrated race horse from Jordan Valley was Bally Beers, who joined the racing circuit and set many records in the West. Bally Beers was by Liberty, a horse of unknown origin, and out of a mare that was half Morgan. Billy Beers' son, Ed, gave Bally to Tom Skinner and Liberty to Frank Swisher. At first Liberty could beat the young Bally, but then Bally began winning, liked being out front, and Liberty never headed him again.

Bally Beers, the most famous race horse in the Owyhees.

Bally was best at the half and quarter mile. He won his early races on the Jordan Valley track, displaying speed, stamina, quality, and intelligence. Probably his finest hour there was against a horse named Shrimp, supposedly unbeatable, but Bally left him eating sod. Bally ran at McDermitt, then went on to Reno and California tracks, for Bally could hold his own with the best bangtails in the business. Tom Skinner had sold him by then. He set many records, the most outstanding the running of the half mile in twenty-two seconds, a mark that stood for many years.

Bally had a particular technique which won him many races. In those days automatic starting gates hadn't been developed. The horses were brought up to a line, sometimes a rope, and the jockeys tried to keep them in check. Many of the animals were nervous and it was sometimes quite an operation manipulating them to the line and set to go. When the starter saw

BALLY BEERS I
DONA LUTIA II
BEAUTIFUL DOLL III

Bally Beers finishing in his usual place — first.

they were all even, he quickly gave the signal and
they were off. Unlike the others, Bally would wait
calmly on the line, registering no outward excitement,
while his competitors jockeyed for positions, pent up,
jittery and putting each other into a state of near-frenzy.
But when the signal was given, Bally charged ahead,
suddenly unwound and not only got a fast start, but
was first across the finish line.

Bally's career became legendary around Jordan
Valley, and many old-timers remember him well.
Frank Swisher said he died in Mexico while being
run on the racing circuit.

Interest in the Jordan Valley track finally declined.
The people who cared about it died off and a new

generation showed little tendency to carry on the tradition. The laws also changed. After racing there finally closed, Ben Swisher took over the site, later selling it to a man named Madariaga. Today the old track land is used as a hay meadow, but you can still see portions of the course that was once known as the fastest in the Northwest.

A race to the finish line — Bally Beers and Shrimp.

MOONSHINE OVER JORDAN

DURING THE Prohibition years, which spanned more than a decade from 1919 to 1933, the manufacture of moonshine became something of an art in certain parts of the country. And nowhere was it practiced with more dexterity than in the Jordan Valley area.

While gangsters made a big time multi-million dollar business out of bootlegging, hard-working and otherwise honest citizens entered the moonshining trade believing that making whisky wasn't exactly breaking the law, since Prohibition was ridiculous anyway. That was largely how folks felt about it in Jordan Valley. The Owyhees had been virtually conquered by the miner, the cowhand, the sheepman, and the trooper, each with his bottle of booze on his hip, so folks weren't at all narrow-minded on the subject. Fact is, there is a story that a local preacher burned his parsonage to the ground while making whisky.

The isolation and remoteness of the three-corner region made it ideal for moonshining, and the govern-

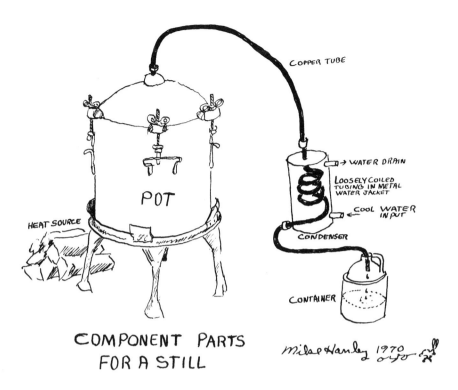

COPPER TUBE

WATER DRAIN

LOOSELY COILED
TUBING IN METAL
WATER JACKET

POT

COOL WATER
INPUT

CONDENSER

HEAT SOURCE

CONTAINER

COMPONENT PARTS
FOR A STILL

Mike Hanley 1970

Moonshine equipment.

ment agents were driven out of their minds trying to cover it all. Every gulch had its still and for every small operator caught by the G-Men, forty others were overlooked. Frank Swisher, who was quite active in the moonshining business, thought he'd been caught for sure one day when Bill Loveland happened to be riding by his operation on Smith Creek in the Junipers. Loveland saw Frank through the open doorway, half submerged in a large keg, busily cleaning it. Bill hobbled his horse and sneaked up behind Frank, who was partly deaf, and clapped him on the back.

"He damned near jumped clear through the other end of the keg, and turned around and came out head first," Loveland chuckled.

Frank Swisher told how he made the stuff:

"The first step is the making of mash. Put grain

in kegs and add sugar, fifty pounds of sugar to every hundred of grain. After the grain and sugar have started to ferment, put it in a copper kettle with a fire under it. You must use a copper kettle because another metal could turn the whisky to poison. The mash starts to let off gas and this is run through a 'worm' which has cold water running around it to condense the alcohol. The worm should be made of copper tubing, with the size of it depending on the size of the operation. The worm should be fifteen to twenty inches long.

"The still I operated was an eighty-five gallon three-quarter worm outfit. I piped water into the worm to keep it cool, because it wouldn't distill into a liquid if it wasn't cool. There were various ways to distill the alcohol. The use of a worm was the most popular, but the thump keg was also used. It was called a thump keg because it made lots of noise. The thump keg consisted of a metal beer keg and had a three-quarter inch tube coming from the top of the kettle running into water, from where it was steamed back into another container as it condensed when cooled."

The stuff could be worked three or four times. Good whisky was run to a high proof and diluted with distilled water. If whisky is run through low proof, it will be poison; and if regular water is used instead of distilled, the whisky will be contaminated by the minerals. Frank ran his to 140 proof and then using distilled water, back to 90 proof.

Many people were poisoned by bad moonshine during Prohibition days, made by unscrupulous operators who were after the dollars rather than concerned for their customers' welfare. Some of them would transport their booze in old milk cans or other metal containers that would turn the liquor to poison. The reckless operators gave the good ones a bad name, too, and the federal government became more concerned about the making of bad booze and its effects on the people than about keeping the Prohibition laws.

The whisky was filtered before it was set to age. The best filter, according to Swisher, was bone charcoal which was placed in three layers, with wool between. After filtering, the whisky was poured into a keg for aging, and coloring was often added. Swisher used burned sugar and cut it back with alcohol. Others used food coloring and some nailed a plug of chewing tobacco to the bottom of the keg. Moonshine that was uncolored often went by the name of "white lightning." Like all moonshine, it could be identified by the charcoal particles in it.

The booze had to be kept in motion to do a good aging job. Big operations would load the kegs on board a ship and after several ocean crossings, the stuff was well aged. The moonshiner used other methods, many

Photo by Jeff Ford

Rancher-author Mike Hanley examines old bottle used during moonshining times of the twenties in the Jordan Valley country. Bottle is a rarity, found at location of a moonshining operation.

of them makeshift with what was handy. Frank Swisher put his kegs in a creek and let the water currents rock them back and forth.

Swisher and his partner, Judd, had an operation just below The Difficulty, on the Middle Fork of the Owyhee River where Ernest Fenwick later homesteaded. Frank tended the day shift and Judd took the evening run. They had been working for quite awhile, and had some two hundred gallons of moonshine stored in a tent. Now they were running it through a second time, which they called "second whisky." Frank had finished his shift and turned over to Judd seventy gallons of seventy proof alcohol from the first run. But Judd had a weakness. He loved to read shoot-'em-ups and became so engrossed in his Western story that he forgot to watch the pot. The stuff boiled over, caught fire and blew up the still and the two hundred gallons in the tent. It was quite a show, like the Fourth of July. The partners had gun powder hanging in a tree, and it went off, too, with a blast that shook the canyon and scared the hell out of the wild things.

"The only thing that didn't burn was Judd's books," added Swisher, "and I threw them in."

But the partners didn't split up, although relations were strained for a time, They moved the operation four miles up the creek, but had only run one batch when they were tipped off that someone had turned them in. They tried to deliver the one batch, but the pick-up man didn't show up.

"We took the hint and quit," Swisher added.

It took real ingenuity and creativeness to transport the booze and dodge the government men. Traveling the public roads was risky business, for they were well patrolled. Swisher and his partner didn't have to take such risks, since their pick-up man had his

Photo courtesy Fred Eiguren family
Not all the moonshine made it safely to the customer. This load was wrecked
near the Sheep Ranch.

own car and would meet them on top of Three Forks.
He took the risk of delivering the booze to Caldwell.

"We made pretty good money," said Frank,
"because it cost one dollar twenty-five cents a gallon
to make and we could get ten to fifteen dollars a gallon
for it. When we moved from The Difficulty to the
rim at Three Forks, we used a hack. Judd rode on
ahead with a saddle horse and gave the high sign if
it was okay to come on. The Government Men used
cars and couldn't follow through the brush and rocks."

Other small operators had their own special
methods of delivery. They resorted to varieties of

camouflage. One man living on Little Butte Creek near Lake Creek, Oregon, did a thriving business delivering his cabbage crop door-to-door. Cabbage brought a good price that year, for he'd hollowed out each head, placing a pint of moonshine inside. A Basque who made moonshine just outside Jordan Valley hauled it in under wagon loads of sagebrush, not only bringing in the whisky, but also getting up the winter's wood.

Some moonshiners were taught by friends and relatives in Tennessee, who were experts by long tradition. Asked about the quality of Basque moonshine, Frank Swisher explained: "The Old Country men were the best moonshiners because they learned fast and became artists at it. They could get away with it because they could pretend (to investigators) that they didn't understand what it was all about."

Two moonshiners had a cellar at Cow Lakes which remains there today. They ran the operation for two years before being closed down. The law hit them when one partner was delivering a batch of stuff to the Stone Hotel, their outlet in Jordan Valley. He met the law on the road, but the officers didn't recognize him, so he got away. His partner was arrested at the still and taken to Vale, to spend four months in jail. The usual sentence was four months and four hundred dollars. But it was almost like a vacation, for the authorities allowed the moonshiner to go to the local restaurant to order his meals, then bring them back to the cell for eating.

A locally famous character was one of the best-known Basque moonshiners. He'd been a sheep-herder, but found operating a still more to his liking. Being caught several times didn't discourage him; it went with the business. Highly superstitious, he never allowed an omen or sign to go unheeded. Once when running a load of booze to LaGrande, the moonshiner saw a black cat crossing the road near Burnt River. He turned onto a side road, bypassing the main highway. Upon delivering his moonshine, he learned that he'd avoided a roadblock. If he wasn't a true believer before, he was from that day forward.

The Basque claimed he carried two pocketbooks. Sometimes the G-Men "would take the big one, other times the little one." But he got his booze supply by whatever method seemed best at the moment. He would steal whisky cached by bootleggers just outside Jordan Valley. He would spy on where bootleggers coming into town would hide their booze, then steal it during the night.

Several cowboys in the Steens Mountain country were facing an extremely dry year and were short on water, but they found a solution. There was a lot of moonshine on hand, so they made coffee with it and mixed it in their sourdough. It was a summer to remember. . . .

The late E. R. Jackman, the well-known author and chronicler of this part of the West, had a favorite yarn about his first visit to Jordan Valley in 1921, when he was traveling for the Oregon State Extension Service. Tired, hot, and dusty, Jackman registered at the Stone Hotel, which was an outlet for the moonshiners. He was conscious of many questions and of being closely studied by the clerk and others in the lobby. Finally, it was decided that he wasn't a lawman.

"Where you traveled from?" asked the clerk.

"Lakeview," replied Jackman.

"That's a long hot road, mister," commented the clerk. "You look like you need a drink." Reaching under the counter, he pulled out a jug and poured Jackman half a water glass of moonshine.

But Sheriff Roy Pearman wound up with the strangest prisoners ever to be housed in the Silver City jail. He'd gone out after some bootleggers, but they'd skipped, leaving their supply. Pearman brought back four kegs of moonshine which he securely imprisoned behind bars of a jail cell. Nobody ever said if the kegs came to trial — in court, that is.

THE COUNTRY DOCTOR

WHEN WALTER WILLIAM JONES was graduated in 1903 from medical school at the University of Iowa, he and his classmates were expected to know a little about everything in medicine, and to be able to diagnose and treat every human ache and pain — and the illness of the local livestock, too. They might even be asked to give practical advice on agriculture, for the local general practitioner was considered the community's sure-fire source of information on any subject because he was a well-educated man with a college degree, he had a huge reference library, and he took many important-looking journals. He was the Country Doctor or the Horse and Buggy Doctor, and in rural communities, words could never be found to express adequately his missionary work.

Dr. Jones was for fifty-three years the only medical practitioner in the Jordan Valley region. He came to the valley a few days before the beginning of 1910 to buy out the somewhat shaky practice of a man named

Douglas. Both Dr. Douglas and his wife, who came to the area in 1907, practiced medicine and were the first permanent physicians in Jordan Valley. Before they hung out their shingle, the nearest doctor had to be imported from DeLamar to treat the sick and wounded, often over bad or nearly impassable roads.

Dr. Douglas was never very popular with the people. Dr. Jones was from another mold — a warm personality who liked people, and therefore the people liked him. He developed a lifetime love affair with Jordan Valley and nothing — not even the opportunity to practice in a large hospital — would pry him loose from the settlement. Except for a period during World War I when he was with the armed forces, Doc Jones remained in the community for over half a century, until his death in 1963 at the age of eighty-seven. His heart and roots were deeply imbedded in historic Baxterville and the surrounding wide open spaces. He served his people well and became a legend in his own lifetime.

In the early years, Doc Jones traveled by horse and buggy, on horseback, or on foot — whatever means was necessary to reach the side of a patient. In the winter he went by snowshoes and skis into the wild and remote corners of the Owyhee country. A house call might mean mushing for seventy miles through muck and snow, often at high risk to himself. In later years, Doc Jones used a jeep to get over the rugged back roads.

Nothing would stop him. Once the good doctor got word that a man named Arthur Drummond had spotted fever. The Owyhee River was running high, for it was early spring. Tom Whitby helped get the doctor across in a boat. They might not have made it in the swift current, but Doc Jones leaped from the craft into waist-deep bone-chilling water to pull the boat ashore. Then taking a saddle horse, he headed for the Junipers through several feet of snow. Drum-

A country doctor and his family. From left to right: Everett Jones, Jr., Everett Jones, Sr., and Dr. Walter William Jones, the physician of Jordan Valley.

mond was nearly dead when the physician reached him, but Doc Jones saved his life.

He had more than one bout with the old Owyhee. He swam the flooding river once with his medical bag to treat a man with a broken leg. Doc Jones constructed a small raft from driftwood, put his clothing and black bag aboard, and pushed it across the river.

Folks never considered Doc Jones' prices "cheaper than at the railroad," when they went to get treatment. After all, he had delivered many of the people who came to see him. Doc Jones delivered babies for twenty-five dollars or a cord of wood. He prescribed and prepared his own remedies in his combination pharmacy and office in Jordan Valley where he treated rashes and fevers, set broken bones, and occasionally patched up a bullet wound. Surgery was performed in the rear of the Jordan Valley Pharmacy. If the doctor

needed assistance, he called in a passerby off the street
or commissioned one of his own children. When the
operation was finished, the patient was taken to the
boarding house next door to be cared for during con-
valescence.

Cowboys, ranchers, miners, Indians, Basques,
merchants and thieves came to him. All received the
best treatment he could offer, for Doc Jones adhered
to the oath he had taken and believed that his primary
reason for being was to help people. Social status or
skin color made no difference to him. Those who had
taken on too much booze or moonshine received not
only his help but his lecture on drunkenness. When
one fellow came to him very drunk, Doc Jones asked
how long he'd been in that condition. His partner
drawled out a quick estimate:

"Well, Doc, I guess about twenty-three years."

Jess Winnemucca, grandson of Chief Winnemucca,
sought out Doc Jones to deliver a baby at the Indian
camp outside of town. The doctor found the woman
lying in the snow inside an enclosure of sagebrush.
He was asked to take the child, which had been dead
several days. Dr. Jones believed the mother would
also die, but four days later, she came into his office
"to pay what was owed" with twelve armloads of wood.

One day two unemployed painters stopped in
Jordan Valley. They were flat broke, desperately in
need of work, but had plenty of paint. Doc Jones
wanted to advertise his pharmacy. He ordered the pair
to paint the word "Pharmacy" across the face of the
huge mound then known as Skinner Butte, just back
of the town. The quality of the paint must have been
top-grade, for the sign remained for many years,
although it has completely faded now. But the name
stuck. To this day, the hill is known as "Pharmacy
Butte."

Sometimes things didn't work out quite as Dr.
Jones expected. One late evening he was talking to

a woman at the drug store. Doc Jones walked her to the door and they both noticed how black it was outside, not a light showing or anyone stirring along the street.

"I wonder what would happen if someone were to ring the fire bell," Dr. Jones remarked.

The woman left and Dr. Jones turned back into his store. A short time later the fire bell began ringing. Doc Jones rushed to the door. There was plenty of activity now; people were running along the street, lights were flashing on, the town was lit up like the Fourth of July. But there was no blaze, and the woman who'd been visiting with Doc Jones was arrested for ringing the fire bell. Later, the court fined her for disturbing the peace, and Dr. Jones, who started it all, was left with a red face.

Doc Jones had a wide variety of interests in this community that he loved. He was an active participant in many community affairs, and a willing counselor on local problems. He was an avid sports fan, too, with a passion for baseball. He played a snappy game with the local nine, but once during the Memorial Day opener, he actually went to sleep during the play. He reached first during the eighth inning and in the lull, began to drowse, not awakening until he was tagged out. Then he was quite embarrassed. Fans surmised he must have been up all night with a patient.

The doctor's hobby was mining, and there was great opportunity to pursue it in the Owyhees. He loved to poke about the old diggings and delighted in pointing out that the sandstone used in construction of his pharmacy contained a certain amount of gold. Another major interest was young people. For years Dr. Jones was the commencement speaker for both the Jordan Valley and Arock elementary schools. And when a new school was built in Arock, it was dedicated to Dr. Walter William Jones.

As a community leader, Doc Jones knew no peers.

He spent much of what spare time he had promoting developments he felt would be good for the area, especially highways and power. The Idaho-Oregon-Nevada cutoff was essentially the same one used by early freighters and stagecoaches. It was practically impassable for the automobile in winter snow, spring mud, and summer dust. Dr. Jones worked hard and long, expending much energy, to have the route improved and paved. It took a lot of time and stubbornness to whip public bureaus into action. He traveled to many towns to raise promotion money for the one hundred twenty-two mile route through Oregon, and met with members of the Oregon State Highway Department to solicit their interest and stress the dire needs for the highway. Finally, in 1944 victory came. The route was oiled and improvements made, and then it was paved. Now a part of U.S. 95, the old I-O-N cutoff is a link in the major route from Canada to Mexico across the inland West. And the victory belongs to Dr. Jones.

When Dr. Jones died, Jordan Valley was left without a physician, the nearest being at Caldwell, sixty-five miles away. But thanks to the good road Dr. Jones helped build, it takes only a short time to cover the distance. It is as though that was what he had in mind: that the day would come when he would no longer be around to watch over the people of Jordan Valley, and that they might need to seek help elsewhere.

Since his death, Dr. Jones' pharmacy has been operated as a gift shop by one of his six children, Everett, and Everett's wife, Mary Alice. But it is more than a gift shop; it's an unusual museum and memorial, not only to the kind Jordan Valley physician, but to country doctors everywhere. All Dr. Jones' medical apparatus is on display in what may well be one of the largest and most extensive exhibits of early phar-

Ellis Lucia Photo

Little pharmacy which was headquarters for many years of Dr. Walter William Jones, colorful country doctor, is still in use today in town of Jordan Valley. He served the community for over fifty years, dying at the age of eighty-seven.

maceutical equipment and medicine bottles anywhere in the Pacific Northwest.

There are nearly sixty large apothecary jars with ground glass stoppers and gold leaf labels held in place with beeswax, resting on the top shelves where Doc Jones left them. There is a great array of bottles, many sizes and shapes: brown, blue and clear, with corks and glass stoppers; bottles of sassafras, larkspur lotion, Dr. Miles Tonic, hemlock oil, oil of tansy, and rhubarb aromatic; bottles of the "barkeeper's friend" — mix it with sour beer and it's great to clean the bar; bottles of asafetida and Stomalix, the latter imported from Spain especially for the Basque sheepherders. The doctor had a hunch that its sixty percent alcoholic con-

Interior of Dr. Jones' pharmacy is today something of a museum of early medicine in rural areas. Shelves contain about sixty large apothecary jars and a great array of medicine bottles. His office in rear of store is much as he left it.

tent was what made Stomalix such a favorite. The collection also contains measuring beakers, mortars and pestals, and three sets of scales used by the doctor in making up his own medical prescriptions. It took lots of equipment and medical supplies to be a country doctor.

Dr. Jones' office in the rear is much as it was when he was practicing. His desk is still there. Three basic medicines were carried by the physician in his black medical bag which is on display. The bag also contained his pathological kit, urinalsysis flask, hypodermic needle, and stethoscope. That bag went everywhere with him, into the rugged back country and when he swam the Owyhee River.

Among the most significant items is the doctor's black leather-bound ledger, which weighs about twelve pounds. Doc Jones recorded literally everything in this book, from births to deaths, and his wholesale accounts and bank deposits. Within its pages is the history of the area and its people for half a century, their joys and sorrows, and also the diary of a country doctor. Among the births recorded there is that of Oregon State Senator Anthony Yturri. At first Doc Jones spelled it Eturri, but then crossed it out to make the correction. He had a most difficult time with Basque names such as Yturriondobeitia, Acordagoitia, and Calzacorta. Payments of bills were made in varied, if not sometimes strange, ways by proud and honest people who were trying to square their accounts. One entry reads: "90 cents by washing, 50 cents by cash, leaving 80 cents in the balance;" and another says, "Wood from an Indian, paid, $3.90". . . .

The story of not only Dr. Jones but all country doctors is contained between the covers of that ledger. They were a special kind, who no longer exist. . . .

BLACKSMITHS WERE A
SPECIAL BREED

THE BLACKSMITH, like the country doctor, was a cornerstone of community life in the West, whether located in mining or ranch areas. Since the Owyhee country had both forms of livelihood, the smith was a dire necessity. He kept the mines open and the wagons rolling.

Every town, mining camp and ranch had its blacksmith. While most of the men could handle some of the work, the blacksmith had special skills and know-how. He was a jack-of-all-trades who, like the doctor, knew something about a lot of things and could cure the ills of a wagon or a piece of machinery from some innate experience and ability; a strong, skillful, friendly and obliging man whose shop with its fiery forge and strange tools was a magic attraction to a small boy, especially if allowed to turn the crank of the forge.

The first blacksmiths in the Owyhees worked

primarily on tools of the mining trade. The blacksmith sharpened picks, drills, and mining gear. He did the heavy work on the big freight wagons, and shod horses, mules, and oxen. As the mines became more sophisticated, he worked on the machinery.

Photo Courtesy Mildretta Adams

Blacksmiths were needed in the mining camps. Here oxen are being shod at Dave Summerville's forge in DeLamar.

When the mines closed down, the blacksmiths were out of business. They lasted far longer on the ranches and farms and in the villages scattered throughout the valleys. Most of them were independent businessmen, although some were employees of certain ranch operations. The ranches and farms always had plenty of work for the smith. Haying and harvest seasons were the busiest times of all, for then everything seemed to break down at once. The smith always got the toughest jobs, for most ranchers were adept at repairing many things themselves. Wagon wheels and plowshares were prime targets for his skills.

Today, plowshares are still sharpened at the forge. Although the automotive age brought an end to the old-time blacksmith, training in the trade is now being taught at some colleges. But generally, the fadeout of the smiths meant an end to the skill of repairing wagon wheels and setting iron wagon "tyres" — as the old-time smiths spelled it — the latter almost an art and a skill that had to be known by the pioneers coming over the Oregon and California Trails. I've

Setting a wagon tyre is an art few are now able to practice as it is done here.

learned to do it, in building my collection of historic Western wagons, but there are few of us around today. Most young fellows prefer working on an automobile. And ask a modern smith and he'll maybe reply:

"I remember helping my father repair wagon wheels, but I never did any of it myself."

Ernest Stites is one of the last living old-time blacksmiths in the West. He plied his trade for years in DeLamar and Jordan Valley. He clearly remembers how to set wagon tyres and how to weld them, using borax and sand for a good flux. The rule in fitting a wagon tyre was to keep the tyre a quarter inch smaller than the wooden rim. If a double tyre was to be set, the outer tyre had to be three-sixteenths smaller than the under-tyre. If too tight, it would break the weld. The tyres were fashioned into the proper curve on a machine called a "tyre bender." When ready, the wooden wheel was placed on a special bench and the tyre expanded by intense heat and slipped over the wheel. It was then doused with water for a quick cooling, to contract or shrink the iron band tightly over the wheel. Stites made his own nails, and also his own horse and mule shoes.

Born on a ranch near Steavensville, Texas, in 1875, Stites came with his folks to Oregon in 1883, to settle originally near Grants Pass. He learned blacksmithing on their farm from an old Britisher. As a young man he attended, and was graduated from, the Oregon Agricultural College at Corvallis. He found that he knew almost as much, or more, about the trade than did the instructor. He and his brother also became involved in politics, stumping Oregon and California for William Jennings Bryan, a relative, in his campaign against William McKinley. Stites remembered that "when Bryan spoke, he could be heard four blocks away — but it didn't win him the election."

In 1900 Stites came to Jordan Valley. He worked for a time at haying, and then bought the blacksmith shop of one of the first Basques to settle there, Antone Azcuenaga. The Basque had operated the shop for several years, but it was at the time of the Spanish-American War. As happens to most minority groups in this country, particularly in times of strife, the Basques were treated roughly. Their connections with Spain didn't help matters. Azcuenaga was no exception, despite the need for his services. One day a Spanish flag was hung outside his shop. It wasn't his doing; someone else unfurled the banner as a cruel joke.

In any case, Stites got the shop and stuck with it for two years. But he was young and restless, so sold the place to a man named Cox, and for a year drove freight wagons from Caldwell to Jordan Valley. Then he acquired the blacksmith business of David Sommerville at DeLamar. That he was a good smith was evidenced by the fact that former customers, learning he was back in the trade, brought their horses to him to be shod. They explained that they not only liked his work but that "Cox talks too much," although I have a hunch that maybe the attractions of DeLamar had something to do with it, too.

Stites put in several years, too, working for the mining companies as a smith. He sharpened tools and handled other repair work, of which there was always quite a lot. But when exchangeable bits were introduced, he lost his job, so turned to installing machinery in the mills. He also did carpentry work. But the trade of blacksmith changed immeasurably in the twentieth century, although he continued following his trade, and adjusting to the requirements of the times. During World War II he worked in the shipyards at Richmond, California, and then in the postwar years as a carpenter, helping to build the famous Mapes Hotel in Reno, Nevada. Today, as this book is published, he lives with his niece, Blanche Miller, near Ontario, Oregon, not far from where he began

Ernest Stites who came to Jordan Valley in 1900 was a member of the dying trade of blacksmith, once among any community's most important occupations. In the early decades of the century he found much work at Jordan Valley and in the Owyhee mines. Later, he worked in the shipyards during World War II and helped build a big hotel at Reno, Nevada.

a trade that is now a part of another age — perhaps the last of the nineteenth century men of the forge, who clearly remembers the art of blacksmithing.

THE BATTLE OF SOLDIER CREEK

DURING THE EARLY 1930s ranchers in the Soldier Creek grazing area near Jordan Valley formed an association to halt the outside flow of sheep from the Snake River Valley which, by their vast numbers, were ravaging the range land.

Passage of the Taylor Grazing Act of 1934 gave the association the power to control unbridled use of the range. In the first year, over one hundred thousand sheep were prevented from grazing on Soldier Creek. The act made such grazing illegal, and the U.S. Government could confiscate the livestock of any law-breakers and fine the owners.

For years, great concern had been expressed by ranchers over the future of the range itself, not only in Jordan Valley but in other parts of this I-O-N territory, which had been "over-grazed to such an extent that the open range was almost a desert." It wasn't merely a problem with sheep, although they were the most noticeable. Cattlemen were also abusers of the range, and so were horse owners who turned their herds onto the public domain. But at least in the beginning, the so-called "tramp operator" was the principal offender. There were tramp cattle operators, called rawhiders, as well as sheep "tramps" and both would be forced out. And while there were many tramp sheep operators, there were other sheepmen who had established ranches; and they — like the established cattlemen — disliked all tramps, be they cattle or sheep.

If some method of protection of the range weren't put into action, there would be no more grazing by anyone. Among those most vitally concerned was Ralph Stanford of the Cow Creek district who worked for passage of a law, through petition, for control of grazing privileges on public lands. This course of action, for which there seemed little other choice, led to the fading out of the traditional "open range" of the frontier West.

The code of the Taylor Grazing Act placed restrictions on the indiscriminate misuse of federal lands. Because of the tramp operator problem, the first item on the agenda for the government men was a requirement that all users of the public range show proof of a *base of operations* for their livestock. This posed a problem more for the sheepmen than for the cattlemen because of the methods by which the two kinds of livestock are handled. With cattle, a "base" is retained — and is necessary — for feeding during the long winters. In contrast, sheep could get by on winter grazing and cheap pasture. Sheepmen lamb in the spring, thus producing a salable lamb later in the summer, and therefore the sheep owner can turn his product faster than the cowman. Furthermore, when the winter-size band "lambs out," the band almost triples in size because many ewes have twin lambs. That means terrific pressure from the great size of the bands on any range where the flocks graze.

Cattlemen must, however, keep their calves much longer than the sheepmen, which means a slower turnover and greater investment. Nowadays, ranchers hold their calves on the average of a year before selling them, but in 1934, they retained them from two to four years. The cowman needed a base property to produce and hold his crop from one year to the next. The vast gap in time between the sheepman's and the cowman's turnover, plus the terrific increase in the size of the sheep band, resulted in over-grazing. This was the basic reason why the cattleman disliked the sheepman so much.

All users of the range, under the new act, were required to show proof of their base of operations. Those who couldn't were forced out of busines. A system of priorities was established, allowing old-time operators seniority in the grazing rights over the late-comers. Armed with these two prerequisites, the Bureau of Land Management began to right the wrongs made by seventy years of indiscriminate use of the range lands.

Following elimination of the tramp operators, the BLM began to adjudicate the range based on the productive capability of the base property and prior use of the federal land. At this point the ranchers saw that it wasn't likely to be as rosy as it had first appeared; that in promoting federal controls, they might have indeed built a Frankenstein's monster. The new range managers were, for the most part, former ranchers who had failed to make it on their own. The active and successful ranchers resented being told how to run their business by men who had failed, and therefore maybe didn't know as much about the operations as those still in business. There was bitterness and many lawsuits ensued, with the ranchers the losers more times than not. Even if they managed to win a decision against the BLM, the lawyer fees were terrific — a major outlay against the years's gross receipts.

The carrying capacity of the Soldier Creek area was based by the advisory board to the BLM on the total demand of Class One Permits. This laid the groundwork for what became known, in Old West terms, as "The Battle of Soldier Creek." In 1943, while the nation was at war, the advisory board and the BLM determined that the Class One Permits — *"ranches which ran livestock during the priority years"* — in the Soldier Creek unit required 77,419 *Animal Unit Months*, which became the measuring stick for the area. This was based on, over a five-year period, on the amount of actual use of the range. Trouble was, some ranchers had not been using their full range privileges. This was called non-use. Thus, when the Class One requests were compared with the range's carrying capacity, the figures didn't jibe. In 1947, for example, the requests totaling 77,419 AUM were more than double the BLM ceiling of 36,356 AUM. The applicants were blocked by the BLM ceiling at a time when World War II was over and the ranchers were restocking to carrying capacity.

The differentials didn't make the BLM popular with the ranchers who felt justifiably that they had priorities on the range. Matters reached a critical stage in 1951 when the advisory board recommended a ceiling of 43,260 AUM. The BLM made additional surveys and concluded there were only 31,284 AUM available and that they would hold to the ceiling of the advisory board, but definitely wouldn't go beyond it. A holler went up; the action not only angered the ranchers, but placed them in a serious bind. The Battle of Soldier Creek hereby began in earnest; not open warfare on the range with Winchester rifles and six-shooters — which might have been the case a few decades earlier — but in the courts. The older ranches which had run at full capacity during the priority years were ordered to reduce their numbers to comply with the advisory board's recommendations. No distinction

The Soldier Creek area became the scene of dispute in the 1930s between sheep and cattle men over grazing rights. Under the Taylor Grazing Act, cattle ranchers formed an association to prevent uncontrolled use of the range. The Bureau of Land Management then took over administration of the range, which brought on "The Battle of Soldier Creek."

was made between Class One and Class Two permits, as was the original intention of the system, and as a result, the Class One ranches were reduced to the same level as Class Two.

The ranchers appealed immediately and it isn't difficult to see why. Mike Hanley (my father) was cut from six hundred thirteen animal units to three hundred eighty-six, with seventy-four listed as "temporary." Ray Gluch was cut from five hundred twelve to two hundred sixty-three, with fifty-one "temporary;" Loveland Brothers two hundred seventy-seven to one hundred thirty-six, with thirty-one "temporary;" Ed Maher cut from one hundred fifty to eighty-nine, with nineteen "temporary;" and

Mike Hanley III, the author's father.

Tex Payne, two hundred twenty-one to one hundred twenty-three, with twenty-four "temporary."

These appellants were represented by George A. Greenfield and the BLM by Dean F. Ratzman, before Dent D. Dalby, hearing examiner for the BLM. Part way through the proceedings, when things looked bad for the appellants, it was discovered that one of them didn't have the attorney's fee. He talked of dropping out, but feeling that there was security in numbers, Mike Hanley convinced him to stay with the ship and, along with the other appellants, covered the fee.

Examiner Dalby supported the Class One users in handing down his decision. He declared:

"After the award of grazing privileges to the extent of the total Class One demand in the Soldier Creek unit, there may be forage available for distribution to Class Two applicants. As previously indicated, each of the applicants here is entitled to an equitable share of this Class Two forage."

The decision left the Class Two holders in a bad

way, for they had lost their right to clear use of the range, and chances were slim of there being any available forage. They were set back to their original status of having to wait until the Class One permits were filled to their holders' satisfaction. But not all was lost, for the Class One ranchers, in a demonstration of good will, agreed to give some of their rights over to the Class Two users so that they could carry on their livelihood.

To the old-time cowmen, the BLM was something they didn't quite understand, for they had been used to full freedom, and not being dictated to from above. The Battle of Soldier Creek opened the eyes of the livestock people to the fact that the federal agency was here to stay, whether they liked it or not. In a way, the ranchers had brought it on themselves, for they had originally solicited government help to protect the range lands. Now it had turned against them. At first, they attempted to fight back, but the expense of the court cases and the difficulty of gaining a favorable decision led them to "throw in the towel." I feel that had they stuck together in the beginning, when the federal government first began dictating to them, they might have altered the course of events. But historically, it is against the better judgement of ranchers to stick together, even on something as important as the BLM actions against them.

Rancher and BLM relations have bettered greatly, however, with the establishment of management programs. These have improved the public range rather than relying solely on the system of merely reducing the numbers of cattle running on them. Oh, we still have our differences and probably always will. One place where we clash is over the policy of "multiple use" incorporating the present-day need for more and more public outdoor recreation areas. This again put the clamps on the ranchers, for it meant that livestock must give way to wild life and lovers of the outdoors.

And the first place that multiple use was introduced into Idaho and Oregon was in the Owyhee region.

But there have been benefits along with the grief. On the range lands there have been brush spray and seeding projects, water improvements, cross fencing, and allotments set up. It has all generally helped for better management of the range. The difference from what it was ten years ago is plainly visible in the Soldier Creek area.

RUNNING OF THE MUSTANGS

WILD HORSES were still plentiful in many sections of the West until a comparatively few years ago. The Owyhee country and the plains of eastern Oregon and northern Nevada vibrated to the thunder of their pounding hoofs, and huge dust clouds could be seen on the far horizons from the herds of free-running mustangs.

There is nothing that catches the human fancy more than the romanticized view of a wild stallion, the leader of his band, surveying the scene from a high ridge, silhouetted against the sky, muscles quavering, nostrils spread, defiantly alert to any and all dangers, symbolizing the kind of complete freedom that human beings strive for and dream about.

Only a few of these wild mustangs still run along the Owyhee River in the breaks above the Owyhee Dam. They are also found in scattering and diminishing numbers, in Nevada, Wyoming, and Montana, where a refuge was established in 1968 in the Pryor

Photo by Bureau of Land Management, Robert D. Hostetter

Small bands of wild horses may still be found in the back country of the Owyhees, although their numbers are diminishing. This pair warily eyes the photographer who got this lucky shot on the open prairie.

Mountain area as a permanent range for the mustang. His history extends far back to the coming of the Conquistadors to central America and he is now recognized along with the buffalo as a distinct part of our Western heritage. And if he is lucky, like the buffalo, he may survive for future generations.

When cattlemen came into the West, they found the great herds of mustangs made for their purposes. They provided a ready-made supply for stock horses when captured and tamed — not always an easy thing — and a means of recreation for fun-loving buckeroos. The Indians found him, too, as useful for hunting, for getting about and moving from place to place, and most important, for waging war against the white invaders. Had Cortes met mounted Indian cavalry when he landed in the New World, the history of the western hemisphere might have been far different.

Mustang comes from the Spanish *mestengo*, meaning wild horse. He is known for his toughness, his spirit, his wild ways, and his endurance. The average mustang was small, weighing about five hundred fifty pounds. When broken, they were either broke plumb gentle or always stayed half wild. And they were smart. When we first came to Jordan Valley, my father bought two from Ambrose Maher and gave them to me for my personal cavaida. The white one we called Pigeon, the black was named Nigger. The black was the better of the pair, for he was spirited and full of little tricks to show his native independence, probably bred into him by generatons of free-ranging forbears. He was easy to catch, except when you had it in mind to ride him. Somehow he could read your thoughts and tell the difference. He had been roped so often, he'd duck his head from the loop and make a break for it. If you were in the way, well, too bad. . . . It seemed to be a game with him. Father tried slowing him down by strapping a lengthy piece of log chain to a front foot, but Nigger would run sideways or in a circle, and jump the chain before it got entangled in his hind legs. Again, if you were in the way, the chain would make a believer out of you.

When you got Nigger saddled, the main show began. He was a great actor. He would suddenly go lame in one or all four legs, and if you didn't know his trick, he'd then be returned to pasture. The moment he was loose, he'd run and jump to show he'd bested you. Another trick was to reach around and bite your toe if you'd been riding him too hard — his own form of protest. Or he'd paw the ground when you'd stopped, as though he were going to lie down on you. But his undoing was an insatiable appetite. Nigger would eat most anything, even beef scraps thrown to the dogs and cats. Once when Jim Elordi and I were camped near Wagontown, exploring the old mines, we paused to eat. Nigger reached over my shoulder, snatching the sandwich right out of my hand.

Nigger was typical of the spirited mustangs. There were thousands of them running at one time in this country, and it was profitable to go after them. There were big horse outfits on the desert, among them the Double Square and Drummond. Bill Loveland remembers that as a boy "there were wild horses all over the country." Not all were mustangs, however. There were other breeds turned loose or having run away from their owners to go wild, many of them bearing faded brands on their rumps.

Photo by Joseph Van Wormer

Spirited mustangs, whose lineage extends back to the Conquistadors, gallop along a rocky defile, trying to escape capture. Note saddled rider in right center. Scenes like this were once commonplace in the West, now are rare as the wild horses have almost vanished from the scene.

"We used to run horses about a month and a half every year," Loveland recalled. "First we would go brand the tame horses, then go mustanging. We put lots of horses into the Deary pasture and in later years, when we started running them with airplanes, the pilot would run them into the pasture, too."

Running the mustangs through rock and brush was dangerous business. A mount could fall and the rider might shatter his arms or legs, or both. When the mustangs were run, there were several different methods. In rough broken country, a trap was built in a blind or box canyon, and the horses run into it, the opening blocked behind them. Another method used on the desert was to guard a waterhole frequented by the horses, keeping them away. When the mustangs got very thirsty, they were allowed to reach the waterhole. They'd drink too much water, get cramped up, and then the mustangers would hit them. A third method, if you wanted just a single horse, was to get close enough to lasso one on his way to water, or by riding into the herd, if you could catch them. A black cowboy in the Midwest had his own special method of bringing in an entire herd of wild horses, while his fellow ranchers were wearing themselves out pursuing the animals for many miles across the plains. His system took time and great patience. He followed a herd all alone until they were used to his being around. He'd "join the herd" with his horse and then finally take over as "leader," bringing the entire bunch right into his corral.

The most widely used — and the most exciting — system for successful mustanging was a *partida*, a bunch of gentle horses into which the mustangs were run to slow them down, and confuse them. The *partida* was the key to the entire operation and was located at a strategic place, usually a big flat where there was plenty of room. The *partida* was held there by the buckeroos, while the rest of the crew ran in a bunch of mustangs.

"We always figured out which way the horses will go, and station men along the route so that they could change off," Bill Loveland said. "This way there was always a fresh horse ahead of them. You couldn't run the mustangs straight into the *partida* because they wouldn't stop and would take the *partida* with them. When they started coming close to the *partida*, the mustangers would begin to circle the herd, and run it into the *partida*. They kept circling the outfit tighter and tighter until they came to a stop."

Leaving the *partida* was the most difficult task.

"When starting the *partida* from a stop," continued Loveland, "you must let them go ahead about two hundred yards the first time, then stop them again. If you don't, the mustangs will all take off to the lead, and you can lose them if this happens. I only let the *partida* run once, and that was when we lost 'em. When leaving the *partida* there should be at least three men in the lead to stop them the first time. One time we were holding five hundred horses on *partida* at Jackie Butte. Bob Wilkenson was *partida* boss and he wanted to run the horses, but the others wanted to let them stand quiet. The whole *partida* took off and we lost the whole outfit."

When the mustangs were started the second time, they were run into a corral or trap. Mustangers of the Owyhees took the horses to Winnemucca, Murphy, and Riverside railheads. It was a five-day push from Loveland's horse camp on Jackie Butte to Riverside.

Loveland and other mustangers later used the airplane to run the wild horses.

"Once a white stud broke out of the bunch and the pilot took after him," Loveland recalled. "He had a big rock tied to the tail of the plane to break up the horses when they kegged up. He took after that stud and turned him. When he did, the rock wrapped around the horse's neck. The pilot felt the plane begin to pull down, so he shot straight up and lifted the stud about six feet off the ground. Then the rope broke. Then he drove the the horses back to the *partida*."

Following World War II, into the 1950s, pressure on the wild horse bands became extremely heavy from sportsmen of various sorts, and also professionals rounding them up to sell to manufacturers for pet food. There were no protection laws and thousands of the animals were being run down, especially in Nevada, through use of the airplane. The wild horse bands didn't have a chance. When the methods and extent of the operations were exposed, there was a widespread public outcry and movement to save the mus-

Photo by Henry D. Sheldon, loaned by Pers Crowell

A small band of mustangs flees from onlooker who came upon them in open country. Wild bands once roamed the West, but their numbers have diminished until now they are an endangered species. Preserves are being established and laws passed to halt the killing of wild horses.

tangs. New laws and restrictions were adopted in the Western states. But the wild horse by then was nearly gone, and probably would be by now, save for that preserve up in Montana. He added pressure to the ranges and when the ranges were fenced up, the horses ran through the wire, so he had to go. . . .

The problem with management plans designed to save the mustang is that there are no clear cut rules provided to control the animals' numbers. I suggest that mustangers be allowed to run them as they once did since these men too, are an important part of our western heritage.

GOINGS ON . . .

THERE ARE COUNTLESS amazing stories, tall tales and exciting legends concerning the I-O-N country. Take Jack Miller, for instance. Miller was a Texan, a tough hombre who had a thriving timber operation in the Blue Mountains. His crew consisted of a half dozen men, among them a cook named Matt Egan.

When Miller fired Egan, the cook took off for Burns in a bitter frame of mind. He swore that Miller canned him for a woman cook, whose company he liked better. He began drinking heavily, and the more he drank, the more he brooded. One day he accosted Miller on a Burns street and all hell broke loose. Egan pulled a gun, there was a struggle, Miller got his own gun free and pumped four bullets into Egan's stomach.

Jack wrenched the weapon from the dead man's hand and brandishing both guns, strode up the street to the saloon where several toughs, possibly friends of Egan, were eyeing him in challenge.

"If any of you sons-of-bitches don't like what I've

done, get right out here and try your hand," Miller declared.

Nobody stepped forward. And the shooting was ruled justifiable homicide.

But a short time later, a warrant was on Miller's head for horse stealing. He got out of Burns ahead of the sheriff, cutting the telegraph lines on the way. He dropped from sight, not to be heard from again until the Klondike Stampede of 1898. Suddenly, he was back in the limelight under a new name — Jack Dalton. He formed a partnership with Ed Hanley, Uncle Bill's brother, and John Malony to drive cattle from eastern Oregon to the Yukon, making them a fortune.

"I got here all right with my cattle," wrote Ed Hanley to his brother and sister in December 1898. "They

Ed Hanley and Jack Dalton with his wife in Alaska, 1898. The route over which Dalton and Hanley drove their cattle to the North became known as the Dalton trail.

averaged three hundred dollars and a little better. We did real well out of them."

The cattle and horse herds bound for the Yukon were put together in eastern Oregon. And the route became known as the famous Dalton Trail. . . .

Charley Loveland and Pearl Duncan were mustanging together. They'd been out several months and were fed up with each other. Only the operation held them together. They were camped at the mouth of a box canyon with their cavaidas trapped inside.

One morning Loveland heard a bell coming, and certain it was Duncan's, just let the horses go on by. After a couple of hours, he mentioned it to his partner. Cursing, Duncan caught his mount and struck out after the ponies. He didn't return till evening, and then without any horses.

"What happened to your bell?" asked Charley.

"They weren't mine," retorted Duncan. "They were your'n."

A sheepherder named Clark and a gambler named Franklin got into an argument in Jordan Valley. Franklin was eating in the dining room of the old Jordan Valley Hotel when someone tipped him that Clark was waiting to ambush him on the stairway from the lobby. The gambler calmly finished his meal, paid the bill, unracked his hat and stepped to the lobby door. As he opened the door he dropped to his knee and pulled his six-shooter. Clark put a Winchester bullet into the door casing where Franklin's head would have been. The gambler killed Clark with two quick shots. Then he went cooly to another spot in town and read a newspaper for several hours.

"Old Man Slaten had a sure fire method for breaking a balky horse," said Jim McEwen. "He was always willing to take on a balky horse and break it. Would lead the horse behind his outfit. When he came to a steep hill, he'd hook the horse up backwards to the wagon with a singletree. On the way down the horse would pull to keep from sliding — had too, or he would be dragged. When he got to the bottom, the horse was broke."

The local bachelors were always vitally concerned about the hiring of a new school marm. The general policy was to sign up only "young, single school marms." Billy Helm, a Jordan Valley businessman, rode herd on the applications. Many of the teachers sent along photographs to prove their qualifications for the job. One year there were eighty applicants. Helm sorted out the huge supply of pictures into two piles, those he felt qualified and those who didn't. Then he leaned back and muttered, "Now let's see what we have."

Helm didn't want a repeat of what happened over in Denio. A teacher sent in an application, but no picture. She indicated, however, that she was young — and single. The stage trip out was long, hot, and dusty. The eager cowboy sent to greet the new school marm was taken aback by the lady, who was obviously well past her prime. And the trip had been rugged on her.

"I feel like I'm ninety years old," she said as she climbed painfully from the stage,

"Why, ma'am," replied the puncher, "you don't look a day over eighty."

When school was dismissed for the day, Frank Swisher and his pals made sport of throwing rocks at the male teacher after he left the building. The teacher quit over this constant harassment. But disgusted parents immediately hired another, who wasn't so much on education, but a stickler for discipline. When the new teacher stepped to his desk the first

Not many people haul wood by this means now, but here the author brings juniper posts from Idaho with a vehicle from the Old West, a six horse team and wagon.

day, he pulled a six-shooter and placed it in plain sight of the young hellions who were studying him intently.

"We'll either have school or funerals," he announced.

Any doubts about that teacher were cleared up fast.

Another teacher was having trouble explaining subtraction to a small boy. He used the illustration of ten cows in a field. If one cow slipped through a hole in the fence, how many would be left?

"None," replied the boy quickly.

The teacher shook his head. "There would be nine. . . ."

"The trouble with you, teacher," replied the boy, "is that you may know arithmetic, but you don't know anything about cattle. If one found that hole, they all would."

Over on Crooked Creek, a family wanted to go

on a picnic. The wife volunteered to stay home, as
Grandmaw needed watching. Grandmaw liked her
whisky and would likely tap a keg of moonshine, if
they left her alone. The Old Man solved the problem
— or thought he did — by raising the keg to the high
limb of a tree. So the missus went along.

When they arrived home, they found Grandmaw
passed out in the sun beneath the tree, a smile on
her face, a rifle beside her. She'd taken a tub, placed
it directly below, put a bullet through the keg, and
let gravity do the rest.

Bill Brown and Uncle Bill Hanley once nearly
caused a female Indian war when they judged a baby
contest. The two jokesters gave the award to an Indian
papoose, just to see what would happen. They found
out; the other ladies were fit to be tied.

Uncle Bill Hanley with his niece Martha at the Bell A ranch.

Vernie High and Raymond Lee, in the winter of
1931/32, were trapping coyotes in the Junipers. They
confused a bottle of squirrel poison with their salt
bottle. When Dewey Weeks found them, both were
dead. The cooking utensils and the half eaten meal
were still there, indicating they had died while eating.
The half starved horses were in the corral. Lee had
managed to write: "We took strychnine for salt."

Observed the *DeLamar Nuggett*: "We are sorry
the dame who, on Monday night, took a shot at the
boys who threw the sow through her window did not
take better aim. A .32 caliber ball in the fleshy part
of the anatomy of such fellows gives them the occasion
to consider that the inmates may be quite as much
entitled to considerate treatment as the men who frequent such places."

And again the *DeLamar Nugget* took note: "By
pulling a six-shooter in Constancin's saloon Thursday,
John Morrison created a stampede which came near
causing injury to several persons who tumbled over
each other in the wild rush for the back door. This
senseless and foolish habit of drawing a gun on every
little occasion will yet lead to serious trouble and then
the *Nugget* will say, 'I told you so'."

A freighter with two wagons of booze stopped at
the Skylight for the night, where some twenty shearers
were working on sheep. The freighter moved all the
kegs to one wagon and slept on top of them as a precaution. But the shearers found a way. They drilled
holes through the bottom of the wagon into two kegs
and had quite a party.

A sheriff from Montana trailed two toughs through
Silver City and down along Sucker Creek. He caught
one man, clapping the cuffs on him. The fugitive asked

The mud wagon type coach, rebuilt by the author, lives up to its name by plunging across the Cow Creek ford at the Ruby Ranch where Hill Beachy once had stables.

to go into his tent for something and the wary sheriff obliged, but followed him inside. The tough pretended he was looking for something and picked up a chunk of chewing tobacco, biting off a huge chaw. Suddenly he turned, spit in the sheriff's eye, and got away.

Three cattle thieves operating out of Sinker had a falling out. One broke it off, setting up camp outside Silver City. The other two went gunning for him, because he knew too much. They emptied their sixshooters into him. Verdict of the coroner's jury was that he died "of lead poisoning." The jury figured it was "good riddance" and let it go at that.

When a stranger to Silver City was arrested for the murder of a vegetable peddler, taking his victim's team and wagon, the verdict was to string him up. The boys all rushed to view the event. Riding by wagon toward the scaffold, the condemned man announced: "No use being in a hurry, boys. There'll be nothing doing till I get there."

Many characters lived alone in the hinterlands of the Owyhees. They would disappear and nobody would know what had happened to them. One month, or one spring or fall, they didn't show up for supplies as was their habit, and that was that. Maybe a partner killed them, or they'd just die, to be found years later. Jeff Anderson found the skeletons of two men in an overhang at Three Forks. Charley Mac who had a dugout on Hard Trigger Creek disappeared without a trace. But they found Joseph Monahan who had the deepest secret of all. Joseph turned out to be a woman.

There was a centennial celebration in 1969 at the White Horse Ranch, an observance of one hundred years of that historic ranch which belonged to John Devine, Miller and Lux, Paul Stewart, and Ted Naftzger. It also celebrated a century of the cattle industry in the country east of the Cascades. The great old ranch is much as it was when the early cattlemen were there. The famous White Horse Barn, dating from Devine's time, is standing, and the blacksmith's shop is one of the best preserved sod houses in the West. The ghosts of a colorful past leap out at you on all sides. In such an atmosphere, it is easy to imagine John Devine striding through the door to tell the smith how he wanted his fine horses shod for the racing season; and Henry Miller arriving from a tour of his Quinn River ranches, picking up a pitchfork which someone had carelessly dropped and leaning it against

Two Owyhee veterans. Omer Stanford "rolls his own" in front of a rebuilt stagecoach.

the wall, muttering, "Mit der tines oop." In such a setting, it all comes very much alive again to those who
care about our heritage and have the imagination to
project their thoughts beyond the "now."

The celebration was a gay time of reminiscing on
those colorful and rugged times. On the way home
to Jordan Valley, I couldn't help but recall another
similar occasion, the big celebration when the railroad
came to Burns and how Uncle Bill felt about it. Bill
Hanley reminisced thoughtfully in his book *Feelin'*
Fine about the changes of an ever-changing world,
and wondering whether a lot of it was worthwhile
in what it did to the old established ways. He wrote:

"Had our big railroad celebration. A trainload
came from the outside to help us rejoice. All we're
happy, big speeches and everything. . . . A fellow
builds a railroad across the plains and we say, 'What
a wonderful thing!' But what is he to the fellow that
made the plains?

"Went out to Section Five in Thirty-One, on the
Bell A where the rails are laid. Had to get off my
horse and go stand on the rails all alone. Seemed like
a mighty lonesome meeting – all my feeling was of
the past. Had worked so much at different times to
bring in the steel rails, and here they were. They had
followed the old trail we drove cattle over so many
times through so many years . . . just backtracked
the cattle. Maybe they wanted to see where all the
cattle came from. Wondered whether I really wanted
it after all, for it made me feel my job was done.

"Anybody can raise cattle and load them into cars.

". . . I thought of the big outfits, the saddle horses,
the herds – how they'd had to move hundreds of miles,
living off the country as they went, the many camps,
and the many years necessary to learn the skill in
handling and moving them. No human would ever
be raised again who could know how to do it. No
reason ever again why he should. The rails had taken

*out the romance and fascination of the life of a
cattleman. My time was done.*

*"They'll be changing our old names that tell people
the whole history of the country: Squaw Flats,
Yaninax, Bake Oven, Rawhide, Stinking Water,
Crooked River, Iron Mountain, Desolation Creek,
Wagontire, Poison Creek, Wild Horse, Summer Lake,
Goose Lake, Chewaucan, Silver Lake, Happy Valley,
Diamond, Mule . . . so many others, given by the boys,
often for things that happened there. All mean some-
thing. Every one a story."*

INDEX

A

Acarregui, Jhonny, 180
Agency Valley, 108, 109*, 110, 112, 148
Alder Gulch, Montana, 203, 204
Alvord, Brig. Gen. Benjamin, 50, 51*
Alvord Ranch, 113
American Federation of Labor, 228
Anderson, James Pickens (Pick), 101, 102*, 103-106, 170, 176
Anderson, William T., 154, 158, 159, 160
Antelope Reservoir, 247-249
Army Camps, 56
Arock Project, 248
Azcuenaga Ranch, 247
Avalanche, The, 25, 26, 36, 54, 57, 62, 68, 69, 207, 208

B

Baldwin, M. A., 216
Ballard, Gov. David M., 199
Bally Beers (famed racehorse), 252, 253*, 254*, 255*

(*Asterisk denotes illustration)

Bank of California, 29, 216
Bannock Indians, 23, 49*, 50, 66*, 127*, 131, 146*, 148
Bannock War, 125*, 131-147, 165
Barren Valley, 32, 135, 143, 165, 170, 171, 172
Basques or Bascos, 9, 178*, 179, 180, 183-193, 194, 247, 248, 262, 263, 268
Baxter, John, 34*, 35, 232, 234, 237, 238
Baxterville, See Jordan Valley (town)
Beachy, Hill, 16, 62*, 203-204
Beers, Billy, 151
Beers, Mrs. William, 238
Bend, Oregon, 122
Bernard, Capt́. Reuben F., 130, 133, 135, 143, 144
Beulah Reservoir, 109*
Bigfoot (Nampuh), See Wilkinson, Starr
Black Jack Mines, 220
Blacksmiths, 274, 275*, 277
Blue Bucket Mine, 23, 24
Blue Mountains, 143, 145, 165, 169, 170, 172, 179, 296
Boise Basin, 24, 39, 158, 204
Boise City, 35, 156, 158, 162, 191, 208

Boise, Nampa and Owyhee Railroad, 220
Boise River, 24, 155, 163
Bonneville, Captain Benjamin, 23
Booneville (Dewey, Idaho), 24, 25*, 26, 28*, 35
Booneville Mine, 220
Brown, Bill, 301
Bruneau Valley, 92, 131, 136
Bryan, William Jennings, 277
"Bull's Head" currency, 106, 111, 112, 113
Buffalo Horn (chief), 13, 127, 128, 129*, 130, 131, 132, 133
Burgess, John W., 162
Burns, Oregon, 122
Bureau of Land Management (U.S.), 10, 33, 195, 282, 283, 285, 288
Bureau of Mines (U.S.), 14

C

Cable, Frank, 232, 234
Caldwell, Idaho, 170, 175, 227, 261, 270, 278
California gold fields (Mother Lode), 23
Camp Henderson, 52
Camp Lyon, 20, 21, 35, site today, 42*, 55*, 56, 67, 70, 131
Camas Prairie, 127, 130
Canter, Alex, 232
Canyon City, Oregon, 145
Carson Mining District, 26
Carson, W. T., 24
Castro, Fred, 104, 105
Catlow, John, 88, 93
Catlow Valley, 93, 95, 96
Cattle companies (early), 85
Cattle rustling (modern), 1-5
Cattlemen vs. Sheepmen, 176-182
Celebrations, 209*, 210*, 211, 231, 240, 241, 251
Central City, Colorado, 206
Charbonneau, Jean Baptiste, 16, 17*
Chico-Ruby City Road, 16, 38*, 40
Childs, S. W., 35
Cherokee Nation, 155, 156
Chinese funerals, 214, 215
Chinese, 15, 53, 68, 211-215, 228
Churches, 208, 242, 243
Civil War, 30, 54, 161, 167
Columbia River, 40, 145, 147
Conquistadors, 289
Cook, Ben, 157

Coppinger, Col. John J., 56, 71*
Cow Creek, 6, 17, 20, 21, 281
Cow Lakes, 17, 18*
Cripple Creek, Colorado, 226
Crook, Gen. George, 128, 130
Crow, Frances, 94*, 95
Crow, James Rankin, 94
Crow, S. H., 96
Curry, Capt. George B., 50, 51, 52
Custer's Last Stand, See Little Bighorn

D

Dalton, Jack, 296, 297*
Dalton Trail, 297*, 298
Dance Hall Girls, 205, 206
Danner, John, 248
Davis, Milt, 169
DeLamar, Idaho, 211, 219, 221, 222*, 226, 230, 251, 266, 277, 278
DeLamar, Joseph L., 221
DeLamar Nugget, 221, 231, 302
Demitt, Ellis, 79, 85
Devine, John, 112-114*, 117, 304
Dewey, Idaho, 217, 220, See also, Booneville
Dewey, Colonel W. H., 25, 26, 34, 35, 217, 218, 220, 230
Dewey Hotels, 220, 221, 230
Diamond Valley, 142, 143
Dog Town, See Jordan Valley (town)
Dodge City, Kansas, 195
Dorsey, Willie (Pawonto), 75*-77
Double-O Ranch, 110, 177, 178
Drake, Capt. John M., 50
Driscoll, Dennis, 83
Driscoll and Lane, 91
Drummond, Arthur, 266
Duck Ponds, 165, 170, 196
Duck Valley, 85, 92, 107, 148, 251
Dwyer-Foy Fight, 210

E

Egan (chief), 53, 128, 131, 143, 147, 212
Egan, Matt, 296
Eiguren, Fred, 162
Elko, Nevada, 89, 131, 169
Elorriga, Ambrosio, 183
Entertainers, show troupes, 207
Epidemics, 244, 245
Eugene, Oregon, 171
Euskaldanak, See Basques

F

Fast horseback ride, 110, 111
First Oregon Cavalry, 21, 54, 70
Fisher, Jack, 199
Fogus, Colonel D. H., 37
Folly Farm, 165
Forest Service (U.S.), 33, 179
Fort Boise, 54, 70, 201
Fort Dalles, 50
Fort Hall, 50, 127, 129, 136, 148
Fort Harney, 56, 141, 143
Fort McDermitt (Indian Reser.), 7, 32, 108, 131, 133, 136, 152
Fort Rock, 23
Fort Walla Walla, 50, 133
Frank, Meyer, 198
French, Peter, 88, 94, 95, 96, 97*, 98, 104, 105, 116, 133, 142, 143

G

Garcia (outlaw), 117, 118
Gates, Lieutenant, 163
Gibbs, Governor A. C., 52
Gilchrist, John, 122
Golconda, Nevada, 103
Golden Chariot Mine, 198, 199, 216
Grande Ronde River, 145
Grande Ronde Valley, 50
Great Depression, 29, 187
Greeley, Horace, 167
Gusman's Ranch, 36, 43, 93, 136, 234

H

Hall's Ranch, 67, 69
Halleck, Maj. Gen. Henry Wager, 56
Hanley, Bill, 149, 175, 176, 177, 178, 301*, 306
Hanley, Ed, 297*
Hanley Family, 11
Hanley, Mike III, 284, 285*
Hanley, Mike IV, 20*, 259*, 276*, 300*, 303*
Happy Valley, 141, 142, 143
Hardin, Colonel, 101
Harney City, 168, 169
Harney County, 5, 122
Harney Valley, 33, 107
Harney, William Selby, 57
Harper Ranch, 123
Hart, artist killed by Bigfoot, 155
Hawes, Willie, 229, 230
Haywood, William (Big Bill), 225, 226, 227*, 228

Hemingway, Ernest, 188, 192
Hillery, Cpl. William, 201, 203
Hoag, George, 162
Hobart, 2nd Lieut. Charles, 54, 57, 58 -60
Home Creek Ranch, 95
Horse racing, 230, 231, 250-255
Horsley, Albert E., See: Orchard, Harry
Howard, James, 199
Howard, Gen. Oliver Otis, 130, 133, 136, 140, 143, 144, 145
Hoyt, Gov. John P., 130
Hudson's Bay Company, 12
Holgate, John C., 198
Holladay, Ben, 116, 212

I

Ida Elmore Mine, 198, 199
Idaho Avalanche, See: Avalanche, The
Idaho Blue Book, 221
Idaho City, 28, 36*, 208
Idaho Stage Company, 16
Idaho Statesman, 69, 144, 160, 199, 203, 211, 230
Idaho Territorial Legislature, 34
Indians at Jordan Valley, 150-152
Indian encounters (personal), 137, 138, 139, 140, 141, 142
Indian tribes, brief history of, 45-47; 48*
Industrial Workers of the World, 228
Inskip, G. W., 61, 62, 67, 70
International Union of Mine, Mill and Smelter Workers, 228
Irish miners, 201, 215
Irrigation project, 247-249
Isaacs, James, 97, 98
Island Ranch, 120

J

Jackman, E. R., 263
Jacksonville, Oregon, 23, 204
John Day River, 145
Johnson, Frank, 157
Jones, Everett, 267*, 270
Jones, Mary Alice, 270
Jones, Dr. Walter William, 151, 193, 265-267*, 271*, 273
Jordan Craters, 18, 19*
Jordan Creek, 9, 15, 16, 26, 35, 38, 65, 247
Jordan, Michael M. (I), 9, discovers gold, 24, 34

Jordan, Mike II, 36, 41
Jordan, Mike III, 37
Jordan Valley — Area: 5-21, 40, 45, 138, 150-152, 161, 204, 250, 256, 265, 280, 290, Bank: 187, *Express*: 238, 245, 246, Hotel: 170, 238*, Pharmacy: 267, 270, 271*, 272*, 273, Town: 7, 10*, 30, 35, 36, 131, 136, 152, 178*, 183, 184, 185, 186, 187, 191, 194, 195, 205, 232-249, 267, 268, 270, 277, 278, 298, 299, 306, Water Users Ass'n: 248
Joseph (chief), 126, 127
Joss houses, 214
Juniper Mountain, 14, 73, 101, 103, 104, 176
"Juniper Mountain Monkeys", 104

K

Kelly, John, 207
Kiger, "Doc", 141, 142
Kimball, Maj. Gorman Gates, 162
Klondike, 206, 297
Knights of Pythias, 225
Kohlhire, Phil, 82, 84, 85
Kreiser, Heinrick Alfred, See: Miller, Henry

L

Last resident of Silver City, 229, 230
Lequerica, John, 193, 194*, 195, 197*
Lequerica, Rufus, 193
Lequerica, Tim, 187, 189*, 193, 194, 195, 196, 197
Lewis and Clark Expedition, 17
Lewis, Joe, 155, 156
Lewiston, Idaho, 145, 203
Lincoln, President Abraham, 52, 53
Little Bighorn, 29, 126
Lockhart, Sam, 199
Lockwood, Jared, 232, 234
Long, Henry, 164
Long, R. A. (Reub), 104
Los Banos, California, 120
Loveland, Charles, 105, 106, 298
Loveland, William (Bill), 257, 291, 292, 293
Lux, Charles, 106, 107
Lyon, Caleb, 56, 57

M

Madams of Tough Town, 221, 222
Magruder, Lloyd, 203

Mahogany Mountains, 6
Mapes Hotel, 278
Marshall, Father Hugh J., 242, 243
McConnell, William J., 74*, 204
McDermitt, Oregon-Nevada border, 7, 165, 186, 240, 251, 253, See also: Fort McDermitt
McEwen, James, 167-173*, 174-176, 179, 180, 181, 182
McEwen, Jemima Scott (Mima), 171, 172, 173*
McKenzie, Donald, 7, 23
McKinley, William, 277
McMahon, James, 239, 241
Mahogany Mountains, 141
Malheur Agency, 128, 143, 148
Malheur County, 5, 6*, 7, 107, 108, 170, 240, 245, 246
Malheur River, 57, 107, 108, 207
Malony, Jack, 297
Maney & Wells, contractors, 248
Marshall, Major L.H., 70, 71, 73, 75
Masonic Lodge, 207, 223
Meek Cutoff, 33
Meek, Stephen, 23, 33
Miles, Capt. Evan, 147
Miller, August, 169
Miller and Lux, See: Miller, Henry
Miller, Charlie, 123
Miller, George T., 79, 84, 85, 88, 101
Miller, Henry, 101, 103, 106-112, 113, 115*-123, 148, 306
Miller, Jack, See: Dalton, Jack
Miners' songs, 201, 202, 206
Missouri River, 164
Monroe, Jim, 86, 87, 88
"Moonshine", 256, 257*, 258, 259*, 261*-264
Moore, Christopher, 28, 80, 82
More, Marion, 199
Morning Star Mine, 26
Morrison-Knudson Co., 247, 248
Moscow, Russia, 228
Murder of Egan, 147
Murphy, Idaho, 27, 195, 229, 293
Mustangs, 288-290

N

Nampa, Idaho, 154, 175, 230
Nevada Gang, 203
New Ulm Massacre, 126
Nez Perce Indians, 128
North West Fur Company, 7
Northwest Vigilantes, 16, 204

O

Odd Fellows (I.O.O.F.) Lodge, 207, 221, 223
Ogden, Peter Skene, 23
Oinkari Dancers, 191
Olsen, Arthur, 122, 123
Ontario, Oregon, 5, 167, 168, 171, 175, 186, 240, 278
Orchard, Harry, 227, 228
Oregon Central Military Road Company, 30
Oregon Humane Society, 177
Oregon State Extension Service, 263
Oregon State Highway Dept., 270
Oregon Steam Navigation Co., 40
Oregon Trail, 23, 50
Oregon Volunteers, 50, 51, 52
Oro Fino Mine, 26
Overfelt, Tom, 107-112
Overfelt and Company, 109, 110, 112
Overmire & Miller Sales and Feed Stables, 88
Owyhee — *Avalanche*: See *Avalanche*,The, Country: 24, 164, 226, 274, 288, County: 14, Crossing: 1, 15, 16*, 38, 40, 135, 162, 163*, 184, 194, 212, Mines: 34, 226, Mountains: 6, 14, 23, River: 6, 7, 9*, 12*, 14*, 21, 24, 74, 101, 266, 267, 273, Volunteers: 13, 63, 64, 73, 75, 131, 132
Oytes (chief), 131

P

Pacific Land and Livestock Co., 2, 104, 114
Paiute Indians, 23, 50, 127, 128, 145, 148
Partida, 292, 293
Pearman, Sheriff Roy, 263
Pelota (Basque handball), 183, 184
Pennoyer, Gov. Sylvester, 7
Pepoon, Lieut., 65, 67, 70
Pharmacy Butte, 243, 268
Plummer Gang, 203
Pocatello (chief), 127
Poorman Mine, 27
Poorman nugget, 27
Portland, Oregon, 35, 171
Pretty Jhonnie, 150, 151
Prineville, Oregon, 171
Prohibition, 256
Pyrenees Mountains, 184, 185

R

Race horses, list, 252
Rambouillet sheep, 176
Reas, Frank, 247
Red light districts, 205, 221, 222, 251, 252
Reno, Nevada, 278
Rinehart, William V., 128, 131, 148
Ringling Brothers Circus, 181
Riverside, 170, 172, 175, 293
Roaring Springs Ranch, 95
Robbins, Col. Orlando "Rube", 133, 136, 143, 144
Rome, Oregon, 1, 15, 16*, 40
Roosevelt, President Theodore, 177
Ruby City, 16, 25, 26, 30, 35, 37, 54, 162, 203, 207
Ruby Ranch, 16, 18, 61, 62*, 63*, trapped by Indians, 67, 137*, 171

S

Sacajawea, 17
Salt Lake City, Utah, 1
Sanford, Ralph, 281
Scales, John, 230
Schnabel, William F., 238, 240, 241
Schoolteachers, 299, 300
Shaniko, Oregon, 164
Shea, Con, 20, 79, 80, 82, 83*, 88, 93, 101, 104
Shea, Jerry, 82
Shea, Tim, 82
Sheaville, 20, 79
Sheep pioneers, 161, 162*-176
Sheep Ranch, 41, 43, 88, 137, 162
Sheep's Head, 103
Sheepherders' Ball, 191
Sheepmen practices, 175, 176, 195,-197
Shirk, David, 41-43, 81*, 82, 84, 85-87*, 88, 89-93, 94*, 95, 97, 98, 99, 100, 103, 162
Shirk, William, 93
Shoshone Indians, 23, 48, 127, 128, 149
Shoun, James, 168
Silver City, Idaho, 26, 29, 56, 74, 77, 80, 82, 84, 85, 131, 133, 152, 158, 163, 198-231, 251, 302, 303, 304
Silver City Nugget, 240, 241
Silver City Volunteers, See: Owyhee Volunteers
Silver Purchase Act, 225
Sinker Creek, 50, 64
Sioux Indians, 126
Sitting Bull (chief), 126, 129

Skinner, Silas (Sam), 34, 36, sketch of early life, 37, 38, 40-44, 88, 232, 233*, 234
Skinner Butte, 268, see also Pharmacy Butte
Skinner Family, 171, 233*
Skinner, Tom, 252, 253
Skinner, William, 180
Smyth, John, 141, 142, 143
Snake Indians, See: Shoshone
Snake River, 12, 33, 35, 82, 92, 101, 155, 157*, 195
Soldier Creek, 56, 280, 283, 284*, 287
South Mountain, 13, 27, 133, 220, 234
South Mountain City (Bullion City), 13
Spain, 184, 187, 188, 190
Spring Mountains, 6
Stagecoach routes, companies, 38-40, 230, 303*, 305*
Stanford, Sheriff, Lyman, 202, 203
Star Valley, 103
Stateline Ranch, 137, 139*
Staufer, Ed, 104
Staufer, Frank (Fritz), 104
Steens Mountain, 52, 96, 133, 135, 162, 186, 263
Steunenberg, Gov. Frank, 226, 227
Stites, Ernest, 277-279*
Stoddard, Jack, 83
Stoddard, J. W., 221
Succor Creek, 8*
Sweetzer, Frank, 104
Swisher, Frank, 104, 150, 222, 223, 252, 254, 257, 258, 259-262, 299
Swisher Place, 139

T

Taylor Grazing Act, 177, 195, 280, 281
Three Forks, 9, 15, 39, 56, 70-72, 261
Tidal Wave, 29
Tombstone, Arizona, 206
"Tough Town", 221
Trade Dollar Mine, 220, 227*, 228
Turnbull, James L., 165
Turnbull, Thomas, 164, 165, 166*, 167, 170, 171, 172, 173, 175, 179

U

Umapine (chief), 147
Umatilla, Oregon, 30, 35

Umatilla Reservation, 145, 146, 147

V

Vale, Oregon, 5, 172, 240
Virginia City, Montana, 203
Virginia City, Nevada, 27
Visher Ranch, 172, 174

W

Wagontire Mountain, 33
Wagontown, 221, 230, 231, 250
Wales, 13
Walsac (chief), 147, 149, 150
War Eagle Mountain, 11, 13, 15, 21, 23, 27, 28, 229*
Warm Springs Ranch, 69
Western Federation of Miners, 225, 226, 227*
Wheeler, John W., 157, 158-160
White Horse Ranch, 95, 113, 304
Whitman Disaster, 156
Wichita, Kansas, 195
Wild Horses, 288, 289*, 291*, 294*, 295
Wilkinson, Starr, 152, 153*-160
Willamette Valley, 23, 33, 171
Willamette Valley-Cascade Mountain Wagon Road Company, 30-33
Williams, Billy, 239
Winnemucca — Chief: 48, 130, 136, 268, Jess: 150, 151, 268, Lee: 135, Nevada town: 13, 29, 95, 103, 105, 175, 176, 191, 234, 293, Sarah: 130, 133, 134*-136, 143, 145, 148, 149, 150, Willie: 151, 152
Winter of 1888-89, 79, 98, 99, 164
Wobblies (I.W.W.), See: Industrial Workers of the World
Wood, John, 165, 170
World War I, 186, 266
World War II, 278, 294
Wrench, The, See: Pacific Land and Livestock Co.
Wright, Gen. George, 54
Wroten, Marshal John W., 241, 243, 251

Y

Yturri, Anthony, 193
Yturriondobeitia, John, 248, 273